From T-2 to Supertanker

Development of the Oil Tanker, 1940–2000

Andrew G. Spyrou

iUniverse, Inc.

New York Lincoln Shanghai

From T-2 to Supertanker
Development of the Oil Tanker, 1940–2000

iUniverse books may be ordered through booksellers or by contacting:

iUniverse
2021 Pine Lake Road, Suite 100
Lincoln, NE 68512
www.iuniverse.com
1-800-Authors (1-800-288-4677)

ISBN-13: 978-0-595-36068-0 (pbk)
ISBN-13: 978-0-595-80604-1 (cloth)
ISBN-13: 978-0-595-80518-1 (ebk)
ISBN-10: 0-595-36068-8 (pbk)
ISBN-10: 0-595-80604-X (cloth)
ISBN-10: 0-595-80518-3 (ebk)

Printed in the United States of America

From T-2 to Supertanker

*Dedicated to the memory of Aristotle S. Onassis,
an inspirational leader, pioneering shipowner,
and a wonderful human being.*

ACKNOWLEDGMENTS

My sincere thanks to Charles W. Wilson of Babcock and Wilcox, U.S.A., for his help to examine the T-2 tanker construction records; to Professor Masaki Mano of Kinki University in Kure, Japan; to Kiyoshi Iwai and T. Murahashi of Hitachi-Zosen Corporation; and to Yasuyo Ishihara of Nippon Kokan Corporation in Tokyo, Japan, for their helpful suggestions.

My special thanks to Eleni Zarocosta for deciphering the enormous amount of handwritten text and typing it; also to Julia Hana for rendering her meticulous computer skills to transform the raw narrative into concise compact disc format.

CREDITS

CONTENTS

TEN

ELEVEN

TWELVE

THIRTEEN

FOURTEEN

Prologue

*The life so short, the art so long
to learn, opportunity fleeting,
experience treacherous, judgment
difficult.*

The above is Hippocrates's aphorism on Medicine (460 BC). The aphorism may be as appropriate to the design and construction of ships, as it was in medicine during Hippocrates' time.

The connection and comparison are made because of the fact that, as in medicine during Hippocrates' time, naval architecture has never been an exact science. As late as in 1960s, while developing the design for the very large crude oil carrier (VLCC)—200,000 to 300,000 deadweight tons (dwt)—there were instances in Europe and in Japan where, upon completion of sea-trials of newly constructed VLCCs by reputable shipyards, they found it necessary to add large amounts of steel to the hull structure, or redistribute existing material in the structure.

Naval architecture lags behind commercial aircraft design and development, and the industry recognizes that ship design and development can benefit from the work of the commercial aviation industry. Today's commercial aircraft design is accomplished in a virtual environment, where the aircraft is developed using the digital design process, with every aspect of the aircraft modeled in three dimensions. This enables all those involved in the design to walk around the proposed design in virtual reality to ensure there are no conflicts in construction details, thus eliminating the need for a physical prototype. This method also ensures the first aircraft off the production line is identical to the others that follow in the series.

Ship design and construction, on the other hand, is a constant learning process, an evolving science. Today's powerful computers have enabled the hull structure designers to develop the *dynamic loading approach* for scantling determination. *Three dimensional computational fluid dynamics method* is used for hydrodynamic refinement of the hull lines prior to model ship testing.

1

Hull-stress monitoring enables the hull structure designer to appreciate more accurately the stresses and strains on the hull structure. The naval architect now makes use of these methods, including risk assessment pioneered by the nuclear industry. All such advantages have made design and construction of commercial ships a more scientific process.

On the ship construction sector, electric welding technology, computer integration, and mechanization of steel prefabrication have resulted in better and more accurate block assembly. This is the result of improved dimensional accuracy, which in turn leads to further improvements in shipyard productivity.

In fact, the advances made in the design and construction of commercial ships during the past sixty years are of greater significance than at any time in the history of naval architecture. The ultimate aim is to develop a commercial ship that will use hydrogen fuel for propulsion instead of fossil fuels. This will help eliminate atmospheric pollution from the exhaust of propulsion machinery that contributes to man-made global disaster.

In the chapters that follow, I have endeavored to place on record the various stages of oil tanker development, starting with the World War II T-2 Tanker of 16,800 dwt to the one-million-dwt tanker. I have enjoyed the experience, and sincerely hope other kindred spirits will derive pleasure reading the book.

Andrew G. Spyrou
Greenwich, Connecticut
October 2005

ONE

The T-2 Tanker during World War II and Beyond

The importance for the strategic deployment of petroleum distribution to meet the energy needs of the Allies became apparent early in World War II. In order to meet the challenge, it was imperative the Allies assemble, as rapidly as possible, a fleet of tankers to carry the oil. The only country that had the resources and the technology was the United States of America. The U.S. Maritime Commission was given the responsibility to develop a design suitable for this purpose and to construct a fleet of oil tankers to meet the needs of the time. This was made possible by the development of what became known as the T-2 tanker, which in turn made possible the transportation of petroleum during the critical war years.

The U.S. Maritime Commission authorized Sun Shipbuilding and Dry Dock Company in Philadelphia, Pennsylvania, to develop a standard tanker for volume production, utilizing readily available machinery components. The resulting design was given the designation T-2-SE-A1, which denoted an oceangoing, single screw oil tanker of about 500 feet waterline length that had turboelectric propulsion, carried less than twelve passengers, and had a dead-weight of 16,000 tons (approximately 141,000 barrels).

The principal specifications of the T-2 tanker, obtained from the archives of the Merchant Marine Academy, King's Point, New York, were:

Length Overall...523' 6"
Beam..68' 0"
Draft, loaded ....30' 2"
Displacement, loaded ....21,800 tons
Deadweight...16,800 tons
Cargo Capacity..141,000 barrels

Pumping Capacity ....8,600 barrels/hr.
Cargo discharge time ....16.5 hrs.
Steaming radius..10,800 nautical miles
Shaft horsepower 6,600
Speed ....14.50 knots
Light ship weight..5,200 tons
Deadweight/Light weight 0.308
Machinery: ....Steam turbines.
Two ....Water tube, two drum boilers, oil burning.
Design pressure...500 PSA
Operating pressure at superheater outlet ....450 PSI.
Operating pressure at the turbine.....................425 PSI.
Fuel rate based on boiler efficiency of 87% and fuel of 18,500 BTU/lb
....0.662 lbs/SHP
Steam conditions: ....425 PSI and 725° F

During this period a total of 536 T-2 tankers were built. The design and construction of the T-2 tanker was part of the U.S. Maritime Commission's World War II emergency program and covered three basic types: T-1, T-2, and T-3. The T-2 design included five variations, the most important being the T-2-SE-A1, A2, and A3. Of these three primary designs, 525 nearly identical tankers were built, but only eleven of the other T-2 designs were constructed.

When the first all-welded merchant ships built in series were launched only in 1937, early in the war, electric welding was a relatively new procedure. Some of the all-welded constructions experienced fractures in the hull structure, attributed to electric welding. The best known case is that of the T-2 tanker *Schenectady*. The tanker had completed sea trials in January 1943 and was tied to a fitting-out berth in Portland, Oregon, when suddenly, with the sound of an explosion, the main deck and both sides fractured just aft of the midship superstructure.

The fracture was total, extending to the turn of the bilge on both sides, while the bottom plating remained intact. The ship jackknifed, with the bow and the stern resting on the bottom of the Willamette River, and no water entered the other cargo holds.

Extensive investigations were carried out by U.S. authorities on hull structures that sustained structural failures during that period. It was established that shipbuilding steel, made at the time, was "notch sensitive" at operating temperatures, a susceptibility that could be caused by high sulfur and phosphorous content. A notch in this sense is a discontinuity in the material that results in high stress concentration.

It was found at the time that although mild steel is normally an extremely ductile material, there were numerous instances recorded where it broke with crystalline fractures with little or no plastic deformation. The factors found to contribute most, to low ductility in test specimens were sharp notches, low temperatures, and high rates of loading. Notches give a high-stress concentration of a complicated nature at the point of fracture. In low temperatures, there is a rapid fall in impact values from about +20 to -50 degrees Celsius.

At the time of the structural failures, engineers and designers were reluctant to admit that it was due to a material problem, although the failure of oil storage tanks and fractures in ships constructed of steel of previously accepted quality did shake industry opinion. Some suggested that the presence of the combined effect of welding stresses and metallurgical changes due to welding accounted for fracture initiation in welded structures.

Professor Constance F. Tipper, a metallurgist at Cambridge University in the U.K., has been credited with the revelation that the fault in the ships lay not in the method of construction and use of welding as had been suspected, but in the material used, which became dangerously brittle under certain conditions.

In a presentation to the British Institute of Welding in 1956, titled "The Brittle Fracture Problem, 1943–1956," Professor Tipper attributed the breaking in two of the T-2 tanker *Schenectady* to the quality of the mild steel used. The investigation also established that design-related structural discontinuities such as hatch openings and other abrupt interruptions in the structure were the source of fractures in the steel.

Until a proper solution to such failures was found, and as a means to prevent the propagation of fractures on the steel that might originate in a hull structure, riveted "crack arrestors" were installed. In addition, structural discontinuities and abrupt section changes were avoided whenever possible. The methods adopted during this time helped reduce considerably the number of structural failures in hulls from brittle fracturing of the steel in an all-welded ship. The record of these rapidly built, all-welded ships more than justified the adoption of electric welding. Considering that more than 5,000 all-welded ships were built in the United States during WWII under difficult conditions, the electric welding procedure was more than satisfactory.

The following brief description of a typical T-2-SE-A1 tanker, built by Sun Shipbuilding and Dry Dock Company, who built 198 of the T-2 tankers, is that of hull number 442, and was the 117th tanker to be completed in her construction group. Sun laid the keel on March 23, 1944, and launched the finished ship on July 7, 1944, but it had not been dry-docked prior to trials. The design is that of an all-welded, single screw, turboelectric propelled tanker.

Hull Structure of the T-2 tanker

The shell is of approved thickness with welded seams and butts. The upper deck and inner bottom are flush plated with welded seams and butts. The longitudinal system of framing is used throughout the cargo spaces. Forward of the No. 1 cargo tank and abaft No. 9 cargo tank, transverse framing was employed. There were two deep web transverses in each tank. Shell and deck longitudinals were bracketed through the transverse bulkheads. except through the pump rooms where brackets were installed on both sides of the bulkheads, instead of passing through.

To further strengthen the ship in longitudinal bending, as well as to support the cargo deck above the upper deck, four continuous longitudinals, 30" x 15" x 172" I-beams with top flanges just below the bottom faces of the transverse beams were incorporated into the structure. These longitudinals extend throughout the tank spaces with centers spaced 10' and 25' port and starboard of the centerline.

The cargo deck forward and aft of the midship house, commonly referred to as the "spar deck," was constructed above the upper deck to the level of the walkway. The structural supporting members of this deck comprised, in the main, 5" x 4" angles with flat plate corner brackets and gussets. The deck itself consisted of movable fore and aft lengths of I sections, and the positions could be adjusted to suit the requirements of the deck cargo to be carried.

One of the most remarkable achievements during WWII by a tanker was that of the T-2 tanker *Ohio,* owned by Texas Oil Company (Texaco). The *Ohio* left the River Clyde in Scotland on August 2, 1942, for Malta carrying 13,000 tons of kerosene and fuel oil, desperately needed by the Allied forces.

The convoy headed for Gibraltar, when on the night of August 8, it experienced its first attack by German planes. On the morning of August 11, about sixty miles off the North African coast, the convoy came under continuous air attack again, and by August the 14 the *Ohio,* her rudder smashed, was towed into Malta with only thirty inches of freeboard. The crew still managed to deliver the badly needed kerosene and fuel oil despite the punishment her hull sustained by the bombing from the German planes.

The T-2 Tanker's Propulsion Machinery

A typical marine turboelectric installation was the arrangement for propulsion of the T-2-SE-A1 tanker. Since the operation of turboelectric equipment is similar for practically all ships, an understanding of the operation of T-2 equipment served as an excellent basis for study.

Although there are two engine-room levels on the T-2 tanker, installation is not particularly difficult. After the pedestal-type bearings are mounted, the propulsion motor is lowered into the lower engine flat as a single unit. The main condenser and lower half of the main turbine are also lowered into the hull as a single unit, so that after the engine-room grating was installed, the condenser and the lower half of the turbine were in the lower engine room, and the upper half of the turbine was in the upper engine room. The turbine rotor, upper casing, and the main generator were then lowered and lined up, and the generator and turbine rotors were coupled. The two boilers were located in the after section of the upper engine room and separated from it by a bulkhead. When the two auxiliary turbogenerator units were installed, practically all of the heavy equipment placement was completed.

The operational efficiency in the T-2 tanker was improved by the use of the main turbogenerator supplying power for the cargo and stripping pumps when the cargo was discharged. Power from the auxiliary sets can also be used for this purpose. Other advantages of the system were that the main turbine is unidirectional and can be warmed up without turning the propeller. The turbine can be left idling in port or at anchorage and so permit departure on a very brief stand-by signal. This procedure was extremely useful in wartime when it was necessary to disperse a convoy of ships because of an approaching air attack. Turboelectric driven ships were rated at 6,000 shaft horsepower, had full horsepower astern, could maneuver with great ease, and cruised at 14.5 knots. Another advantage of an electric-drive system was that the failures that occurred could usually be repaired at sea, whereas certain types of gear troubles that occasionally occur on ships with other drives may necessitate a shutdown and tow to port.

A disadvantage of electrical drive was the high initial cost of the installation. Electric-drive installations are also heavier in weight per horsepower than other types of propulsion equipment, but the layout of the installation required less deck and overhead space, and therefore permits more convenient and efficient use of the available space. The running efficiency is slightly less than that of the geared-turbine drive, owing to a loss of approximately three percent in the form of heat losses in the motor and generator windings. The flexibility of the installation is better, and no astern turbine is required. It is important, however, that operating personnel must be able to cope with the complexity of the electrical controls and have a good understanding of alternating current technique.

The majority of marine turboelectric propulsion systems employ alternating current. A single-screw installation of this type may consist of a single, variable-speed, non-reversible turbine operating at approximately 3,600 revolutions per minute and directly connected to a three-phase, two-pole, high-speed alternator. The alternator supplied alternating current to either an induction motor or a multipole synchronous propulsion motor mounted on the propeller shaft. The installation further included an exciter for furnishing direct current to the generator and motor fields and the necessary control equipment.

It is worth noting that, in the years 1940 to 1948, 739 oceangoing tankers were built in the United States of America. Seventy-two percent of these tankers had turboelectric propulsion, eighteen percent had geared-steam turbines, eight percent had steam-reciprocating machinery, and two percent had direct-diesel propulsion.

The lack of manufacturing facilities for mechanical reduction gears during the war was the main reason for the extensive use of turboelectric machinery, rather than its inherent superiority. Since the end of 1945, no turboelectric machinery has been installed. After 1945, all tankers built in the United States have had geared-steam turbine machinery.

The T-2 tanker attained, in addition to numerical supremacy, statistical supremacy by being used as a yardstick in oil transport statistics, as "T-2 equivalents" of about 140,000 barrels. The years immediately after the war, were years of growth, and change in the tanker industry, and the T-2 tanker was used as specimen vessel in the business of trading tankers worldwide. To simplify the trade, a standard measure of cost called "Worldscale" was used for many years. It provided a comparatively straightforward reference gauge for tanker owners and charterers. It was a simple index for a complex market. It evolved from a system set up in November 1952 by two major oil companies and was called the London Tanker Nominal Freight Scales, published by the World Scale Association.

As the size of tankers increased, the T-2 scale became too small, and in 1989, a "New World Scale" was introduced, where the basic reference was a 75,000 dwt tanker with a speed of 14.5 knots using heavy fuel oil of 38 cst at a daily consumption of fifty-five tons. The charter rate was priced in U.S. dollars per ton, for round voyages between stated load or discharge ports.

For the casual observer it is difficult to grasp the difference in size when comparing the linear dimensions, that is, length, breadth, and depth, of the T-2 tanker, with those of today's very large crude oil carriers (VLCCs). By doubling the linear dimensions of a T-2 tanker, the deadweight increase is 14.5 times larger. The 16,800 dwt of the T-2 tanker becomes a VLCC of 240,000 tons.

A prime factor in maintaining today's massive oil flows necessary for today's world requirements is the world fleet of giant tankers that are the direct descendants of the T-2 tanker of World War II. It was during this time that the technology was developed, to design and build today's tanker fleets of VLCCs and ULCCs, described in the chapters that follow.

Phoenix: The Largest All-Welded Tanker, Built during World War II

In 1944, an interesting change occurred in the shipbuilding industry in the United States of America, near the end of the war.

D.K. Ludwig, president of the National Bulk Carriers, Inc., placed an order with the Welding Shipyard, Inc. of Norfolk, Virginia, for the construction of an oil tanker with a deadweight capacity of 23,600 tons.

This was the largest oil tanker of all-welded construction ever built, the design of which was developed by the New York office of Sir Joseph Isherwood, who had introduced the longitudinal framing for tankers in the 1930s.

Model tests were carried out at the National Physical Laboratory at Teddington in the U.K., where consideration was given to investigate the value of a bulbous bow for this particular design, to determine whether the results warranted the additional cost involved. The results of the tests indicated the reduction in resistance was minimal even at seventeen knots, and it was decided to abandon the idea of a bulb at the bow.

The shipyard at Norfolk, Virginia, had a 600-foot building birth and had gained experience in the building of T-2 tankers, with an output of five such tankers per year.

The Ludwig order was for a larger tanker and the first of this size to be built by this shipyard. The time required from keel laying to launching was seventy-six days, with twenty-seven additional days until the commissioning of the tanker.

The shipyard, with the exception of two fifty-ton cranes, had the normal shipyard equipment of that period. It had four automatic welding machines that were used only for the shell, deck panels, and longitudinal and transverse bulkheads.

The remaining welding was done manually. The yard had no riveting equipment available.

The tanker was named *Phoenix,* and it had the following particulars:

Length, Overall	556' 0"
Length, B.P.	541' 0"
Beam	80' 0"
Depth	40" 0"
Draft	31" 4.5"
Deadweight	23,600 tons
Displacement	29,270 tons

Block Coefficient...0.7545
Tank Capacity...217,000 barrels
Speed ....17 knots
Propeller speed...105 rpm
Total time to discharge the cargo ....14 hours
Machinery:
High pressure steam turbines,
High pressure water tube boilers.
Steam conditions ....525 psi
....750° F
Shaft Horse Power..13,200

*The "Inglewood Hills," a T-2 tanker,
one of more than 500 built to carry
fuels to Allied nations.*

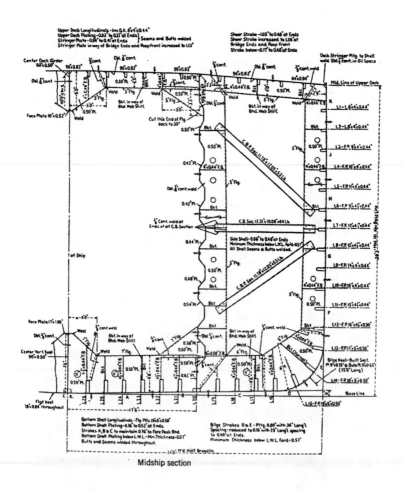

Midship section

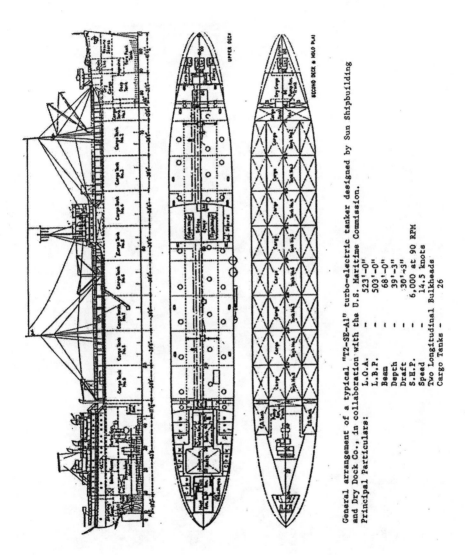

General arrangement of a typical "T2-SE-A1" turbo-electric tanker designed by Sun Shipbuilding and Dry Dock Co., in collaboration with the U.S. Maritime Commission.

Principal Particulars:

L.O.A.	—	523'-0"
L.B.P.	—	503'-0"
Beam	—	68'-0"
Depth	—	39'-3"
Draft	—	30'-3"
S.H.P.	—	6,000 at 90 RPM
Speed	—	14.5 knots
Two Longitudinal Bulkheads		
Cargo Tanks —		26

—View of S. S. *Schenectady* after splitting in two at her outfitting dock.

-S. S. *Schenectady*, view inside crack showing complete fracture of longitudinal bulkheads.

—Aerial view of failure of *S. S. Esso Manhattan* taken from one of two blimps convoying vessel.

TWO

The Suez Canal—Its Influence on Oil Tanker Size

The idea of a canal linking the Mediterranean Sea to the Red Sea dates back to 600 BC. The first Canal was dug during the Pharaoh Necho period and was apparently completed during the Persian invasion of Egypt by King Darius I.

The Suez Canal consists of two parts, the first linking the Gulf of Suez to the Great Bitter Lake, and the second connecting the Lake to one of branches of the Nile delta. Over the years, it fell into disrepair and was completely abandoned when the trade route around Africa was discovered.

In 1854, by a French initiative, the viceroy of Egypt, Said Pasha, decided to build a canal connecting the Mediterranean Sea with the Red Sea that would shorten the route to India. A final attempt to dig the canal was undertaken by Ferdinand de Lesseps, who was granted a decree to operate the Canal for ninety-nine years after it was completed.

In 1858, La Compagnie Universelle du Canal Maritime de Suez was formed to construct the canal. The company was owned by French and Egyptian interests, and administered the canal for ninety-nine years.

Construction of the Canal started in April 1859 and by November 1869, the canal was opened for navigation, having a width at the bottom of the Canal of twenty-two meters, a surface width of fifty-eight meters, and a depth of eight meters. The length of the Canal is 163 km, and it has no locks.

Proceeding south from Port Said, it runs in an almost straight line to Lake Timsah. From there, a cutting leads to the Bitter Lake and reaches the Gulf of Suez, thus connecting the Mediterranean Sea with the Gulf of Suez and thence with the Red Sea.

In 1875 the British Government purchased the Egyptian interest and became the largest shareholder.

In 1888, all major European powers signed the Constantinople Convention, declaring the canal neutral and guaranteeing free passage to all in time of peace and war, with Britain being the guarantor of the neutrality of the canal. Over the years, the canal was dredged and widened.

In 1936, through a treaty, the British obtained the right to keep military forces in the canal zone.

In June 1956, all British troops left the canal zone and the Egyptian military moved into British installations.

In July 1956, Egypt nationalized the canal, and in October 1956, France and Britain attacked Egypt under the pretext that they wanted to open the canal to all vessels. Egypt answered with the sinking of forty ships that were inside the canal at the time.

In March 1957, the canal was reopened following United Nations action to remove the wrecks.

In June 1967, as a result of the Six-Day War with Israel, Egypt closed the canal for the second time in a decade. It was during this time that the tanker industry, in order to meet the demand for oil transportation, designed and built the much larger tankers. The tankers were too large for the Suez Canal and alternate sea routes increasingly were used.

The Suez Canal, after being closed for 8 years, reopened in June 1975. The reopening made little difference, because most of the tankers were now too large to use the canal. Another reason that contributed to the reduced Suez Canal use by tankers was the growth of offshore oil fields in the North Sea, Alaska, and the Gulf of Mexico.

The closing of the Suez Canal on two occasions provided the impetus for Europe to deepen its oil ports such as Genoa, Foss-Sur-Mer, and Rotterdam, and to locate new refineries at deep water sites, effectively removing all restraints on growth in tanker size.

It is worth noting that, although the Suez Canal was first opened for navigation in November 1867 when eighty full-fledged oil tankers were sailing transatlantic routes, the first oil tanker allowed to transit the canal was the steam tanker *Murex*. This was a 4,950 dwt-tanker built in 1892 in the U.K. for Messrs. Marcus Samuel & Co. of London, now Shell Oil. The *Murex* sailed through the Suez Canal on August 24, 1892, carrying a cargo of Russian kerosene in bulk, from the Black Sea part of Batum to Thailand. The *Murex*, because of her design, has also been credited with satisfying all safety requirements by the Suez Canal Authorities at the time, enabling the tanker to make the passage in loaded condition carrying oil in bulk.

Increase in Tanker Size and Change in Profile

An important development in tanker hull structure design occurred in 1906 when the transverse framing of the hull in the way of the cargo tanks was changed to longitudinal framing. The change resulted in far greater longitudinal strength and became known as the Joseph Isherwood system of cargo tank configuration. The structural modifications introduced by Isherwood in 1906, and again in 1925, resulted in the construction of tankers in excess of 20,000 dwt. In 1938, the total world's tanker fleet was 16.6 million tons without one tanker being more than 25,000 dwt. By 1945, the United States of America, had the largest tanker fleet in the world.

The post-World War II demand for oil increased dramatically, and by 1950, the world tanker fleet had grown to 27.6 million dwt, yet of that total only 1.5 million tons was being transported on tankers larger than 25,000 tons. This however was not because larger tankers could not be built. Tanker size limitation factors were neither technological nor design-influenced; the primary limitation was the size of the Suez Canal.

Another significant change was that of the tanker profile. The oceangoing tankers of the 1940s and 1950s were of the *three islands* configuration, with forecastle, midship, and poop deckhouses, and with catwalks providing access between the three islands as well as housing piping and electric cables between the three islands. The navigation bridge and deck officers' quarters were located in the midship deckhouse, while the engineers and remaining crew, the galley, mess rooms, and recreation rooms were located aft at the poop deckhouse. Two of the supertankers of the time, the *Tina Onassis* and the *Al-Malik Saud Al-Awal,* built with the three islands arrangement.

Both tankers were built in Hamburg, Germany. The *Tina Onassis,* with a capacity of 45,000 dwt, entered service in 1953, and was the largest crude oil carrier in service at that time. The tanker, in addition to having a robust structure that was well above classification rule requirements, was described in the U.K. maritime press as, "one that deserves a place in maritime history, in being the most outstanding handsome tanker the world had seen—or indeed is ever likely to see."

The *Al-Malik Saud Al-Awal,* with a capacity of 47,000 dwt and of similar appearance and construction, was not strictly a sister ship, because a fractional increase in the tanker's beam gave this tanker, which entered service in 1954, the edge on tonnage over the *Tina Onassis.* It was during this period that Mr. Onassis was discussing a form of cooperation with the Saudi Arabian authorities and this was upsetting the major oil companies who issued the famous cautionary note, *Quo Vadis Onassis*.

In the late 1950s, the configuration changed, and the navigation bridge and midship accommodation were moved aft and became part of the poop super structure. The change made good sense, because it reduced construction as well as maintenance costs, and allowed access to mess and recreation rooms, irrespective of weather conditions outside.

It was during this period when the ocean tanker profile was streamlined, and several items in the design that belonged to a different age were eliminated or simplified. Tankers were originally designed specifically for long haul crude oil service. The aim of the newer tanker designer was to obtain a more functional design without detracting from the safety, reliability, and good performance of the tanker.

Cargo handling was arranged through one cargo pump room, located forward of the engine room, with the driving units located in the engine room. The changes made were necessary, because as the number of tankers increased, the availability of properly trained officers and crew to man the tankers became an important consideration.

Despite the structural changes that resulted in a more robust structure, tankers of more than 25,000 dwt were very rare and remained so well into the 1950s. The reason for the reluctance to build larger tankers was the question of profitability. In theory, it is more profitable to move large amounts of oil in single tankers across the oceans. The question of economics of scale did not apply, because ports were limited in their ability to handle large tankers. Tanker owners had no incentive to build larger tankers, and no one who wished to carry oil profitably between Europe and the Far East would consider going around the Cape of Good Hope. The passage through the Suez Canal was still the most direct and cost-efficient route. That in turn meant the optimum tanker size was the size suitable to transit the Suez Canal.

By 1954, the Suez Canal was deepened and widened, which allowed tankers of 32,000 dwt to transit the canal. Closing the canal for several months in 1956 created problems for the industrialized free world, and the question was how to bring the oil from the Persian/Arabian Gulf to a suitable point in the Mediterranean.

One thought was by pipeline through Syria. The other way, was around the Cape of Good Hope. A pipeline through Syria was considered vulnerable to sabotage. The Cape of Good Hope alternative meant a long voyage, and although more secure than the pipeline idea, using smaller tankers for such a voyage was not economical.

To overcome the problem of draft limitation and still be able to use the Suez Canal, some carriers would take a partial cargo of Persian Gulf crude oil through the canal then top off their load in the Eastern Mediterranean at Tripoli or Banias. This of course was dependent upon the availability of crude oil at these ports.

The notion that the Suez Canal may open in the near future necessitated that the tanker industry do some careful and complex arithmetic on the economics of using the Suez Canal versus the Cape of Good Hope route. It should be noted that the Suez Canal dues are based on the tanker's Suez Canal tonnage, which was close to the tanker's net tonnage.

In the case of an oil tanker the two factors that affected the use of the Suez Canal equation was the price of bunkers, which had increased dramatically since 1967. This had also contributed to making those extra days of steaming around the Cape of Good Hope less attractive.

The other factor was the increase in the value of cargoes. Every extra day of steaming meant more interest must be paid. Never before had there been such a need for big tankers. The time of the supertanker had arrived.

Closing the Suez Canal on two occasions provided the impetus for Europe to deepen its oil ports such as Genoa, Foss-Sur-Mer, and Rotterdam and to locate new refineries at deep water sites effectively removing all restraints on growth in crude oil carrier size.

In building up the free world's tanker fleet, the emphasis was on the size of the tankers and the ability of ports, like Genoa in Italy or Foss-Sur-Mer in France, to service VLCCs that took the Cape of Good Hope route. Tanker activity through the Suez Canal was not as hectic as in the pre-1967 period.

Development of the Supertanker

The problems associated with this size of tanker at the early stages of its development including the following:

- Determination of the principal dimensions, particularly draft requirements at loading and discharging ports. For Europe, the tanker terminals in Foss-Sur-Mer in Southern France and Le Havre in Northern France were able in 1975 to accept tankers with a draft of twenty-five meters. By 1978 tankers with a draft of twenty-eight meters could be also accepted. Rotterdam, at Europort, was designed to accept a draft of around twenty-nine meters, even with the rather limited water depth in the English Channel and the North Sea near the Hook of Holland. For North America, new cargo transfer stations (CTS) were being planned, capable of handling tankers with a draft of twenty-five to thirty meters.

- Consideration of the economic efficiency of the new design. Developers had to keep in mind compliance with regulatory requirements, of IMO and other governing bodies for cargo and ballast tank configuration, such as the Segregated Ballast Rule.

- The speed and power requirements, which in turn would decide whether single or twin screw arrangement.

- Maneuverability, especially in confined waters. Our company's experience with large tankers was that handling them was different from handling smaller tankers but not difficult. Therefore handling large tankers presented no difficulty or greater risk.

- Extent of automation for the propulsion plant, navigation, as well as cargo handling, all of which would affect the manning of the large tankers.

- Availability of existing or planned dry docks and repair facilities.

- Economy of scale. This was an important consideration aimed at reducing the per-ton cost of building the larger tanker.

It is for the above reasons that the naval architect has more influence on ship economics and ship safety than any other profession.

It is also important to recognize the fact that irrespective of a shipbuilder's or classification society's reputation, the owner must take an active interest in the details of the design and follow closely the design and construction of the tanker, considering the enormity of the investment.

The tanker industry has seen tremendous increases in tanker size since World War II particularly with the crude oil carrier. This necessitated change in the design, construction and in the operation of these large tankers, in order to meet the demands of the times for crude oil transportation.

Tanker structures became progressively more complex, requiring design and optimization techniques to achieve innovative approaches to cost effective improvements. Unfortunately, developments in the building of these large structures happened faster than the experience gained. This has left many questions to be answered, and presents demanding new challenges to preventing oil pollution of the seas by oil tanker accidents.

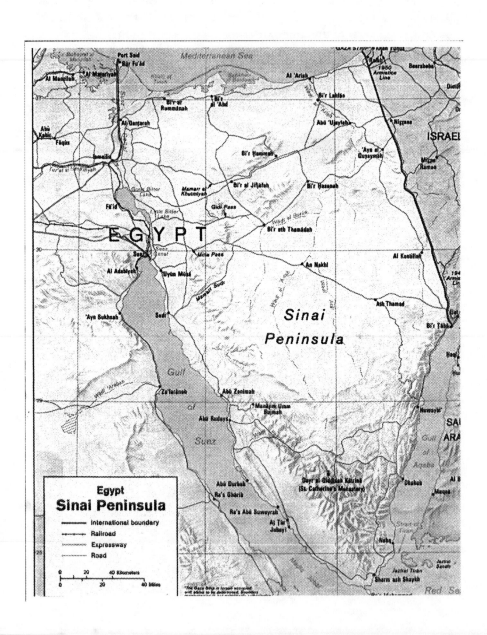

Egypt
Sinai Peninsula

International boundary
Railroad
Expressway
Road

0   20   40 Kilometers
0   20   40 Miles

SUEZ CANAL

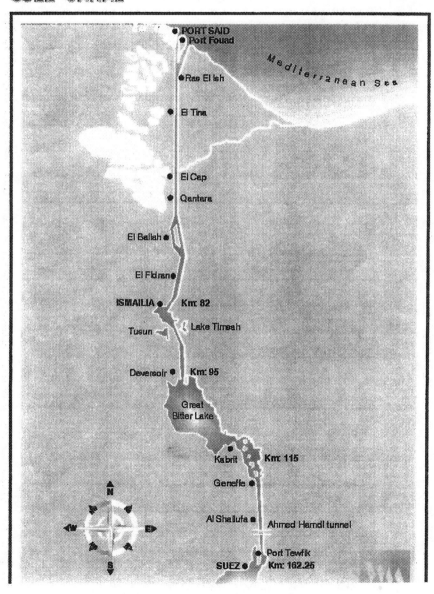

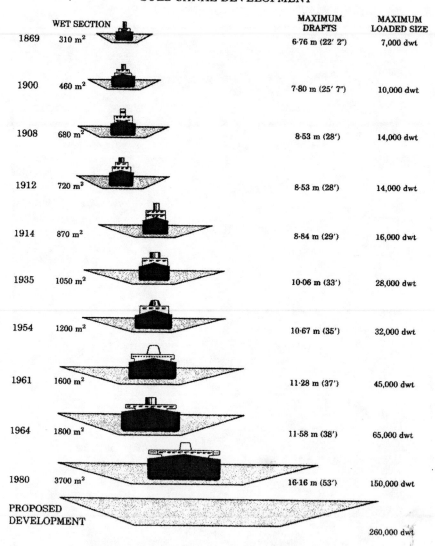

SUEZ CANAL DEVELOPMENT

	WET SECTION		MAXIMUM DRAFTS	MAXIMUM LOADED SIZE
1869	310 m²		6·76 m (22' 2")	7,000 dwt
1900	460 m²		7·80 m (25' 7")	10,000 dwt
1908	680 m²		8·53 m (28')	14,000 dwt
1912	720 m²		8·53 m (28')	14,000 dwt
1914	870 m²		8·84 m (29')	16,000 dwt
1935	1050 m²		10·06 m (33')	28,000 dwt
1954	1200 m²		10·67 m (35')	32,000 dwt
1961	1600 m²		11·28 m (37')	45,000 dwt
1964	1800 m²		11·58 m (38')	65,000 dwt
1980	3700 m²		16·16 m (53')	150,000 dwt
PROPOSED DEVELOPMENT				260,000 dwt

THE CANAL WAS CLOSED TWICE
FIRST IN OCTOBER 1956 TO MARCH 1957
AND AGAIN IN JUNE 1967 TO JUNE 1975

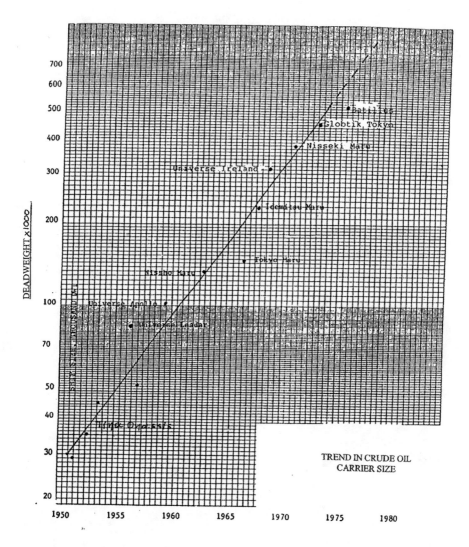

TREND IN CRUDE OIL
CARRIER SIZE

YEAR DELIVERED TO OWNERS

PROFILE OF CRUDE OIL CARRIERS

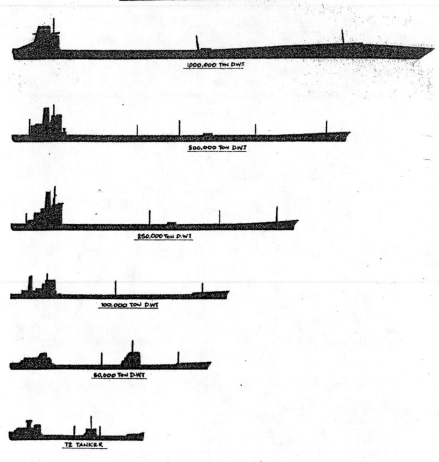

DEVELOPMENT OF THE CRUDE OIL CARRIER
1940 – 1975

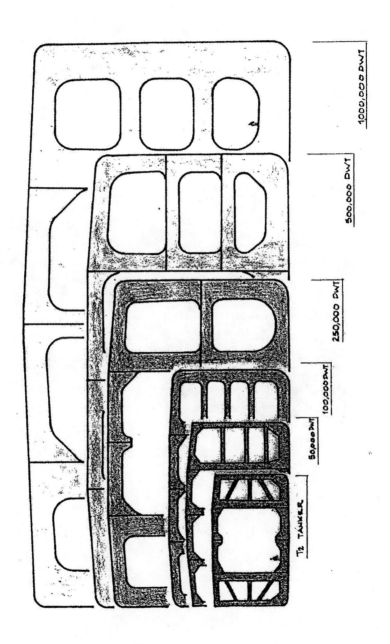

MID-SHIP SECTION OF CRUDE OIL CARRIERS

Above; the supertanker "TINA ONASSIS" of 45,000 dwt., discharging at Rotterdam – Holland in 1956.

On the left, the Author (wearing beret), discussing with Lloyds' Register of Shipping representatives, Tom Bunyon and Simon Archer, the sea-trial results of the "TINA ONASSIS", in Hamburg – Germany in 1953.

The tanker SS *Manhattan*: length 940 ft, beam 132 ft, deadweight 108,590 tons. Delivered in 1962, the *Manhattan* has twin propellers and rudders, a cargo capacity of more than 38 million gallons, and a top speed of 19 knots.

THE VLCC "OLYMPIC ARMOUR" OF 219,000 DWT. IN BALLAST CONDITION

THE VLCC "OLYMPIC BOND" OF 265,000 DWT. IN LOADED CONDITION

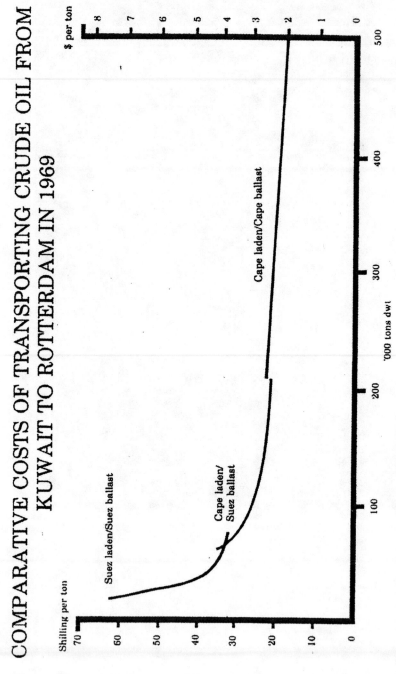

COMPARATIVE COSTS OF TRANSPORTING CRUDE OIL FROM
KUWAIT TO ROTTERDAM IN 1969

Source: *Royal Dutch Shell Group — "Shell Briefing Service"*

The Author in conversation with Mr. Onassis and son Alexander Onassis attending naming ceremony of the VLCC "OLYMPIC ANTHEM" in 1969 at ST. NAZAIR – FRANCE.

THREE

The Million-Ton Crude Oil Carrier (Projected)

The period between 1950 and 1973 was a time of accelerated world economic growth, a period which the economists refer to as The Golden Age. This growth enabled the shipyards in Japan and in Europe to press the upper limits of tanker size, so that by the late 1960s and early 1970s, the very large, ultra large, and the half-million-deadweight crude oil carriers were a reality.

During this period, the economics of oil transportation favored heavily the use of much larger tankers than the quarter- or half-million-dwt crude oil carriers. It was calculated that the pure economic advantage of a half million-tonner against the quarter million was fairly marginal, and could be offset by the greater flexibility in operation. This is because there were a number of important trading routes that would be practically denied to much bigger tankers. It was during this period that Mr. Onassis, having built sixteen very large crude oil carriers (VLCCs), negotiated the construction of two half-million-dwt carriers in France at Saint-Nazaire shipyard, and was seriously considering building the one-million-dwt crude oil carrier.

Preliminary discussions, for the basic design started in August 1973. In January 1974, the first Super Ocean Carrier Conference (SOCCO) was held in New York, where the author made a presentation titled, "Million-Ton Tanker Fleets." Prior to this presentation, research had been carried out by our office to identify the sea routes and ports that would accommodate this size of tanker, including dry dock availability. A decision also had to be made regarding the hull design and cargo tank configuration to comply with what was then known as IMCO, now IMO. Also, we had to decide whether it should be single-hull with two longitudinal bulkheads; single-hull with three longitudinal bulkheads or double-hull with two longitudinal bulkheads. OPA 90 legislation was not around at that time.

Notwithstanding the economics involved, we had to contemplate other very important considerations with respect to larger tankers. Our office developed a world map identifying the various sea routes and deep water ports that could accommodate these tankers. It was during this time that serious studies were underway to bypass the Suez Canal by providing suitable pipe line to serve Europe. Some also investigated how the Malacca and Lombok Strait might be bypassed by using the Isthmus of Kra in southern Thailand, a route that would better serve Japan.

The main constraint in employing the million-tonner would be the routes and port facilities that could physically accommodate these enormous tankers, and by the reception facilities at the oil terminals. Because of its large draft— around thirty-five meters—this size tanker would be excluded from certain routes to northwestern Europe. The tanker would not be able to enter the North Sea through the English Channel in order to approach the Continent. It may however enter the Mediterranean via the Strait of Gibraltar. This would leave three choices open to the European countries, either create another Bantry Bay to supply northwestern Europe, or make Fos-Sur-Mer, France or Genoa, Italy, what Rotterdam is to northwestern Europe today. For Japan, the million-tonner would have to use the Lombok strait. For the United States of America, there would be no limitations around the Cape of Good Hope.

There were also operational and other problems that had to be resolved, such as the hull structure, because classification societies' rules did not cover a structure of such length, and this was of concern. Could the rules, which at that time covered tanker lengths up to 300 meters, be stretched to cover a tanker 500 meters in length or longer? The scantlings for tankers larger than 300 meters in length must be determined by direct calculation. The accuracy of the direct calculation, which is of paramount importance, could only be verified by stress measurements on board the actual tanker, and if necessary corrective steps would have to be taken on the actual tanker. Therefore at this point experience was most important in the determination of the scantlings.

All of these factors affecting the decision on this important subject were raised and discussed with Mr. Onassis. After some deliberation, the green light was given to initiate discussions with the shipyard in France, and arrangements were made to prepare outline specifications for the million-ton tanker.

Hull Design and Cargo Tank Configuration

The design for the million-tonner was based on a twin screw, twin rudder arrangement and a service speed of sixteen knots. Tank size was to be in accordance with the 1971 IMCO Regulations: no segregated ballast tanks; single-hull, with three longitudinal, oil tight bulkheads; higher tensile steels for deck and bottom plating and for the longitudinal stringers. This structure had no corrosion margin allowance.

Consideration was given to single-screw, single rudder, as well as triple-screw twin-rudder arrangements. For the single-screw single-rudder, the designers found that hull performance was satisfactory, including directional stability. However, because of the size of the rudder, it would have been extremely difficult to handle, erect, and dismantle for removal. The required size of the steering gear was problematic as well. Dry-docking of the single-screw design would result in excessive weight on the keel blocks in the dry dock. For a triple-screw arrangement, the hull lines presented serious problems that affected hull performance.

The twin-screw, twin-rudder, slightly canted, twin-skeg arrangement was considered to give a good hull performance. The arrangement simplified dry-docking and gave a realistic size of the rudder and steering gear equipment. With regard to dry-docking these million-ton tankers, careful consideration was given to the compressive stresses that would be imposed on the ship's structure. Particular attention was given to the loads on the two skegs. Dry dock representatives were consulted in an effort to determine the reaction forces on the supporting blocks in the dry dock, particularly the keel block forces.

The three-longitudinal oil tight bulkhead arrangement would contribute to the hull strength. This arrangement resulted in thirty-four wing tanks, twenty center tanks, and four slop tanks, giving a total of fifty-eight tanks. The length of the wing tanks was the IMCO Regulation length of twenty meters, which was also suitable for the construction and production facilities of the shipyard at Saint-Nazaire. It was considered very important to ensure and maintain continuity of the longitudinal members of the structure from bow to stern.

The strength and stiffening arrangements of the bow were also carefully considered, and the designers decided that vertical stiffening would be better than horizontal for the main stiffening members in the bow area. This was particularly important, because, the bow shape and bow height would be arranged to minimize "deck wetness," and to provide additional reserve buoyancy, which would influence the pitching motion in extreme seas.

The study to determine the economical speed for this design resulted in a service speed of sixteen knots. However, with fuel oil prices as of August 1973, the most economical speed would be around fourteen knots.

The principal dimensions of the basic design were:

Length B.P.:..476.00 m
Breadth: ....80.00 m
Depth:..43.00 m
Draft: ....35.00 m
Deadweight:..1,000,000 tons
Block Coefficient:...0.86
L/B: 5.95
Net steel weight (no corrosion margin)............140,000 tons metric.
Steel weight/Deadweight 0.140
Twin Screw Arrangement
Total shaft Horse Power:..................................82,000

Structurally, the design was considered to be superior to the VLCCs and ULCCs in existence at the time and much stronger than the designs that entered service after the 1950s. The reason was that the tank configuration, with its three longitudinal oil tight bulkhead arrangement, would provide much better support to the hull girder, resulting in a more robust structure.

From the point of view of hull vibrations, consideration was given to the possibility of having to face such a problem. After preliminary studies of the masses and forces involved, designers concluded that the question of hull vibrations should be of no concern. The twin screw arrangement was especially helpful in this regard. The propellers are arranged away from the hull structure, and the exciting forces are not large enough to create problems, particularly since the propulsion power would be shared between the two propellers. Some minor panel vibrations could be created, but this would be local, of no consequence, and would be dealt with easily if and when they occurred.

During the period this study was underway, and because of the increase in propulsion power, engineers encountered propeller shaft alignment problems as a result of structural deflection of engine room's double bottom structure. Here again careful thought was given to the structural arrangement of the propeller shaft bearing supporting structure. There were also problems with the stern tube seals. It was known at the time that such seals, particularly seals made in Europe, could be used successfully up to a power of 60,000 on one shaft. We could therefore use the European seals and expect no problems. But of course, there will always be doubts associated with anything as visionary as this project, and only a shipyard with superior technical competence could be entrusted to undertake such a project.

Another question that caused some concern was that of maneuvering. The feeling was that large tankers are unwieldy and consequently at greater risk. After carefully studying the subject, engineers decided that the handling of big tankers is different, but not necessarily difficult. Provided this difference is appreciated by the handler, and the tanker is operated in a safe environment, no greater risk should ensue. Designers concluded that problems arise when tanker size begins to outgrow the operating environment such as estuaries, port facilities, and so forth, but this can happen to any size of tanker.

An item to which we gave some thought was the location of the draft marks. On a tanker with a B.P. length of almost half a kilometer, determining the displacement from the drafts at the traditional location would not be accurate because of the longitudinal deflection of the elastic hull. A more suitable location to position the draft marks had to be determined.

Other items of concern, where there was no previous experience included the following:

- Mooring, anchoring, and emergency stopping.

Designers carefully considered the means for operating and handling the mooring arrangements, specifically that the mooring ropes would have to be handled mechanically because of their size. An alternative method of securing this size of tanker at her berth would be to use tugs that will hold the tanker at a predetermined location while loading or discharging. With regard to anchoring, using the conventional means of handling the anchor windlass might not be suitable because of the size of the anchors and cables. Designers considered hydraulic or other means to handle the anchor.

Emergency stopping was one of the questions that occupied our thoughts for some time, and we had decided to carry out research work on three possibilities.

(a) Provide controllable fins or flaps housed at either side of the tanker. The fins or flaps would be operated in an emergency, which would act as a brake on the hull.

(b) Design in the bulb at the bow, an arrangement of gate valves that would open, flooding the bulb space, providing a braking effect on the hull.

(c) Use of parachutes, located at the stern and released in the water, thus providing a braking effect to assist in slowing or stopping the tanker in an emergency.

- Survey and dry-docking:

We had concluded that surveying the million-ton tanker would differ little in procedure from similar surveys on a VLCC, ULCC, or even smaller tankers. It is only the physical size of these tankers that will make survey work a problem. It was necessary therefore that, careful and serious thought was given during the design stage so that survey work could be done safely, effectively, and rapidly. At a seminar arranged by the American Bureau of Shipping in February 1992 in Houston, Texas, the subject was "Tanker Designs for the 21st Century." The seminar was attended by representatives of three major oil companies, the U.S. Coast Guard, as well as shipowners and operators.

One of the items discussed at this seminar was some owners' philosophy with respect to maintenance, inspection, and repair in the design of double hull tankers, and there was agreement that a double hull tanker design should be "surveyor friendly." It was pointed out during this gathering that one possible solution to this problem would be to construct side stringers in the wing tanks forming inspection walkways that would permit all coatings and structures in the wing ballast tanks to be closely and easily inspected. Also maintenance of the coatings and of the steel structure could be carried out without staging the tanks. It was also pointed out that in very large crude oil carriers having wing ballast tanks, it may not be practical to fit stringers extending the full width of the tanks. In such cases, extended or oversized longitudinals with a protective guardrail should be fitted. What was not mentioned at the seminar was the problem of inspecting the deckhead structure, both in the ballast and in the cargo tanks.

This was one of the subjects we discussed extensively with Mr. Onassis in the late 1960s when we were developing the design for the one million ton tanker. We decided to engage someone who could help us develop a design for a portable, removable arrangement that could be inserted into the tanks through the cargo hatch and move around using the butterworth openings on deck. This portable arrangement could cover the entire deckhead area or any part of the tank structure for close inspection, without tank staging or tank flooding.

Dr. Henry J. Modrey of Stamford, Connecticut, was engaged to develop such an arrangement, and he visited several of our VLCCs in service and under construction in Japan and Europe, which enabled him to understand what I really had in mind for the inspection of the structure to be accomplished by those who had to do the job safely and in comfort. The result was the "Tank Inspection Carousel" for which a U.S. patent was awarded in November 1969. During the development of the million-tonner, there were two other items that were troubling me. The propulsion machinery was to be steam turbines, and that meant water tube condensing equipment. I wanted to be able to effect repairs to condenser tubing, if it became necessary, without dry-docking the ship, should there be a problem with securing the sea chest valve that supplied circulating seawater to the condensers.

The other item was to find a solution to the painting of the outside of the hull by the crew. In the case of our other tankers, the crew would arrange staging, which was secured from the deck rails and put over the side where painting was done by the crew. Further discussions were arranged again with Dr. Modrey, who produced a design for the condenser sea valve, which we named "temporary sea valve closure". This was to be used in the event the sea chest valve could not be made tight from the engine room. Additionally, without having to dry-dock the tanker, a diver could insert the specially designed plug in the sea chest valve that would prevent sea water from entering the condenser. When repairs to the condenser were completed, the diver could remove the plug and replace the sea chest grating. A U.S. patent was also awarded for this idea in November 1969.

On the question of painting both the vertical sides and the flat bottom of the hull of the tanker, a remotely controlled, automatic paint applicator was developed to enable the crew to paint the hull while the tanker was afloat. The advantage of the paint applicator was its ability to automatically produce paint pressure by the action of magnets, independently from the operator. The principle of magnetic adhesion was used to its advantage, and it greatly improved painting process when compared to manual painting. The U.S. patent application for this device was entered in December 1968.

So far as the million-tonner was concerned, by the end of 1976, at least four dry-docking facilities were to be available to accommodate this size of tanker, and by 1980 three more dry docks for this size of tanker would be in service. All of these facilities would be available in locations around the world, such as the Persian Gulf, West Africa, the Mediterranean, northwest Europe, the southern United States, South America, and Southeast Asia.

Despite the fact that there is an inherent risk of damage in and high cost of dry-docking these large vessels, it is the best and quickest way to carry out survey work and any difficult ship "surgery" that may be required. Is there another way to carry out repairs to these large tankers other than in a dry dock? There is such a method, and we called it, "repairs in the afloat" condition. We used just such a method very successfully on two of our tankers, the *Olympic Runner* and the *Olympic Rider* in 1966. These were sister ships, 48,100 dwt each, built in Japan in November 1959 and January 1960 respectively. The tankers were cut athwartship into two sections through cargo tank no. 3. The main deck was raised to the level of the poop house deck, by cutting horizontally through the second strake below the sheer strake and inserting a newly fabricated belt. The existing forecastle was also raised. This afloat enlargement increased the dead-weight of each tanker by 10,000 tons. Because of this experience, I felt confident if need be, we could undertake important repair work to the hull of the million-tonner without going in dry dock.

With regard to survey work of the underwater part of the hull while afloat, there are available facilities, using high-resolution video to examine the entire hull area and appendages. To facilitate such survey work, we planned to paint hull markings so that different locations of the ship's hull could be readily identified by a diver or when using remotely controlled video equipment.

I had the opportunity to successfully use high-resolution video equipment when our company decided to take over a VLCC that was abandoned by the original owner, prior to taking delivery from the shipyard. We agreed not to dry-dock the tanker before taking delivery, provided the video examination of the underwater parts of the hull showed no signs of any problems on the hull structure or the appendages. In fact when we took over the tanker, it was named *Aristotle S. Onassis*.

The Million-Tonner and the "Squat Phenomenon"

Engineers were concerned about the effects of the "squat phenomenon," and how it would affect this size of tanker. Squatting is the bodily sinkage that results in loss of under-keel clearance as the tanker sails forward in confined and shallow waters, compared with the keel clearance when the tanker is stationary.

"Squat" is directly related to the ship's block coefficient and varies with the ship's speed. Also, full-form ships, such as tankers, squat more than finer-form ships, such as container carriers. The question was, "What should be the allowed minimum keel-clearance for the safe navigation of the million-ton tanker?"

The squat-phenomenon was one of the subjects we discussed with our VLCC captains during our regular meetings to analyze their experiences in the handling of these large tankers. The company owned nineteen VLCCs; the largest one was the 260,000 dwt *Olympic Bond*. We learned that the pilots who assisted with navigation on our VLCCs only knew enough to caution the captains about squat, but not about preventing it. It was one of the subjects placed in our agenda for thorough research, in order to understand and be able to determine the effects of ship squat.

Since the early 1970s, a great deal of research has been done worldwide, to understand more fully this phenomenon, and the results of the latest efforts to measure and quantify ship squat in shallow waters and confined channels were presented at an international gathering in Elsfleth, Oldenburg, Germany, in March of 2004.

Aesthetics: Deciding the Tanker's Profile

A well-known American tanker owner, when asked to consider the shape of the smoke stack for his tankers, responded, "How much oil can we carry in a smoke stack?" With some imagination and a little ingenuity, the cost a achieving a pleasant profile is reasonable. Two items in which Mr. Onassis took personal interest were the tanker's profile and the crew accommodations. For these, I made arrangements with the designer of the interior of the U.S. Space Capsule to meet in Paris. I spent several hours explaining to the designer what an oil tanker does and what Mr. Onassis would like to see in the profile. The profile for the million tonner is shown at the end of this Chapter.

Because the overall length is in excess of 500 meters, the main-deck sheer appears to be a negative sheer. This effect was achieved by increasing the height of the bulwark at the fore end. This would also serve as protection, helping to reduce the amount of "green seas" landing on the main deck forward, which could cause damage to main deck fittings. The enormous mass of this tanker traveling at a speed of fifteen knots would sail through a head sea rather than rise on a wave.

To some people in the late 1960s, the idea of the million-ton tanker was little more than a sensational headline in the mass media, and there were predictions of the likely difficulties that would be faced in this quantum leap-forward in crude oil carrier size. This was the period when technological progress in the design and construction of commercial ships was considered to be equal to all progress made in the previous 200 years, particularly in the crude oil and bulk carrier class of ships. Even during this time, our ignorance exceeded our knowledge.

The economics of ocean transportation and the increasing and continuing demand for energy supplies were shaping and propelling this development. During the early 1970s, the implications of oil price increases were so enormous that in the judgment of some experts, they threatened the economic and monetary stability of the world. It was felt at the time that price, not embargo, was the key political issue. The energy problem transcends national boundaries. The Western world had to think bigger and bigger in terms of appropriate solutions, and the transportation of crude oil would be important to these solutions. In order to succeed, radical technological improvements and innovations in the shipping industry were needed, and such changes and innovations were bound to create problems. The idea, however, was to succeed and to make building and operating these very large crude oil carriers an asset, not a liability.

An important reason to go for the large size tankers is the lower building cost per deadweight ton, reflected in the cost of transporting the oil. Also, instead of thirty-one T-2 tankers, you could have one half-million-tonner, or instead of sixty-two T-2 tankers, you could have one million-tonner.

With the T-2s, then, you would require thirty-one or sixty-two times as many seafarers as you might have on one of the larger tankers. Deaths or accident risks on board the T-2 tanker may be considered to be about the same as for the seafarers on board the large tankers. And with respect to pollution of the seas and atmospheric pollution, more ships would produce more pollution.

By the middle 1970s, the tanker freight market had collapsed, and the decision was made to abandon our plans for this project. We terminated negotiations for the building of the two half-million-tonners at Saint-Nazaire in France. Mr. Onassis died in March 1975.

The ULCC *Jahre Viking*

The 564,763 dwt *Jahre Viking* is the largest tanker afloat today. The tanker was originally ordered by the Nomikos Group in Japan as a 400,000 dwt tanker in the early 1970s. The collapse of the freight market in mid-1974 forced the Nomikos Group to abandon the contract, which was taken over by the C.Y. Tung Group.

The new owners lengthened the tanker at N.K.K.'s Tsu shipyard in Japan, which resulted in the new deadweight rating, making the tanker the largest mobile steel structure. The ship was named *Seawise Giant*. In 1978, during the Iran-Iraq war, the tanker was heavily damaged. It was later taken over by the Jahre Group of Norway, repaired at the Keppel shipyard in Singapore in 1991, and was renamed *Jahre Viking*.

The ULCC *Batillus*

In Europe, the largest crude oil carrier built is the 500,001 dwt *Batillus*, built in 1976 by Chantiers De L'Atlantique, in Saint-Nazaire, France, for Shell Oil.

The tanker's measurements are:

Length Over All	414.21 m
Length Between Perpendiculars	401.07 m
Breadth	63.01 m
Depth	35.90 m
Draft	28.50 m

Twin Screw, Twin Rudder arrangement

Transporting Crude Oil Using the "Delta" System

The draft restrictions preventing the million-ton tanker from bringing crude oil to oil terminals in northwestern Europe were considered a challenge. My office, with the approval of Mr. Onassis, set out to research and if possible overcome the draft obstacles. The result was the genesis of the "Delta" system of sea transportation shown at the end of this Chapter. The design, for which patents were obtained in the United States, Europe, and Japan in 1972–73, consists of a "mother ship," that accommodates four "caissons" of identical dimensions and tank configuration, each capable of carrying 250,000 tons of crude oil.

The principle of the system is this: upon arrival, loaded at a suitable offshore anchorage, each caisson would be detached from the mother ship, and towed to the oil terminal to discharge the cargo of oil. Discharging of the cargo would be accomplished by the diesel-electric pumping arrangement installed on each caisson through the assistance of on-shore personnel. The same personnel would then crude-oil-wash the cargo tanks, ballast the caissons, then it would be towed back to the mother ship.

By suitably adjusting the ballast of the mother ship, the caissons would be secured onto the mother ship for the return trip to the loading port. The mother ship would be riding on the caissons, while providing the necessary propulsion power and other navigational requirements to complete the voyage. The crew for navigation and handling of the system would be accommodated on the mother ship.

Building the caissons, would have presented no problem because there were several shipyards in Europe and the Far East with suitable building facilities. The challenge was the construction of the mother ship. The only way to build such a structure would have been by constructing the prefabricated sections in existing building facilities, then join them in an afloat condition using the same method we had used for the enlargement of our tankers *Olympic Runner* and *Olympic Rider* in Yokohama, Japan, in 1966. The method was fully described in a presentation by the Mitsubishi Heavy Industries representatives to members of the U.S. Welding Institute in 1968. A brief description of the method is given in the following pages.

A Two-Dimensional Enlargement of Crude Oil Carriers while Afloat

The purpose of adopting this method of enlargement, also known as the T-type enlargement, was to minimize the number of days necessary for the tanker to be in dry dock.

After discussing the idea with Mr. Onassis, and despite his reservations on the success of this type of enlargement, he agreed we should proceed. Two sister ships were selected from our fleet of tankers, the *Olympic Runner* and *Olympic Rider* built in Japan in November 1959 and January 1960 respectively, each having a deadweight of 48,100 tons.

In the meantime, consultations were carried out with the Classification Society—in this case Lloyd's Register of Shipping—and the Welding Institute of Japan. We also consulted with the builders of these two tankers who were to carry out the modifications to the hull structure in order to increase the tanker's deadweight afloat, instead in a dry dock. This was a new and rather unique way to carry out such an extensive and important hull structure modification afloat, and there were some doubts as to the success of the undertaking.

Prefabrication of the new parallel mid-body started soon after the technical specifications and the building contract were signed on March 2, 1966. Early in June 1966, both tankers were brought to the port of Yokohama in gas free condition and ready for hot work.

The *Olympic Runner* and *Olympic Rider* were of the three island arrangement, that is, poop house, midship house, and forecastle, which was typical of this vintage of tankers. The tankers were cut athwartship into two sections through cargo tank No. 3. The main deck was raised to the level of the poop house deck, that is 2.5 m, by cutting horizontally through the second strake below the sheer strake, and inserting a newly fabricated belt 2.5 m wide. The existing forecastle was also raised 2.5 m. Additional local stiffening and other primary hull-strength reinforcements were provided in accordance with the classification society's requirements. All such work was carried out in the afloat condition.

The rudder, rudder stock, and the steering gear were not affected by the increase in the principal dimensions. Anchors, anchor chains, and mooring lines, however, were replaced, and cargo and stripping lines were modified accordingly.

Upon completion of the modifications and changes, Suez and Panama Canal Navigational Rules as well as International Load Line and Safety of Life at Sea Convention 1960 requirements were met with respect to the larger size of the tanker.

The following table compares the original with the enlarged principal particulars of these two tankers.

	Original	Enlarged
L.B.P.	204.00 m	240.26 m
Breadth	28.80 m	28.80 m
Depth	14.70 m	17.20 m
Draft	10.79 m	12.50 m
Deadweight	48,112.00 LT	58,900.00 LT

An increase of 10,788 long tons in deadweight was the result of this effort. The parallel midbody had added a length of thirty-six meters. During this time, the opportunity was taken to carry out steel renewals of the existing hull structure as found necessary, and after successful sea trials, both tankers sailed from Yokohama at the end of September 1966.

The cost of this enlargement was US$1,482,500 for each tanker, or $137.42 per long ton deadweight increase. After the enlargement, both tankers traded successfully for many years, until it was decided by the owners their useful life was over. The *Olympic Runner* was brought to the breakers' yard for recycling in August 1978, and the *Olympic. Rider* in March 1979.

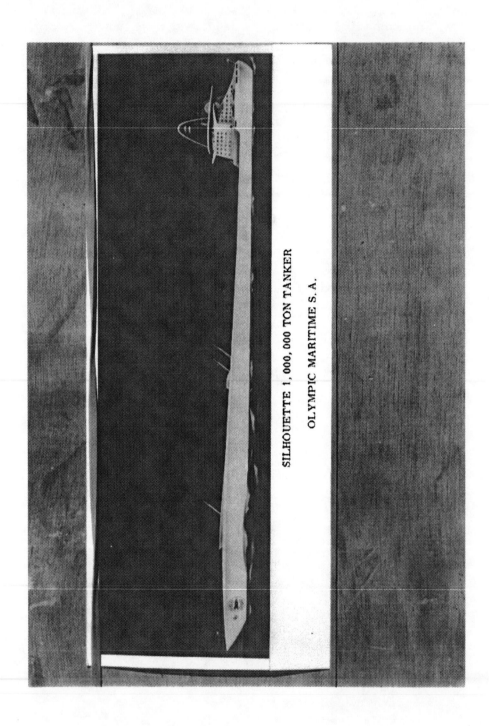

SILHOUETTE 1,000,000 TON TANKER

OLYMPIC MARITIME S.A.

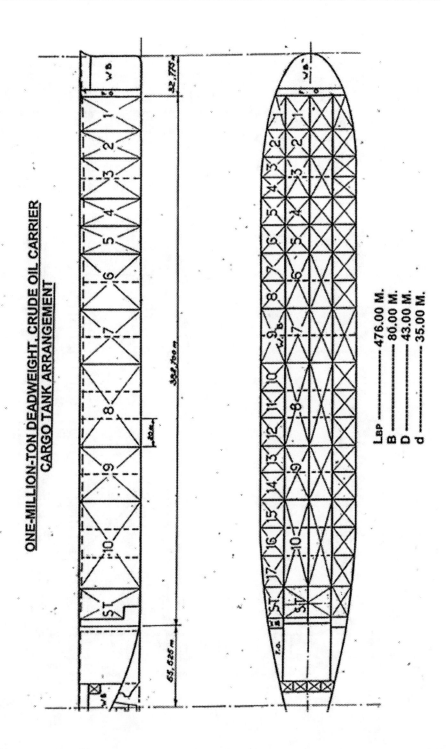

ONE-MILLION-TON DEADWEIGHT CRUDE OIL CARRIER
CARGO TANK ARRANGEMENT

L$_{BP}$	476.00 M.
B	80.00 M.
D	43.00 M.
d	35.00 M.

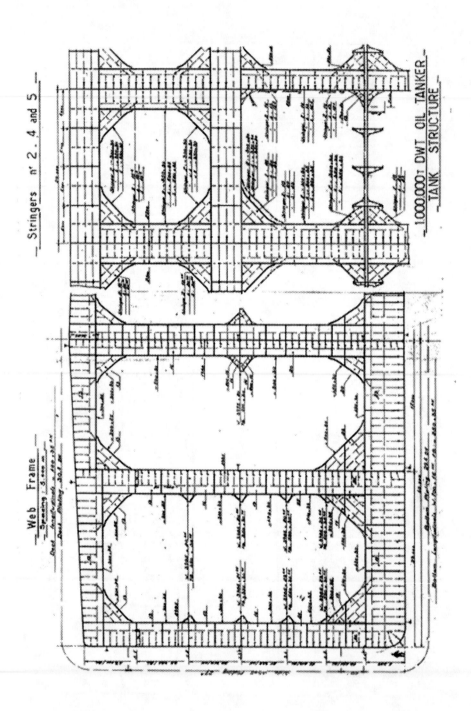

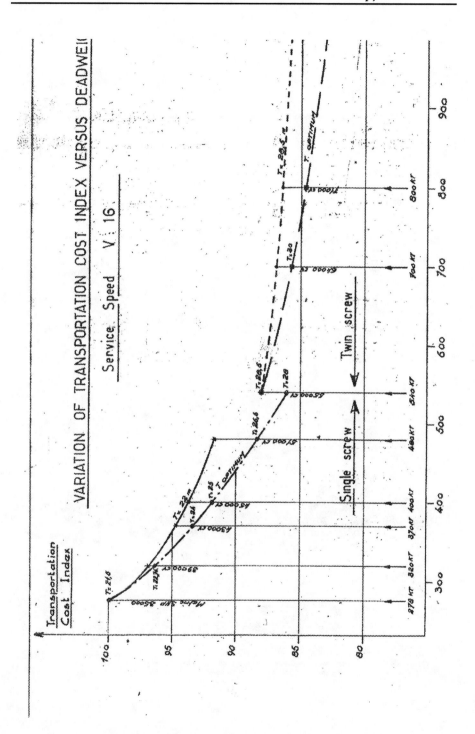

VARIATION OF TRANSPORTATION COST INDEX VERSUS DEADWEI

Service Speed   V : 16

The "DELTA" Million Tonner

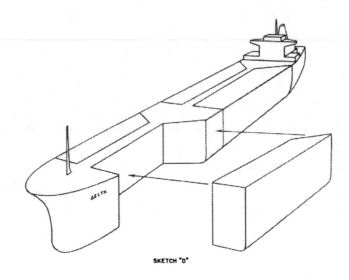

SKETCH "D"

SKETCH "E"—The one-million-ton tanker is not intended to enter a port for loading or discharging. Ballast is adjusted offshore, which enables the "mother" ship to detach itself from the "caissons." The "caissons" are then pulled away from the "mother" by tugs and towed to the discharging or loading berth.

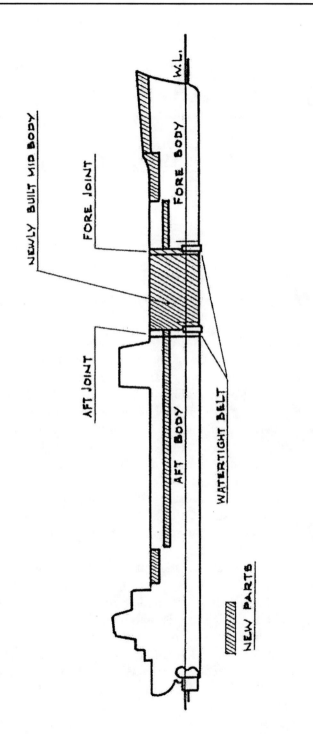

"OLYMPIC RUNNER" — "OLYMPIC RIDER"
TWO DIMENSIONAL ENLARGEMENT USING AFLOAT CONDITION METHOD

FOUR

Crude Oil (Petroleum) and the Oil Industry

A Brief History of the Nature of Crude Oil

Crude oil (petroleum) can be found all over the world, beneath land and sea at various depths. It is the accumulation of hydrocarbon, formed long ago by decomposition of animal and vegetation remains. It is a mixture of many substances from which various by-products are manufactured, such as liquefied petroleum-gas, gasoline, kerosene, gas oil, fuel oil, lubricating oil, wax, and asphaltic bitumen. These substances are mainly compounds of only two elements, carbon (C) and hydrogen (H), hence the term hydrocarbons. The simplest of these hydrocarbons is methane, consisting of one carbon atom and four hydrogen atoms (CH_4). Hydrocarbons at normal temperatures and pressures may be gaseous, liquid, or solid, according to the complexity of their molecules. Petroleum is normally restricted to the liquid deposits known as crude oil, the gaseous ones are know as natural gas, and the solid ones as bitumen, asphalt, or wax.

Crude oil and natural gas are the raw materials of the petroleum industry. These companies locate the resources, harvest them from the ground, and manufacture and sell the products in the world market. To ensure future supplies to meet increasing demands, the industry is continuously working to discover new sources of oil, in long-term operations. Finding petroleum involves great effort and expense. When oil is found, it requires complex processing to produce technically useful and marketable products. One division of the petroleum industry deals with the transportation of crude oil and its products between the refinery and the world market.

During the industrial revolution, the petroleum products people wanted were for lubrication of machinery. Petroleum products were by far much better than lard. Illuminating oils, particularly kerosene (paraffin), provided it was handled properly, gave safer, brighter, and more reliable light. In 1850, James Young of Glasgow introduced a process for the production of lamp oil by the distillation of coal or shale. Young's idea was taken up in the United States, where by 1855 several factories were making coal oil, now preferred over lard, for use in lamps.

The start of the modern petroleum industry happened in 1859. A well was sunk specifically for oil and struck it at 69.5 feet in Pennsylvania. Around the same period small amounts of petroleum were being produced in Russia and Romania.

When oil is found, it requires complex processing to produce useful by-products that require specialized transport. Outside the United States, oil fields are mostly far from the main consuming countries, so long-haul transportation means are essential. As a result, an international trade has evolved that deals with transporting oil.

Crude Oil Production

Crude oil can hardly be considered a new resource, and the problems of transporting it at sea were just as old. Despite its antiquity, crude oil did not become a globally available commodity until well into the Industrial Revolution. Today, crude oil is the lifeblood of the industrialized world, and because of its superior qualities and the ease with which is can be transported and handled, it has assumed a most important role as an energy source.

The dire predictions that the world would soon run out of oil proved to be emotional and political reactions, although at the time, oil experts knew that they had no scientific basis. Oil exploration technology surprised many people. Drill bits now come with sensors that, linked to a computer on the surface, more or less smell their way to the oil. In fact, the average distance an oil company must drill to produce a barrel of oil has fallen sharply, because oil drillers can now drill horizontally from the bottom of a well. Vertical depths have indeed increased, but radial and horizontal drilling allow the driller reach more oil with less shaft in old and new oil fields alike. Because of such advances in exploration, global proved reserves have almost doubled since 1973.

Although world petroleum reserves cannot be assessed accurately, the best estimate given so far is that the reserves are between 250 to 300 gigatons—that is the equivalent of 1.5 to 1.9 trillion barrels of oil. At the end of 2000 proven oil reserves were 1.05 trillion barrels. If all reserves are recoverable, it is estimated, petroleum will last until the end of the twenty-first century. It must be kept in mind, however, that the world's economy is based on a finite resource.

Even if we assume that only fifty percent of petroleum in the ground can be recovered, the world will have petroleum for the next fifty years, at the present rate of world consumption. In the meantime, conservation efforts are continuing, and other sources of energy are being used or are under development.

Against that, world population growth is increasing at the rate of 80 million per year. (At the end of the year 2000, world population was estimated at six billion). By the year 2050, the estimated world population will be ten billion.

A presentation by Shell International, Limited, titled "The Evolution of the World's Energy Systems," published in London in 1996 has this to offer:

> Over the last hundred years, energy demand per capita has more than trebled, from 4 to 13 barrels of oil equivalent/year, spurred by growth. However, major parts of the world's population have still little or no access to the comfort provided by electricity, nor the wider range of choices and opportunities

linked to mobility. Meeting these needs, for today and tomorrow will require increased and sustainable energy supplies.

During the 1800s and 1900s, coal was king. Coal was dethroned in the late 1900s and oil has become king. By 2100, oil will most likely have abdicated because known oil reserves will be exhausted by that time, and hopefully alternative renewable and economical resources for power will have been developed. This makes oil a 200-year phenomenon.

In the early part of the twentieth century, the United States was huge exporter of crude oil; today is a huge importer. In a recent study by the U.S. Department of Energy, titled "International Energy Outlook," published in 1996, they project that worldwide oil consumption will continue to rise over the next two decades, increasing by 44 percent, adding 30 million barrels a day to the international oil flow. According to the study, world oil demand will increase from the present level of about 69 million barrels daily to 99 million by the year 2015. The study anticipates that world oil supplies will be able to meet the growing demand, although there will be cost increases as well as an increase in carbon emissions resulting from the greater use of oil. The study mentions that forty-one to fifty-two percent of the world's oil requirements (37.8 to 53.5 million barrels per day) will come from future oil production of Arabian Gulf OPEC members.

As regards oil reserves, the U.S. study states that "more than 350 billion barrels of crude oil reserves were added worldwide in the late 1980s. The additions were made predominantly by the OPEC nations." (Members of OPEC at the end of 1988 were: Algeria, Ecuador, Gabon, Indonesia, Iran, Iraq, Kuwait, Libya, Nigeria, Qatar, Saudi Arabia, United Arab Emirates, and Venezuela.) In this swelling flood of oil, the ideological content has, to a large extent, been drained out of the oil business. In the old days, oil-producing countries were throwing out the big foreign oil companies. Today, most of the same countries are welcoming them back.

New technologies such as horizontal drilling have reduced production costs considerably. In the North Sea, the cost per barrel of oil produced has been reduced from US$11.00 in 1981 to US$5.00 in 1996. The Norwegian oil fields in the North Sea have operating costs of under US$1.00 per barrel which means it costs little more to produce oil in this harsh environment than to produce it from the placid sands of Saudi Arabia.

In the Caspian Sea area, the proven oil reserves are estimated at 28 billion barrels with talk of 200 billion barrels of oil in that area. Western oil companies have started oil explorations in this region. Russia produces approximately ten percent of the world's oil. Saudi Arabia has twenty-five percent of the world's total oil reserves, estimated at 260 billion barrels, and Iraq's known reserves of 110 billion barrels is approximately eleven percent of the world's total oil. That is more oil than the reserves in Europe and South America put together, and more than Africa and the Asia-Pacific region combined. The oil in those regions has global, strategic, political, and economic significance.

U.S. deposits are increasingly depleted, and many other non-OPEC oil fields are beginning to run dry. The bulk of future oil supplies will have to come from the Arabian Gulf region. As of the year 2003, the region accounted for thirty percent of global oil production, but has sixty-five percent of the world's known oil reserves, and is the only region able to satisfy any substantial rise in world oil demand. In January 2003, the U.S. Department of Energy warned that the United States would have to increase its oil imports sharply in the next twenty-five years to meet rising domestic demand. The Department said the U.S. net oil imports could account for as much as seventy percent of total domestic demand by 2025, up from fifty-five percent in 2001. The increased demand for oil, particularly in the United States, will require more tanker tonnage to carry it. This is where tanker size and economy of scale will become important if the cost of transportation is to be kept under control.

NOTE:

Depending upon the specific gravity of crude oil;

1 barrel per day is approximately 50 metric tons of oil per year.

1 barrel is 42 U.S. gallons.

1 barrel is 35 U.K. gallons.

1 barrel is 160 liters.

Ocean Transportation of Crude Oil

Ocean transportation of crude oil began in 1861 when Philadelphia, PA, became the premier port for the shipment of oil to the U.K. In November of that year the brig *Elizabeth Watts* of 224 tons was chartered and successfully crossed the Atlantic bringing the cargo of oil to London. As the export market gradually grew, so did transportation of crude oil in bulk. Bulk transport is the most cost-effective mode to transport the oil, using large tanks and pumps. This is the primary characteristic of the modern crude oil carrier.

The first oceangoing tanker designed and built in the U.K. for the carriage of petroleum in bulk was the Belgian owned *SS Vaderland* of the Red Star Line in 1872. The ship's length was 320' 0", with a beam of 38' 0" and 2,748 GRT. In 1879, the Norwegians started a new phase by sending their first tanker, the *Stat,* to Philadelphia to load a bulk cargo of crude oil.

Meanwhile, in the Caspian region, Robert and Ludwig Nobel of Sweden (brothers of Alfred Nobel of explosives fame) were transporting refined petroleum products in barges and sailing vessels fitted with iron tanks or in holds lined with cement. These vessels operated from Baku to the mouth of the river Volga, and later continued up the various rivers. In 1885, the Black Sea Navigation Co. (a Nobel concern) ordered several steamers from British and Swedish shipyards. Each steamer was to be fitted with petroleum tanks with a total capacity of 1,500 deadweight tons. These tankers were intended to compete with the Americans in the shipment of crude oil to Europe.

Toward the end of 1885, a tanker of greatly improved design, the *Sviet,* was delivered by the Swedish yard Lindholmen to the Russian Steam Navigation and Trading Co. of Odessa. This new design had a length of 274' 0" and a beam of 35' 0" with 1,830 GRT. Notable features of this new design were the one longitudinal bulkhead and five transverse bulkheads that resulted in configuration of four pairs of cargo tanks. The transverse bulkheads did not extend to the side shell. Instead they finished approximately on an inner shell 0.5 m from the outer shell. The tank head had a clearance of few centimeters from the deck, while the bottom of the cargo tanks was supported by a cellular double bottom. The design was the equivalent of today's double hull tanker.

The 1870s and early 1880s were years when several designs of oil carriers were constructed, and it is fair to call these early carriers developmental designs of small carrying capacity. The first dedicated steam driven ocean going oil tanker built was the *SS Gluckauf,* designed by Henry F. Swan and built in the U.K. in 1886 for the German-American Petroleum Company. This oil tanker has a unique position in the history of tanker development, regarded as the prototype of all existing tankers, because it incorporated the best ideas found in earlier experimental tankers, in addition to many that were quite new. This tanker can also claim to be the first crude oil carrier constructed using the "horizontal bulkhead" concept, which is the equivalent to today's "mid-deck" principle.

The length of the tanker was 300.5 feet, its beam was 37.2 feet, and had a GRT of 2,307. The transverse bulkheads extended to the side shell, and there was no double bottom, (except in the machinery space), because it was considered that a double bottom through the cargo tanks was a dangerous arrangement where accumulation of dangerous gases could result. The tanker operated successfully until 1893, when it ran aground on Fire Island near New York.

By 1888, there was a great deal of activity for those involved in the tanker industry because of the exportation of American oil to the U.K. and Europe. By now the American shipyards had become interested in building this type of vessel. In 1889, A. & J. Inglis started to build their first tanker, the SS Bayonne, for the Anglo-American Oil Co., Ltd. The tanker was 330 feet long, 42.2 feet wide, had cargo carrying capacity of 4,000 tons, and carried petroleum in bulk from the United States to London.

The next steam tanker built was the Murex, built in the U.K. for Messrs. Samuel and Co. of London, (which later became Shell Oil). It was launched on May 28, 1892, had an overall length of 349 feet, a beam of 43 feet, and depth of 28 feet. It had a rating of 4,950 dwt, and was capable of discharging her entire cargo in twelve hours. The design of this tanker required closely spaced riveting of the shell plating to ensure oil tightness. She was built with a view to transport crude oil in bulk through the Suez Canal and became the first tanker that was allowed to sail in Suez Canal.

It is worth noting, that even during the early years of tanker development, it was not unusual for tankers to take petroleum one way and dry cargo the other. An early example of such a voyage was performed by the Anglo-American's tanker Seminole, 417 feet long and 7,000 dwt, and built in the U.K. In 1904, its maiden voyage began by sailing from the river Tyne on July 27 for Novorossisk to load a cargo of crude oil for Calcutta. On completion of discharge, the tanks were cleaned and a cargo of jute was loaded for Dundee in Scotland, where she discharged in November of that year. That is a round trip of less than four months.

By early 1900, naval architects and shipbuilders were faced with a major design problem as a result of the growing increase in the length of tankers. Some designers advocated placing the propulsion machinery amidships. It was argued that there would be less strain in the ship's structure when in ballast or when experiencing heavy weather, and that the hull could be trimmed more easily. The additional building cost and loss of cargo space resulting from a long propeller shaft tunnel caused the naval architects to find another solution to the problem.

Transporting Crude Oil by Tankers is a technically complex and capital-intensive business that is of vital importance to the growth of world economy. The industry is international and has standards influenced by the tanker builder, the shipowner, the classification societies, the International Maritime Organization, as well as the administration of the flag state and the charterer.

The oil-consuming countries without oil resources require the oil to be trans-ported to them, and where there is no oil pipeline, the only way to transport it in bulk is by sea. The industry's perennial problem, however, is that tonnage supply and demand have been out of balance. What is disturbing is that statistics on tonnage supply and demand, tanker freight rates, and new building costs indi-cate that the tanker industry has been forced to cope with aged tanker tonnage for a long time. This is the result of constant economic pressures during the 1980s that resulted in a general decline in the tanker industry's standards. Such conditions forced some tanker owners to look into ways of prolonging the life of their existing tankers. One such measure was the "Life Extension Programme" and more recently, the "Enhanced Survey Programme." Guidelines for these pro-grams were prepared by the International Association of Classification Societies and submitted to the International Maritime Organization.

Having recognized the fact that the world's shipyards do not have the capacity to scrap and replace all existing tankers in the near future (there are presently some 3,250 oceangoing tankers), both the U.S. Coast Guard and IMO have adopted a twenty-five to thirty year mandatory phase-out age, pro-vided these aged tankers are properly maintained in accordance with approved "Life Extension" and "Enhanced Survey" standards. However, the reliability of a tanker hull structure and the tanker's equipment is less a function of age than how well the structure and equipment have been maintained. Aging, poorly operated tankers and ill-trained crews have given the tanker industry a bad name. The fact that among tanker owners there are the "stingy bargain hunters," otherwise known as the "cowboys" of the industry, has not enhanced the industry's reputation. In addition, regulatory burdens on an already underpaid industry have not helped the situation.

Carrying oil in bulk by ship is a service that has been in existence for more than a century, and it is impossible to legislate the risk of marine pollution out of existence. Despite comprehensive regulations from international agree-ments, oil pollution of the seas by oil tankers continues to be a significant international problem. The Arctic, Southern Pacific, and Atlantic Oceans, as well as in the North and Mediterranean Seas, have all experienced in the past few years oil spills of catastrophic proportions from oil tanker accidents. As no acceptable energy substitutes for oil are forthcoming in the foreseeable future, and transportation of the oil can only be done by oil tankers, accidents must be expected, just as they are in other industries such as commercial aviation, coal mining, and the nuclear industry.

The tanker industry's problem is an international problem that requires an international solution. The underlying question, however, remains: "Are the present efforts and arrangements as now made satisfactory." Clearly, they are not. The following chapters discuss the issues involved and highlight the weaknesses of the procedures adopted in the recent past efforts to ameliorate the situation.

NOTE: As of January 2004, the world oil tanker fleet represented just over 19 percent of the world's commercial ships of 300 GRT and over, with an estimated growth of 7.6 percent over the next five years.

Global Sea Transportation of Crude Oil

The size of crude oil carriers appears to have reached its optimum economic profitability considering today's regulatory requirements. The speed factor is crucial as well, given the distance of the three major oil consumers from the Arabian Gulf (Europe, 11,300 nautical miles; United States, 11, 900 nautical miles;, and Japan, 6,800 nautical miles). Any increase in demand for tanker tonnage will have to be met by an increase in the number of carriers, not larger tankers.

Tanker freight rates have been subject to wild variations over the years. The price for new tankers has, however, followed a reasonable pattern, reflecting the increased cost of labor and materials as well as currency fluctuations, until the entry of South Korean shipbuilders in the international shipbuilding arena. The South Korean entry forced the dominant Japanese shipbuilding industry into a defensive position for many years. But today, the South Koreans have actually overtaken the Japanese in terms of annual tonnage building, particularly in the tanker sector. The Chinese shipbuilding industry's entry into the international market has made shipbuilding more competitive still, and China has become a strong competitor with both Japan and South Korea.

The independent tanker-owner who has survived the harsh economic pressures of the past decades is now conditioned to expect ships of greatly increased productivity. The improvement in overall ship efficiency is not achieved simply by economics of scale, but rather by a vastly increased flexibility. The period from 1950 to 1970 saw the development in the size of the crude oil carrier from what was then known as the supertanker of around 45,000 dwt, to the very large crude carrier of 300,000 dwt, to the ultra large crude carrier of 500,000 dwt. Some shipbuilders considered building the megatanker of 1,000,000 dwt. The largest crude oil carrier afloat today is the *Yahre Viking* of 564,000 dwt.

The development of cargo access and transfer systems continues to focus on improvement of the handling efficiency and safety of existing tanker types as well as promoting the evolution of new marine transport concepts. The most effective route to meet the challenges ahead is a continuing dialogue between tanker owner, builder, and the classification societies from the early stage of a project. An example of such cooperation is the development by South Korean builder Concordia Maritime. The result has been a double-hull, twin screw VLCC with a deadweight of 314,000 tons at a scantling draft of nineteen meters. Other principal dimensions of this design are:

Length B.P...320.00 m
Breadth ....70.00 m

```
Depth..................................................................25.60 m
Service Speed...................................................16.90 knots
Design Draft....................................................16.75 m
```

The wider hull apparently necessitated a twin-skeg arrangement to obtain better flow to the propellers.

The Japanese shipbuilder NKK recently developed and built what is now known as the Malacca-Max VLCC, 300,000 dwt, at a draft of 20.84 meters, which is the maximum permitted to sail through the Strait of Malacca. The design incorporates the "ax bow," claimed to greatly reduce wave resistance under rough sea conditions. The other principal dimensions of the design are:

```
Length...........................................................333.0 m
Breadth .........................................................60.0 m
Depth.............................................................29.6 m
```

Early in 1970, the Dutch authorities of Rotterdam seriously considered the development of a restricted draft ULCC of 425,000 dwt. The purpose of the study was to explore the economic viability of the restricted draft tanker concept in competition with tankers of normal design. This particular study was limited to the carriage of crude oil from Arabian Gulf via the Cape of Good Hope to Rotterdam, and Libya to Rotterdam.

The optimum dimensions that resulted from the study, for a single screw tanker, with a service speed of sixteen knots were:

```
BP Length .....................................................395.00 m
Breadth .........................................................66.50 m
Depth.............................................................27.35 m
Draft .............................................................22.00 m
Total Block Coefficient ..................................0.825
Deadweight....................................................425,000 tons
```

The steam turbine machinery required 55,000 hp from the shaft.

The design was to be a single-hull construction and higher strength steel was also considered. Based upon D.N.V. Rules, the calculated steel weight was 61,780 tons, of which 14,800 tons was high strength steel (H-30). Had the design used mild steel throughout, the estimated steel weight was 66,000 tons. At that time, designers concluded that a safe draft for a loaded tanker in the area around and approaching the port of Rotterdam could be 22.5 meters. No tankers of this design were ever constructed.

Proved reserves at end 2000

Thousand million barrels

North America
64.4

Former Soviet Union
65.3

Europe

Asia Pacific

Africa
74.8

Middle East
683.6

S. & Cent. America
95.2

The world's proved oil reserves
continue to be dominated by
the Middle East which holds
65.3% of the total

Major trade movements

Trade flows worldwide (million tonnes)

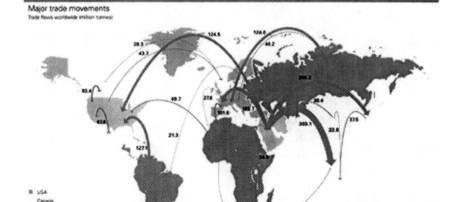

- USA
- Canada
- Mexico
- S. & Cent. America
- Europe
- Former Soviet Union
- Middle East
- Africa
- Asia Pacific

World's top oil exporters, 2003
In millions of barrels per day

Country	millions of barrels per day
Saudi Arabia	8.38
Russia	5.81
Norway	3.02
Iran	2.48
U.A.E.	2.29
Venezuela	2.23
Kuwait	2.00
Nigeria	1.93
Mexico	1.74
Algeria	1.64

OPEC
Non-OPEC

SOURCE: ENERGY INFORMATION ADMINISTRATION

Petroleum Flow Chart from the Well through the Refinery

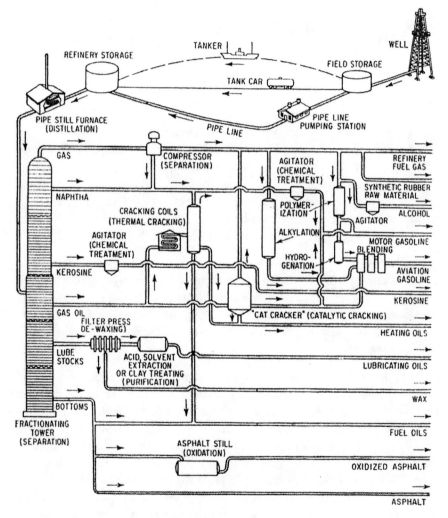

(Courtesy of Humble Oil & Refining Co., Esso Standard, Eastern Region.)

FIVE

Anatomy of an Oil Spill at Sea

The disasters of the tanker *Erika* in December 1999, and *Prestige* in February 2002 were high profile casualties that caused public outcry in France and Spain. They also proved that public sensitivity to environmental damage has increased vastly over the past two decades. These disasters created the public perception that every tanker is an accident waiting to happen, causing marine pollution. The U.N. Conference on Human Environment, held in Stockholm in June 1992, defined marine pollution as the following:

> The introduction by man, directly or indirectly, of substances of energy into the marine environment, (including estuaries), resulting in such deleterious effects as harm to living resources, hazards to human health, hindrance to marine activities including fishing, impairment of quality for use of sea water.

The tanker industry's image remains vulnerable to the fallout of the consequences of tanker accidents that result in damage to the marine environment. The major oil companies remain sensitive to such accidents involving their own tankers. Because their core business is exploration, production, refining, and selling the crude oil's byproducts, transporting the crude oil in tankers is perceived as an unfortunate necessity. Oil companies prefer pipelines over tankers for the movement of crude oil. Their marine transportation division is a touchy subject because of the public's sensitivity to oil spills at sea. The oil companies believe, therefore, that no one can operate oil tankers as well as they can. They are determined that the nightmare scenario of a major oil pollution event, with the resultant costs, fines, and adverse publicity, must not happen to them. They are careful about how their own tankers are designed, maintained, and operated.

The most published oil spill at sea has been that of the *Exxon Valdez*. The single-hull, 269,000 dwt VLCC is a U.S. designed, built, manned, owned, and operated crude oil carrier. The tanker was owned by Exxon Co. of the United States. In March 1989, the tanker went aground on the eastern edge of Prince William Sound in Alaska while on a loaded voyage from Terminal Valdez. From the information obtained from Exxon, the U.S. fisheries and WildLife Services, and the Alaska Department of Environmental Conservation, the results of that grounding included the following:

- Oil spilled: 10,836,000 gallons
- Shoreline Contaminated by oil: 1,090 miles
- Shoreline Treated by Exxon (up through September 1989): 1,087 miles
- Shoreline still needing to be cleaned after September 1989, according to the state of Alaska: At least 1,000 miles
- Number of dead birds: 33,126
- Number of dead Eagles: 138
- Number of dead Otters: 980
- Cost of cleaning up to Exxon: US$1.28 billion. (After tax cost; insurance companies were expected to reimburse Exxon US$400 million).
- People involved in the clean up: 12,000
- Vessels and planes used in the clean up: 1,385
- Oil recovered: 2,604,000 gallons
- Waste from oil clean up: 24,000 tons
- Law suits filed against Exxon: 145

The Nature of the Cargo Carried by Tankers

Crude oil is a mix of hydrocarbons, an arrangement of hydrogen and carbon molecules that requires physical or chemical processing to be turned into useable products. It contains varying proportions of the different hydrocarbons, known as fractions, and the refining process separates these hydrocarbons out into useful by-products. The densest byproducts are asphalt and tar; the lighter (in descending order of specific gravity) are heating oil, diesel fuel, kerosene/paraffin, naptha, and gasoline; and the lightest and most volatile are petroleum gases, butane and propane, and the important natural gas methane.

When oil is spilled at sea, it undergoes a number of physical and chemical changes, some of which lead to its disappearance from the sea surface, while others cause it to persist. The overall fate of an oil spill depends upon the climatic conditions and the physical characteristics of the oil, such as specific gravity, viscosity, and distillation characteristics. Sedimentation and biodegradation determines the ultimate fate of an oil spill. An appreciation of the likely fate of the spilled oil is therefore an important element in the preparation of contingency plan, in order to determine whether any response at all is necessary beyond monitoring the spills dissipation.

A thorough understanding of the natural fate of spilled oil is critical for coping with accidental spills. During an oil spill several processes interact to alter the distribution and composition of crude oil released into the marine environment.

- Spreading is the first, most significant process, and it is controlled by the physical and chemical properties of the oil and environmental conditions into which it is released. Although related to chemical composition and processes, spreading is a physical phenomenon.

- Drift or advection is the movement of the center of mass of an oil slick. This is controlled by wind, waves, and surface currents and is independent of spreading and spill volume.

- Evaporation and dissolution are the first two processes of degradation of oil released onto the water. It is the mass transfer of the oil hydrocarbons from the liquid oil to the vapor phase. The composition, surface area, and physical properties of the oil, wind velocity, air and sea temperatures, sea state, and intensity of solar radiation affect hydrocarbon evaporation rates. It is the most substantial initial degradative process.

- Dissolution, which is similar to evaporation, is the mass transfer of hydrocarbons from the floating or suspended oil into the water column. The rate and extent of dissolution depend on the composition and physical properties of the oil, extent of spreading, water temperature, turbulence, and amount of dispersion.

- Dispersion is the incorporation of small particles or globules of oil into the water column. Natural or chemically induced dispersion soon after the oil spill may result in high dissolved hydrocarbon concentrations in the water column for a short time.

- Emulsification, like dispersion depends on oil composition and sea state. It is the evaporation of volatile hydrocarbons within the first ten hours after the oil spill, and subsequent increases in density and viscosity initiate the formation of emulsions.

- Sedimentation. There are two sedimentation types, adhesion and absorption. Sedimentation increases in shallow, near-shore areas, and depends on the amount and type of particulate matter in the water column. The fate of oil or oil hydrocarbons, once sedimented, varies according to local conditions. Oil stranded on low-energy beaches has little chance of reexposure. A high energy beach profile undergoes drastic changes with seasons or major storms. Oil is frequently buried, re-exposed, and reintroduced into the littoral environment.

- Biodegradation is the natural process through which bacteria or other microorganisms alter and decompose organic molecules into various substances such as fatty acids and carbon dioxide.

In contingency planning for oil spills careful planning and preparation is essential for any successful operation. The first processes acting on an oil spill are all physical, involving distribution of the oil and partitioning of its components among the sea surface, air, water column, and sediments. Physical weathering greatly alters the destructive potential of an oil spill by changing its physical properties, redistributing toxic components, and determining its location. After extensive alterations, however, many oil hydrocarbons persist unchanged. Their toxic nature is diluted but not diminished. No crude oil is subject to complete biodegradation. The many components in the oil differ considerably in solubility, volatility, and susceptibility to biodegradation. It makes it difficult and possibly misleading to speak in terms of an overall biodegradation rate.

Some hours after an oil spill, the biological and chemical degradative processes become increasingly significant. Because marine microorganisms ingest, metabolize, and utilize the oil as a carbon source. Without the organisms, the abundance would increase at great rates. The rate and extent of biodegradation depend on the nature and abundance of the indigenous microbial predators available in organic nutrients, oxygen, ambient temperature, and oil distribution and composition.

• Auto-oxidation is the degradative process of hydrocarbons in floating and dispersed oil reacting with oxygen molecules in the water column. The extent and by-products of oxidation reactions vary depending on oil properties and composition, water temperatures, solar radiation intensity, abundance of various inorganic components in the water or oil and extent of diffusion and spreading of the oil.

Effective cleanup efforts are contingent on a good estimate of the dominant physical, chemical, and biological processes acting on the oil spill at any given time. Spreading dominates earliest, while the most critical intermediate time processes, such as evaporation, emulsification, and dispersion, alter the composition and physical state of the oil. Sedimentation and biodegradation largely determine the ultimate fate of the spilled oil and may be active for years after the spill.

In November 1992, I was involved in the establishment, of a company to guide and assist foreign flag owners operating in U.S. waters, in the event of an oil spill by one of their tankers. The company, located in Virginia, was capable of providing quick response and qualified individuals in order to minimize the environmental damage of oil spill. The company's philosophy was, no matter what, and no matter where, an oil spill should get a best-effort response.

The U.S. Oil Pollution Act of 1990 requires oil tankers operating in U.S. waters to have in place by February 1993 vessel response plans with their other requirements, including contingency plans, environmental audits, and rapid response teams. Establishing the company enabled me to understand better the damage an oil spill might cause to the marine environment. It is therefore essential to understand oils. There are occasions where mounting a clean-up response becomes unnecessary. If it can be confidently predicted that the oil will drift away from vulnerable resources or dissipate naturally before reaching them, no further action is required. Often however, an active response will be necessary aimed at accelerating the natural processes through the use of dispersants or limiting spreading by containment methods.

The first figure at the end of this Chapter shows schematically the physical and chemical changes of a typical medium crude oil under moderate sea conditions. Given sufficient time, natural processes such as evaporation, biodegradation, and sedimentation, effectively reduce the destructive potential of an oil spill. Acceleration of the natural process is enhanced by the efforts of the oil spill response teams.

THE WORLD'S BIGGEST OIL SPILLS

Tanker's Name	Year	Location	Tons
Torrey Canyon	1967	Scilly Isles U.K.	119,000
Jakob Maersk	1975	Oporto Portugal	88,000
Urquiola	1976	La Coruna, Spain	100,000
Hawaiian Patriot	1977	300 Miles off Honolulu, HI, U.S.	95,000
Amoco Cadiz	1978	off Brittany, France	223,000
Atlantic Empress	1979	off Tobago, West Indies	287,000
Independentza	1979	Bosphorus, Turkey	95,000
Castillo de Bellver	1983	off Saidanha Bay, S. Africa	252,000
Odyssey	1988	off Nova Scotia, Canada	132,000
Kharg 5	1989	off Atlantic Coast of Morocco	80,000
Exxon Valdez	1989	Alaska, U.S.	35,000
Haven	1991	Genoa, Italy	144,000
ABT Summer	1991	700 Miles off Angola	260,000
Aegean Sea	1992	La Coruna, Spain	74,000
Braer	1993	Shetland Islands, U.K.	85,000
Sea Empress	1996	Milford Haven, U.K.	72,000
Erika	1999	Brittany, France	30,000
Prestige	2002	La Coruna, Spain	77,000

Source: International Tanker Owners Pollution Federation

The Case for the U.S.A. Oil Pollution Act of 1990, OPA '90

Background; Purpose; Regulatory History.
Background:

Our Western society had taken for granted that the marine environment had an infinite capacity to absorb the waste generated by the oil industry. Sometimes however, there was a heavy price to pay in terms of environmental damage, example of which is the tanker *Torrey Canyon*, which went aground in loaded condition on the rocks off Land's End in the U.K. in 1967, broke its back, and spilled the entire cargo of crude oil the tanker was carrying. It was the first major oil pollution disaster in shipping history, and led to an expansion of IMO's work in the environmental and legal fields. This disaster also led to the creation of the Oil Companies International Marine Forum (OCIMF) in 1970. The OCIMF is responsible for the establishment of the Ship Inspection Report that became known as "SIRE" Programme. It is a computerized data base of technical information about the condition of oil tankers, and it covers a significant proportion of the world's tanker fleet. This readily accessible pool of technical information covering the condition and operational procedures of tankers is available to charterers and to port authorities.

During the early 1970s, there was a long and sometimes heated controversy over the need to build double bottoms into tankers as a means of curbing oil spills in the event of an accident. In October 1973, the double bottom question was debated at great length in London by the seventy-nine nation Inter-Governmental Maritime Consultative Organization (IMCO), now the International Maritime Organization (IMO). They drafted the International Convention for the Prevention of Pollution from Ships in 1973. The U.S. measure for double bottom was rejected soundly by IMCO. Opposition to mandatory double bottom requirements was at that time, frequently attributed solely to oil interests and shipping, who were described in the United States of America as being "motivated only by economic concerns, and as having a callous disregard for environmental protection."

The Honorable Russel Train, who lead the U.S. delegation to the 1973 IMCO Marine Pollution Conference, in an appearance before the U.S. Senate Commerce Committee after his return from the London meeting, summed up why the double bottom proposal was not adopted:

> There were those who feel for example, that with double bottoms, if a ship goes on a reef and the double bottom is breached

and fills with water, even though this is not mixing with oil and there may be no discharge of oil at that point, the ship will settle more positively, if that is the phrase, upon the reef and be that much more difficult to get off. It may well be that the use of the double bottom in such cases could be a detriment rather than an advantage in terms of protecting the seas.

On March 24, 1989, the 211,000 dwt tanker *Exxon Valdez*, a VLCC designed, built, manned, operated, and owned by Exxon Oil Company, ground to a halt on Bligh Reef in Prince William Sound, Alaska, shortly after leaving the Port of Valdez in loaded condition. This grounding resulted in the largest oil spill to occur in U.S. waters.

Public outcry in the United States demanded that, U.S. shores need to be protected against oil spills, and ships need to be protected against the oil tank punctures that cause oil spills. Such protection should be mandated now, not 25 years from now.

In January 1990, the state-appointed Alaska Oil Spill Commission issued its report. The commission drafted eight fundamental conclusions about the dangers of oil transport, as listed below:

1. Moving oil by sea involves a complex, high-risk megasystem whose breakdown can threaten the welfare of entire coast lines.

2. Risk is unavoidable in modern oil transportation. It can be reduced but not eliminated.

3. Prevention of major oil spills must be a fundamental goal in the oil trade, since cleanup and response methods remain primitive and inadequate.

4. In government as well as industry, enforcement zeal declined, alertness sagged, and complacency took root in the years preceding the *Exxon Valdez* disaster. Prevention was neglected.

5. Without continuing focus on the safety of the entire system by government and industry leaders, the oil transportation system poses an increasing risk to the environment and people of Alaska.

6. The State of Alaska has primary responsibility for protecting the resources of the State and the welfare of its people, who bear the risk of unsafe conditions in oil transportation.

7. Privatization and self-regulation in oil transportation contributed to the complacency and neglect that helped cause the wreck of the *Exxon Valdez*.

8. The safety of oil transportation demands review and overhaul. Not just new technology, but new institutions and new attitudes in old institutions are required.

As part of the process to improve the situation, relevant technical data on tankers were generated by experts in the maritime industry for consideration by the U.S. Congress in their preparation of legislation. The U.S. National Academy of Sciences was charged with the responsibility of submitting the relevant data to Congress.

On August 18, 1990, the United States took a definitive stance on the prevention of oil pollution at sea by mandating double-hulls on all tankers operating in U.S. territorial waters, including the Exclusive Economic Zone, when President Bush signed the Oil Pollution Act of 1990 (OPA '90) into law, (Public Law 110-380). The Act addresses oil pollution and removal of spilled oil, as well as the wide ranging problems associated with preventing, responding to, and paying for oil spills.

The focal point of the pollution prevention topic was the requirement of double-hulls for all tankers for which a building contract, or a contract for a major conversion, was placed after June 30, 1990, or for tankers delivered after June 1, 1994. Existing tankers are also subject to OPA '90 requirements. "Existing tankers" is defined as any construction or major conversion for which contracts were signed before June 30 1990, and delivered under those contracts prior to January 1, 1994.

Another significant rule increases the liability limits on the owner or operator of the tanker that spilled oil, but provides for individual States to maintain their authority to impose unlimited liability, and to implement their own compensation plan. The United States Coast Guard (USCG), supports the idea of State imposed fines, and works closely with local and state governments, encouraging them to actively participate in its regulatory process. Consequently, state and federal law, should not conflict. However, to the extent there is such a conflict, federal law remains supreme (*U.S. Constitution*, Article VI, clause 2).

The introduction of OPA '90 legislation was at first vigorously opposed by some international oil companies, some independent tanker owners, and some shipyards. The tanker industry, however, was told in no uncertain terms that, "OPA '90 is not a bad dream that will fade away with the morning mist." The industry was also told that the U.S. Secretary of Transportation is charged with conducting a study to determine whether effective alternatives to double-hull construction exist, but he is not empowered to simply approve such systems. The Secretary of Transportation has to base his determination on the recommendations of the U.S. National Academy of Sciences and other organizations. All he can do with his recommendations is present them to the U.S. Congress for legislative action. Therefore, any changes may take quite a long time.

Regulatory History:

Double-hull standards for vessels carrying oil in bulk are established by the United States Coast Guard (USCG), an agency of the United States Department of Transportation. Details of the proposed standards were made available to all interested parties at home and abroad, who in turn were invited to participate in the rule making process through written comments, attending public meetings organized by USCG, or both.

On December 5, 1990, USCG published a notice of proposed rule making titled "Double-hull Standards for Tank Vessels Carrying Oil," in the *Federal Register* (55 FR, 50192).

On August 29, 1991, USCG published a notice in the *Federal Register* (56 FR, 42763) announcing a public meeting to obtain the views of interested parties regarding the scope of the environmental assessment. The meeting was held on September 26, 1991.

On September 6, 1991, the USCG published a notice in the *Federal Register* (56 FR 44051), reopening the comment period until October 7, 1991.

On January 15, 1992, the USCG published a notice in the *Federal Register* (57 FR 1854) announcing the availability of the Interim Regulatory Impact Analysis and Environmental Assessment. In response to the IRIA and EA, USCG received a total of 112 letters commenting on this rule making.

On August 12, 1992, the USCG published an Interim Final Rule titled, "Double-hull Standards for Vessels Carrying Oil in Bulk" in the *Federal Register* (57 FR 36222), which requested comments be received on or before October 12, 1992.

On December 18, 1992, the USCG opened a second comment period for the Interim Final Rule, by publishing a notice in the *Federal Register* (57 FR 60402). The Coast Guard received sixty-one letters during the IFR comment period when all comments were duly considered, up to the close of the second comment period on February 26, 1993. A public hearing was not requested and none was held.

On April 10, 1995, the Interim Final Rule, published on August 12, 1992, which established regulations for the design standards of double-hull tankers pursuant to the requirements of section 4115 of the Oil Pollution Act of 1990, (Public Law 101-390), became final and effective with minor changes to definitions.

In November 1990, the USCG, who represents the United States at IMO deliberations, submitted a proposal to IMO's thirtieth session of the Maritime Environment Protection Committee (MEPC 30) for international standards requiring oil tankers to have double-hulls. The proposal resulted in a draft Regulation 13F of Annex I to MARPOL 73/78.

In July 1991, MEPC 31 approved draft Regulation 13F for circulation to IMO member states for their consideration.

In November 1991, an MEPC working group refined Regulation 13F, which was further refined and formally adopted at MEPC 32 on March 6, 1992. The United States reserves its position during the adoption of Regulation 13F due to technical differences with OPA '90 regarding the applicability of double-hull requirements to certain categories of tankers, and the allowance of mid-deck concept as an alternative to a double-hull.

The two major technical differences between the United States and international standards are the following:

- The acceptance by IMO of the mid-deck tanker design as an alternative to the double-hull.

- Variances in phase-out schedules for existing single-hull tankers. The double-hull dimensions prescribed in the USCG Interim and Final Rule are consistent with those in Regulation 13F, as adopted at MEPC 32 on March 6, 1992.

During MEPC 32, Regulation 13G to Annex I of MARPOL 73/78 was also adopted. This Regulation contains a schedule for retrofitting single-hulled tankers with double-hulls or retiring single-hull tankers at twenty-five or thirty years after delivery. Regulation 13G, also requires tankers built prior to requirements for Protectively Located Segregated Ballast Tanks (Pre-MARPOL tankers), to convert tanks protecting thirty percent of the sides or thirty percent of the bottom to non-oil-carrying wing tanks or double bottom spaces, no later than twenty-five years after delivery.

The United States also reversed its position during the adoption of regulation 13G of Annex I to MARPOL 73/78, when on December 23, 1992, the United States deposited a declaration with IMO regarding the U.S. acceptance and enforcement of Regulations 13F and 13G. This declaration stated that the express approval of the U.S. Government would be necessary before Regulations 13F and 13G would enter into force within the United States of America.

Purpose:

A substantial amount of oil (approximately fifty percent of the country's oil consumption), imported into the United States is transported on board foreign flag tankers. Since OPA '90 legislation applies to all vessels in U.S. waters, including foreign flag vessels, the USCG recognized that U.S. double-hull regulations would have a significant global impact, and has worked at the international level and with the International Maritime Organization (IMO) to establish the following:

- Double hull standards
- Structural and operational measures to reduce oil spills from existing tank vessels without double-hulls
- Requirements for longitudinal strength
- Plating thickness and periodic gauging of tankers
- Operational measures to reduce oil spills from existing tankers without double-hulls
- Designation of lightering zones

As a United Nations agency, IMO oversees international maritime affairs. They are responsible for developing various international conventions such as the International Convention for the Safety of Life at Sea, 1974 (SOLAS '74), and the "International Convention for Prevention of Pollution from Ships, 1973, as modified by the Protocol of 1978 relating thereto (MARPOL 73/78).[1]"

USCG Definitions:

Tank vessel means a vessel that is constructed or adapted primarily to carry, or that carries oil or hazardous material in bulk as cargo or cargo residue, and that meets the following criteria:

- It is a vessel of the United States.
- It operates on the navigable waters of the United States.
- It transfers oil or hazardous material in a port or place subject to the jurisdiction of the United States. This does not include offshore supply vessels fishing vessels, or fish tender vessels of not more than 750 gross tons when engaged only in fishing industry.

Cargo tank length means the length from the forward bulkhead of the foremost cargo tanks, to the after bulkhead of the aftermost cargo tanks.

The USCG has not identified equivalent designs to the double-hull tanker for the prevention of oil outflow due to grounding. Section 4115 of OPA '90 accepts only the double-hull design. Amendments to OPA '90 would be needed to allow for acceptance of any alterative tanker designs.

Due to the global nature of oil transportation by sea, the USCG considers international consistency an essential element in the successful adoption of the double-hull concept. The required design standards submitted by USCG have received strong public support, and have been incorporated in IMO's accepted

Regulation 13F of Annex I of MARPOL 73/78 for international vessel double-hull design standards.

Requirements for Longitudinal Strength, Plate Thickness, and Periodic Gauging for Certain Tank Vessels

On March 23, 1993, the USCG issued a notice of proposed rule making in the *Federal Register* that requires the issuance of regulations on two matters related to the structural integrity of vessels that carry oil in bulk as cargo or cargo residue. The new regulations are as follows:

- Establish minimum standards for plate thickness

- Require periodic gauging of the plate thickness

- Apply to all tankers over thirty years old operating on the navigable waters of the United States or the waters of the Exclusive Economic Zone.

The purpose of the regulations was to ensure adequate structural integrity of oil tankers throughout their service life. The statute also requires the regulations to be consistent with generally recognized principles of international law and stipulated that the USCG should consider gaugings by classification societies "if equivalent to the Secretary's requirements, to be acceptable evidence of compliance."

Prior to the "Final Rule," the USCG invited public comments and received 26 such comments for consideration. As a result of these comments, the "Final Rule" was issued on October 8, 1993, (Part VI), with an effective date November 8, 1993.

The "Final Rule," includes revisions and changes to the originally proposed rule making of March 23, 1993.

Public comments are a valuable source to USCG in testing public reaction to rule making notices and result in better understanding of the notices. In this case, two of the leading classification societies commented on the above rule making, which resulted in the following:

- The change of the proposed minimum section modulus and thickness standards, from the original "as built" construction of the vessel, to the "as required" standards of the appropriate rules for the vessel's present service route. The reason for the change is that some tanker owners, including the company I work for, provided a larger corrosion margin in the scantlings than required by classification rules.

- Other classification societies, in addition to the American Bureau of Shipping, can be approved for purposes of the structural evaluations required by the new regulations.

USCG Requirements for Operational Measures To Reduce Oil Spills From Existing Tankers Without Double-hulls. (Part 33 CFR Part 157; 46 CFR Parts 31 and 35):

On November 3, 1995, the USCG proposed regulations that would require the owners, masters, or operators of tankers of 5,000 gross tons or more that do not have double-hulls and that carry oil in bulk as cargo to comply with certain operational measures. The proposed regulations contain requirements for bridge resource management training, rest hour minimums, enhanced surveys, maneuvering performance capability requirements, and other measures aimed at reducing the likelihood of an oil discharge from these tankers. Additionally, the USCG proposed to amend requirements for the carriage of onboard emergency lightering equipment. These proposed regulations represent the second step in the USCG's three-step effort to establish structural and operational measures for tankers without double-hulls as required by OPA '90.

A public meeting was held on January 20, 1994, to obtain information on the proposed regulations related to certain structural measures, particularly their reliance on Regulation 13G of Annex I of MARPOL 73/78.

On January 4, 1993, the USCG submitted a report to Congress on the "Alternative to Double-hull Tank Vessel Design" based upon the findings of an independent consultant in the United States, Herbert Engineering Corp., who completed their study in July 1992. The USCG report to Congress concluded that:

> At this time, the Coast Guard has not identified equivalent designs to the double-hull tanker for the prevention of oil outflow due to grounding. Shortcomings exist in the tanker evaluation methodology. Environmental performance standards on a specific methodology for evaluation of alternative designs in terms other than oil outflow are not fully developed. USCG recommended to Congress that, no changes in OPA '90 be made concerning the acceptance of other tanker designs at this time.

Designation of Lightering Zones:

On August 29, 1995, USCG issued a final rule titled "Designation of Lightering Zones" (60 FR 45006), which established four lightering zones in the Gulf of Mexico. Under the provisions of the final rule, tankers without double-hulls may lighter in the Exclusive Economic Zone, including the existing tankers affected by this rulemaking. These tankers would be allowed to continue conducting lightering operations in these zones after they are phased out of service under the provisions of section 4115(a) of OPA '90 until the year 2015. However, under section 4115(b) of OPA '90, these tankers would also be required to meet any structural and operational measures for tankers without double-hulls.

It should be noted that OPA '90 has reinforced the need for tougher and more restricted controls over oil transportation.

Summary of the U.S. Initiative:

For several years, the United States of America pursued a policy to introduce requirements for oil tankers as a means to minimize oil spills. The most significant effort occurred in 1976 when the U.S. Coast Guard was instructed by the U.S. Government to develop regulations for double bottoms on all tankers over 20,000 dwt. This resulted in IMO holding a conference in 1978, when the U.S. proposal was rejected. Instead, requirements for protectively located (PL) segregated ballast tanks (SBT), and inert gas systems (IGS) were developed. During this time, the requirements for crude oil washing (COW) were also developed for all new tankers over 20,000 dwt carrying crude oil, was made one of the options for existing crude oil carriers to facilitate implementation of MARPOL 73/78.

Having been thwarted in the past at IMO, and considering the length of time necessary to implement IMO requirements, the *Exxon Valdez* and damage its grounding and spill did to the environment in Alaska in March 1989 inspired the OPA '90. The legislation rendered all existing tanker designs obsolete.

The U.S. attitude on the adoption of the double-hull, versus other designs offered to the industry, was at the time characterized by some as dogmatic, bureaucratic interference and an emotional solution. The act's passage sparked a series of dramatic hearings, discussions, debates, and complex rule making processes. The act itself seeks to improve tanker safety, reduce the chances of major oil spills, and improve the response to any such spills. It is important to keep in mind that the U.S. market accounts for approximately thirty percent of total world seaborne oil movements, and tanker owners cannot afford to ignore such a vast market. The size of tankers suitable for trading in the U.S. waters—50,000 dwt, 80,000 dwt, VLCCs and ULCCs—is another important consideration.

The oil price shocks of 1974 and 1979 caused the major oil companies to reduce sharply their involvement in tanker ownership. As a result, independent tanker owners increased their tanker tonnage to the point where they now dominate the U.S. oil trade. An independent tanker owner, if he chooses to involve himself in the U.S. market and abide by OPA '90 regulations, faces a new and complex compensation system if one of his tankers is involved in an oil spill accident. The overall implication is that the tanker owner's liability under OPA '90 is effectively unlimited. With such a prospect, he greatly increases the risks of trading in U.S. waters. An oil spill in U.S. waters can entail catastrophic business consequences for a tanker owner—in addition to virtually unquantifiable liabilities, the owner could be subject to fines, penalties, and prison terms. The enormous liabilities and severe criminal penalties in a proven case of negligence attached to pollution incidents have forced all concerned to focus on the absolute need to minimize accidental oil outflow under all circumstances.

It is now recognized that the double-hull configuration provides protection in low energy collisions and groundings. The U.S. Government believes that the rule represents a major initiative to reduce oil pollution of the seas. The disaster in European waters, caused by the tanker *Erika* and *Prestige* in the years 1999 and 2002, respectively, may be food for thought.

The Council has already sharply criticized the implementation of OPA '90 as being "too weak" to fulfill the mandates of OPA '90. The Council has attacked specifically the double-hull construction mandate and failure of USCG to provide much needed guidance on hull strength and corrosion protection.

Technology and techniques in the shipping industry change very rapidly. Especially today, forward planning is essential, whether developing a new design or operating an existing tanker. It is vital to be aware of any impending regulatory changes that could necessitate structural changes at a late stage of construction. For existing tankers, delay in becoming aware of changes will create problems, as a consequence of outdated certificates. Shipowners and builders must consult regularly with appropriate authorities concerning interpretation of OPA '90 legislation and rule making process, because requirements to satisfy OPA '90 are continuously refined or updated by the U.S. Coast Guard.

It is also important to appreciate that OPA '90 has created a dynamic evolving situation. An owner navigating the U.S. waters must be kept constantly informed and kept up to date with developments. Frequent changes are introduced by the U.S. Coast Guard to the requirements of OPA '90 that necessitate close contact with the U.S. authorities to ensure that the "Vessel Response Plan" is kept up to date. Each response plan is custom-made, because what is good for one owner/operator may not be suitable for another. The consequences of an oil spill in the U.S. territorial waters are too serious to be left to chance, so don't find out by accident.

Single-Hulls, Double-Hulls, and OPA '90

As mentioned earlier, the focal point of OPA '90 prevention is the requirement of double-hulls for tankers. Specifically, double-hulls are required for all tankers for which a building or major conversion contract was placed after June 30, 1990, and delivered under that contract prior to January 1, 1994. In general, OPA '90 legislation requires all single-hull tankers to be retrofitted with double-hulls or phased out of the trade by the year 2010. However, to avoid the potential impact of a large number of tankers reaching a legislated obsolescence on January 1, 2010, a phase out schedule based on vessel deadweight and age is included in the OPA '90 Legislation.

Tankers engaged in offshore unloading, that is tankers delivering oil to a lightering operation more than sixty miles offshore or unloading at a licensed deepwater port, such as the Louisiana Offshore Oil Port (LOOP), are exempt from the double-hull requirement until January 1, 2015.

Epilogue to OPA '90

For almost twenty years, the U.S. Congress has been trying to enact legislation that will protect the marine environment from oil pollution by tankers. Since OPA '90 became law, various groups, both within the United States and internationally, have been studying the technical issues surrounding the design of an oil tanker that will minimize oil pollution in the event of an accident. The intent of OPA '90 legislation is to encourage the development of innovative and cost-effective approaches to oil spill problems.

The design for an oil-spill-free tanker is a utopian goal. The wording of the legislative intent makes it clear that the choice of the double-hull concept offered a reasonable solution to the oil spill problem and presented a logically acceptable starting point for further research and development. The passage of the Oil Pollution Act of 1990 greatly broadened the authority of the federal government to regulate the transportation of oil and oil products within the jurisdiction of the United States of America, to prevent oil spills, to clean up those spills that do occur, and to compensate affected parties for damages resulting from spills.

The law places expanded regulatory and financial responsibilities on the owners and operators of oil port facilities and tankers used to transport oil. Liability limits and standards are now more stringent, and penalties are more severe. The strict liability scheme imposed by the Comprehensive Environmental Response Compensation and Liability Act (CERCLA) and many state counterparts can have severe consequences for owners and operators of oil tankers operating in

U.S. waters. President Bush's signing of OPA '90 is the most significant event in the history of the tanker industry to this point.

The European Union's Phase Out of Single-Hull Tankers

In March 2003, the European Union's Transport Council reached unanimous agreement to introduce a mandatory age limit for single-hull tankers regardless of their condition. They officially adopted a unilateral plan for accelerated phase out of single-hull tankers. The regulation was published in the October 1, 2003, edition of the *Official Journal of the European Union* and came into effect on October 21, 2003. It provides for, among other things, the immediate ban on transport of heavy grades of oil in single-hull oil tankers of 5,000 dwt or above to or from European Union ports. At the same time, they implemented an accelerated phase out of single-hull oil tankers on a schedule tied to the tanker's MARPOL category.

The tanker industry viewed the E.U.'s move as a demonstration of their decisiveness after the *Prestige* disaster by introducing amendments to the MARPOL 73/78 Pollution Convention. They ignored IMO's concerted efforts to arrive at an international framework to deal with matters affecting international shipping.

The international tanker industry was upset with the way the European Union rushed into the accelerated phase out schedule. Even Japan, a major shipbuilder who could gain much from the need to replace tankers, described the 2010 cutoff date as "lacking a logical basis." The mandatory age limit provided for the effective and retroactive devaluation of a tanker's value for no reason other than a date of construction.

The international tanker community felt the E.U.'s measures would have negative repercussions on the shipping industry generally. Due to the international nature of E.U.'s regulations, it is imperative that safety, security, and environmental standards must be established on the basis that they would be applied globally. Serious-minded shipping representatives, however, considered that a more flexible phase out timetable must not compromise the need to minimize or eliminate major disasters. The E.U. did not want to take any more chances that tanker hull structure failure and the resultant oil spills would continue to plague their ecology.

In the light of what happened to the marine environment by the sinking of the tankers *Erika* and *Prestige*, the E.U.'s anger and frustration was understandable. E.U. Regulation 1726/2003 prescribed the phasing out of single-hull tankers was, however, a disturbing precedent. On the other hand, it made sense that the following should be implemented:

- Certain grades of oil transported by sea should be carried on board oil tankers that are structurally and mechanically in top-class condition
- Older single-hull tankers should be subjected to the most rigorous scrutiny at more regular intervals
- Oil should be carried in double-hull tankers on the grounds that, in certain scenarios, the risk of polluting the seas with oil is reduced

However, the E.U.'s hasty move was disturbing for the following reasons:

- It preempted the *Prestige* inquiry by the flag states by making assumptions about the cause for the sinking of this tanker.
- It introduced unnecessary unilateralism and regionalism into the operations of an international industry.

IMO's disappointment was obvious because of the E.U.'s decision to reject them at the international forum for consideration and adoption of such measures. The IMO was further disappointed because of the fact that they had already agreed to adopt a fast-track approach to accommodate European Union environmental concerns arising from the *Prestige* sinking, particularly to consider the accelerated phasing out of the single-hull tankers.

The meeting that took place at IMO in London during the first week of December 2003 was to address the demands of the European Union, submitted by all fifteen E.U. member states, for further acceleration to an agreed single-hull phase out timetable. On December 4, 2003, IMO's Marine Environment Protection Committee agreed to a global compromise on single-hull tanker phase out requiring exceptional leeway for regional interests. The new rules restricting the movement of heavy grades of oil in single-hull tankers and accelerating the phase out of the vessel type came into force on April 5, 2005.

In the light of the way E.U. administrations have already implemented their own package of post-*Prestige* measures, high significance was attached to reaching concessions on their intentions over early implementation. The new rules envisage a first cutoff date for single-hull tankers of above 5,000 dwt, delivered in 1984 or later, at 2010. Agreement, however, was reached so that the flag states could allow the operation of single-hull tankers to 2015, or to the tanker's twenty-fifth anniversary of build, whichever came first, so long as they are subject to the newly strengthened Condition Assessment Scheme (CAS). From April 2005, tankers fifteen years or older must undergo a CAS at their next scheduled intermediate or renewal survey. The compromise rests on the ability of individual administrations to deny entry into ports or offshore terminals under their jurisdiction.

There were congratulations all around for achieving a compromise agreement on single-hull tankers at the IMO this time. Some expressed fears that the new rules might prove messy in practice, and could lead to considerable confusion. Others viewed the adoption of the accelerated phasing out of single-hull by the European Union as taking a page from the OPA '90 legislation. The United States' delegation at IMO reserved its position over these rules.

1. Immediately after oil is spilt on the sea, it spreads over the water surface and begins 'to weather'. How long it persists depends on its physical properties and the weather conditions.

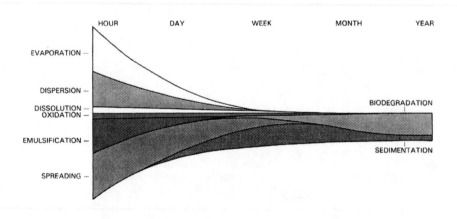

Figure 1. A schematic representation of the fate of a crude oil spill showing changes in the relative importance of weathering processes with time — the width of each band indicates the importance of the process.

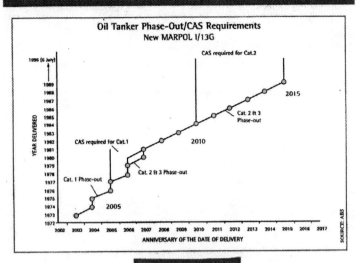

REVISED MARPOL 13G: EFFECTS

Oil Tanker Phase-Out/CAS Requirements
New MARPOL I/13G

DEFINITIONS

Category 1 tankers ('Pre-Marpol'): pre SBT/PL, 30,000 dwt and above plus 20-30,000 dwt vessels carrying oil/dirty products. Any vessels continuing to trade after their anniversary date in 2005 until their phaseout, must submit to the Condition Assessment Scheme - a stricter form of special survey. Such ships must trade either in SBT/PL (Segregated Ballast Tanks/Protectively Located) or in hydrostatically balanced loading mode after their 25th birthday as per the old 13 G regulation.

Category 2 tankers ('Marpol tankers'): crude/dirty products carriers with SBT/PL 20,000 dwt and above plus other products carriers 30,000 dwt and above. They must submit to CAS from 2010 onwards.

Category 3 covers crude/dirty products carriers from 5-20,000 dwt and other products carriers up to 30,000 dwt. They are unaffected by CAS.

November/December 2001

TOP 20 WORLD TANKER FLEETS BY COUNTRY OF OWNER

Self-Propelled Oceangoing Tankers 1,000 GRT and over.
Tonnage in Thousands

	Country	Tanker No.	DWT.
1.	Greece	780	61,995
2.	Japan	768	37,137
3.	Norway	479	33,361
4.	United States	417	33,271
5.	China	316	7,501
6.	Germany	196	7,388
7.	Hong Kong	137	16,042
8.	Korea (South)	223	8,242
9.	Taiwan	42	3,232
10.	United Kingdom	159	7,648
11.	Singapore	309	11,662
12.	Denmark	149	7,122
13.	Russia	386	7,564
14.	Saudi Arabia	77	11,024
15.	Italy	227	4,883
16.	India	113	6,340
17.	Turkey	93	1,318
18.	Iran	35	5,459
19.	Switzerland	36	1,313
20.	Malaysia	94	2,809
	All other Countries	2286	66,099
	TOTAL	7322	341,409

Based on parent company nationality.
Source: U.S. Maritime Administration. November 2003

10 Largest Oil Co./State Oil Co./State Tanker Owners

Owner	No. Tankers	Mil. DWT
Vela	18	4.9
China	104	4.6
NITC	23	3.6
Exxon-Mobil Group	22	3.3
Petrobras	50	3.2
Shipping Corp. of India	43	3.1
KOTC	17	2.9
Sovcomflot	32	2.8
Nat. Shipping of Saudi Arabia	11	2.8
Shell	19	2.5
Totals	339	33.7
Independent Fleet	716	59.5

Source: INTERTANKO Annual Review & Report 2002

10 Largest Independent Owners

Owner	No. Tankers	Mil. DWT
Frontline	73	17.0
Mitsui OSK Lines	78	10.6
Teekay Shipping	90	9.2
WorldWide	29	7.1
Overseas Shipholding	40	6.4
Bergesen d.y. A/S	17	5.0
Tanker Pacific Mgmt.	42	5.0
AP Moller	28	4.9
NYK	25	4.7
Angelicoussis Shiphld	18	3.9
Totals	440	73.8
Independent Fleet	2,846	246.3

SIX

The Quest for the Environment Friendly Oil Tanker

The notion of environmentally sustainable development has still to be fully recognized by the maritime community. Implementing the solutions to the environmental concerns is the shipping industry's responsibility, and this includes the following:

- Reduction in atmospheric pollution
- Ballast water treatment to prevent harming aquatic organisms via tanker's ballast water
- Ban on the use of tin-based antifouling hull paints
- Ship recycling, with a view to recycling ninety-five percent of a scrapped ship

The IMO, leading classification societies, and other independent organizations are endeavoring to find both regulatory and technical solutions for the environmental problems. The difficulty is ensuring long-term benefits and consequences of currently proposed solutions are favorable if elimination of environmental damage is realized, and to ensure that today's solution does not become a future problem.

Atmospheric Pollution by Ships

Since the industrial revolution 150 years ago, it has been taken for granted that the environment has an infinite capacity to absorb the waste generated by man's industry. Any concern for the environment's safety or consequences of the unrestrained consumption of finite fossil fuel consumption has been expressed until comparatively recently only by a minority. Depletion of the ozone layer, global warming, and water pollution have now become pressing issues and have been placed near the top of the international political agenda. The debate whether human activity was altering the global climate has shifted. Specifically, is the release of hothouse gases into our atmosphere to blame?

Some studies indicate that since the beginning of the industrial revolution, and primarily as a result of burning fossil fuels, the concentration of carbon dioxide in the atmosphere has risen by almost one third, from 280 to 370 parts per million. In fact in the 1990s, as a result of human activities, the annual discharge of CO_2 into the atmosphere has been 1.5 parts per million, and with each passing year, this rate has increased.

Even though humans release other hot-house gases, such as methane and nitrous oxide (NOx), it is estimated that CO_2 emissions will account for about two-thirds of potential global warming global carbon dioxide. Carbon dioxide is heavier than air.

As apprehension has grown regarding the possible hazards of a changing global climate, environmental groups, governments, and certain industries are trying to reduce the level of hothouse gases in the atmosphere by promoting energy efficiency and alternative energy sources, such as wind and solar power. Despite such efforts, more than eighty-five percent of the world's commercial energy needs are supplied by fossil fuels today. In efforts to limit the damage to the environment, IMO's Marine Environment Protection Committee had to consider protective measures. Classification societies and independent organizations initiated studies to obtain reliable information to be used during discussions at the IMO. Ships operating around the world will be expected to meet increasingly stringent environmental regulations, and many governments have comprehensive shipboard pollution abatement programs that will enable ships to be environmentally sound.

Amongst the more serious pollutants from ships' exhaust emissions are carbon monoxide (CO), carbon dioxide (CO_2), nitrogen oxide (NO_x), sulfur oxide (SO_x), Freon and other halogens, and cargo vapors. Freon and halons cause depletion of the earth's ozone layer. The stratospheric ozone layer is about 19 km—12 miles—above the earth's surface. Icy clouds provide the unusual conditions that activate chlorine from chlorofluorocarbons (CFCs). The stray chlorine atoms from ozone—a three oxygen molecules. As the ozone is destroyed, the earth loses much of its protection against harmful ultra violet radiation that can promote skin cancer and damage crops. It is believed that ozone depletion over the midlatitudes from CFCs is only a matter of time. Acid rain, in part a result of natural and manmade NO_x and SO_x in the atmosphere, continues to be a concern as well.

Little information on the significance of exhaust emissions from ships was scant, and any data available were dated and unreliable. Lloyd's Register of Shipping, in a major research program titled, "Marine Exhaust Emissions Research Program" completed in early 1995, provided the shipping community with a reliable set of generalized exhaust emission factors into estimates of general levels of emission and distribution of gases into the atmosphere by ships.

Many of the air pollutants, including the chlorofluorocarbons (CFCs, manmade chemicals used for refrigeration, some cleaning processes, and aerosol propellants), halons, and volatile organic compounds (VOC), were targeted by the IMO, and they focused their interest primarily on proposals for the restriction of the exhaust gases nitrogen oxide (NO_x) and sulfur dioxide (SO_2). This was an important program, because before any major action was considered on the restriction of exhaust emissions from ships, a realistic assessment was needed of the magnitude of the gases' distribution around the world.

Funding for the program was provided by Lloyd's Register, the Dutch authorities, the European Commission, and the U.K. Marine Safety Agency. Part of the program focused on particulate emission rates from marine diesel engines under typical service conditions and the quantification of regional exhaust emissions from ships. During these trials, NO_x, SO_2, CO, CO_2, and HC emissions were measured to assess the particulate findings in the context of steady gaseous emissions data obtained previously. The findings revealed that all of the fuel oil burning engines exhibited higher particulate emission rates of four to twelve kg/ton of fuel compared with the gas oil fueled engines, the rates of which were below two kg/ton. On the question of quantification of regional exhaust emissions from ships, the highest emission rates were found in the English Channel, the southern North Sea, and the Strait of Gibraltar.

The Ship and Ocean Foundation (SOF) of Japan—a non-profit organization—also carried out comprehensive research on the Reduction of CO_2 emissions into the atmosphere from ships. The project was sponsored by the Nippon Foundation. The SOF findings were presented at the IMO, during the Forty-Fifth Session of the Marine Environment Protection Committee in October 2000. The survey established that the total CO_2 emissions from ocean shipping were 400 million tons each year, based on a CO_2 measurement. This was derived from world transport patterns, vessel type, and bunker fuel consumed.

- Tankers accounted for thirty-one percent of the total CO_2 emitted by oceangoing cargo vessels, or 12.40 million tons per year.

- Container carriers accounted for thirty-three percent of the total CO_2 emitted, or 13.20 million tons per year.

- Bulk Carriers accounted for thirty-six percent of the total CO_2 emitted or 14.40 million tons per year.

Based on the results of this research, the Foundation was able to predict the annual increase of CO_2 emissions from tankers to be one percent; bulk carriers, two percent; and container carriers, six percent.

These estimates were based on an analysis of actual transportation volume over the previous five years.

The Norwegian Shipping and Research Organization embarked, in early 1991, on a research and development program called the Green Ships Programme. Their goal was to encourage the construction of environment friendly ships.

Their aim has been to develop and put into effect technological improvements to systems and equipment as well as putting themselves at the forefront of environment friendly ship development. Vapors from cargoes are particularly relevant to Norway because of the fleets of shuttle tankers operating in the North Sea. Developing a technology to eliminate atmospheric pollution from cargo vapors will also reduce loss of oil cargo.

A "green ship" has been defined as one which, during normal operations, does not discharge environment hostile substances to the sea or air and which, in the event of damage from a grounding or collision, has adequate built-in protection to prevent any such discharge. One of the objectives of the program was to contribute to and influence future environmental legislation at the IMO.

It would appear the Norwegian program inspired the establishment of the Green Award Foundation. This foundation was originally set up as a subsidiary of the Rotterdam Municipal Port Authority in Holland in 1994, but since 1998 has been operating as a fully independent body. The Dutch foundation, as its name implies, awards certificates to tankers. That in effect means more inspections and more inspectors.

The Diesel Engine Onboard Ships

Annex VI, Regulation 13 of MARPOL 1973/78, which deals with a wide range of air pollution matters, including ozone-depleting substances and acid deposition materials, is due to take effect soon. This amendment created the realization among diesel engine builders that it is more than likely that "dirty" engines will eventually become unsalable as much stricter legislation takes effect. Recognizing that exhaust emission requirements will become more stringent over time, diesel engine builders have been investigating a number of emission-reduction techniques. The requirements may sound daunting to the shipowner, but most of the compliance work falls on the engine builders, who are now developing diesel engines with lower exhaust emissions. Engine builders realize that good environmental performance will be an important sales factor in the future. This can be achieved without reduction in the performance of the engines they build and without incurring extra running costs for additives to fuel used by the engines.

The requirements for testing, survey, and certification to demonstrate emissions compliance are set by the Technical Code on Control of Emissions of NO_x from marine diesel engines. The code was drawn-up by IMO's Marine Environmental Protection Committee and governs all diesels with more than 130 KW output, except those installed solely for emergency use.

When Regulation 13 comes into force, it will be applied retroactively to the engines installed in ships built after December 31, 1999. The regulation also has the "engine group" concept, where only the parent engine in the group is required to take the certification test. The other engines belonging to the group are certified without NO_x measurement tests.

In the case of diesel engines on ships built prior to January 1, 2000, there should be two sets of emission measurements performed onboard while going through the approval process before an Engine International Air Pollution Prevention (EIAPP) Certificate is issued. In the interim period, a statement of compliance with the NO_x Technical Code will be issued instead. The feeling of those involved in the development of Regulation 13 of Annex VI is that this regulation will create many questions from administrations, shipowners, engine builders, and classification societies before the issue of exhaust emissions from ships is finally settled.

All diesel engines for installation on board ships fall within the scope of Annex VI, Regulation 13 requirements for installation on ships built on or after January 1, 2000, will generally be expected to have an Engine International Air Pollution Prevention Certificate. The actual engine certification process depends on the principle that NO_x emissions do not increase over the service life of the engine. More recent studies on pollutant emissions from commercial ships globally, carried out by the diesel engine builders MAN B&W, have achieved an up-to-date situation by adopting realistic average loads and engine running hours in one year, across the existing world merchant fleet ships above 100 dwt during the year 2001.

The results of the earlier studies in annual NO_x emission released by the world's commercial ships was in the order of ten million tons of NO_x, based on a total global marine fuel consumption of about 140 to 150 million tons per year. Further investigation has revealed that bunker oil consumption is much higher, resulting in a corresponding increase in NO_x, SO_x, CO_2, hydrocarbons, and particulate matter, including soot. The effects on atmospheric pollution therefore are more severe than previously suggested.

The MAN B&W study has taken into account a total of 90,000 oceangoing ships with a total installed main engine output of 286,000 MW. Emissions produced by the auxiliary engine equipment were calculated on the basis of thirteen percent of the installed main engine output. The study took into account NO_x emissions from port and coastal traffic. The total consumed bunker fuel for the year 2001, including the auxiliary engines was 281 million tons, of which 191 million tons was heavy fuel oil, and 90 million tons marine diesel oil and marine gas oil.

The total NO_x emissions, including the emissions from the auxiliary engines during 2001, was estimated to be twenty-two million tons. This is more than twice the NO_x emissions reported in previous studies.

It is of importance to note that for new ships whose keel was laid in January 2000, their diesel propulsion machinery must comply with IMO's requirement for NO_x limits. The diesel engines onboard these ships produced emissions as low as six to eight g/KW/h.

Is the Climate Change a Threat to Shipping?

Global warming affecting the oceans and the atmosphere has already unleashed a fury of energy, feeding and intensifying series of weather disasters at sea and along the coasts. The International Panel on Climate Change (IPCC), a United Nations Meteorological Organization based in Geneva, warned recently that coastal areas in many parts of the world are among the most affected by the destructive power of storms, and it is estimated, a three to four degrees Celsius rise in sea surface temperatures could produce hurricanes with more destructive power than current ones, sustained by winds up to 350 kilometers an hour (approximately 217.5 miles per hour). Such hurricanes may well grow stronger and more frequent due to the increased energy generated by the interaction between the warming sea surface and the atmosphere.

Atmospheric Pollution from Emissions

Fuel combustion quality is indicated by the smoke intensity visible in the exhaust gases as they leave the smoke stack. The content of particulate matter and nitrogen oxide (NO_x) in an engine's emissions must be controlled to meet IMO's pollution control standards. In a modern diesel engine installation on a tanker, emissions control is achieved by the following:

- Optimization of fuel valves and nozzles
- Water emulsification
- Installation of a selective catalytic reduction device

Particulate emissions in the exhaust gas may originate from the following:

- Formation of very small particles of partly burned fuel
- Partly burned lubrication oil
- Ash content of fuel oil and lubrication oil
- Sulfate and water

The sulfur content in fuel oil used has a large impact on the particulate level in the exhaust gas. Tests and analyses of exhaust gas have shown that a high-sulfur fuel produces a much higher level of particulate levels than gas oil.

MARPOL Annex VI on Air Pollution Prevention, entered into force in May 2005. Now all new and existing ships with diesel engines having a power output of 130 kW or more engaged on international voyages need to be certified to the requirements contained in the mandatory NO_x Technical Code.

Establishment of HELMEPA

In June 1982, representatives of the Union of Greek Shipowners and the Greek Seaman's Federation formed HELMEPA, an organization whose goal was to eliminate ship-generated pollution. They wrote and signed a "Declaration To Save The Seas," endorsed by the following agencies:

- The International Union for the Conservation of Nature and Natural Resources
- The Worldwide Fund for Nature
- The International Ocean Institute
- The International Institute for Environment and Development
- The Club of Rome

The aims of HELMEPA are promoted through training seminars and publicity campaigns. Their promotional materials relate studies of marine accidents to a pollution-free vessel's handling and safety. Such studies do help avoid making the same mistakes in the future, because past marine casualties involving pollution can reveal patterns and trends that are invaluable to organizations like HELMEPA.

The result of this initiative has led to the establishment of a Federation of Mediterranean Coastal States, with the object of eliminating waste from the Mediterranean Sea and coastal areas.

Fouling of the Underwater Hull Surface

Fouling of a tanker's hull is an unwanted growth of biological material on the under water part of the hull. If the hull is not protected by antifouling systems, it may gather up to 100 kg of marine growth per square meter in less than six months of being at sea. On a VLCC with a wetted surface of 40,000 square meters, such fouling could add up to 4,000 tons of marine growth. This increases the tanker's frictional resistance enormously and seriously affects speed and fuel consumption.

Biofouling of the tanker's underwater part and seawater pipe works, including sea chests, arises when barnacles and other types of marine organisms attach onto the steel surface as larvae and grow. An effective way to minimize biofouling was the use of TBT antifouling systems. As a biocide, TBT needed to be toxic to be effective in killing off the marine organisms that would attach to the hull. The main problem with TBT was its persistence in the marine environment. As TBT began to be used widely in antifouling paints, increasingly high concentrations of TBT were found in areas with high concentrations of yachts and ships, such as marinas, ports, and harbors. In the open seas and oceanic waters, TBT contamination was seen as less of a problem, although some studies showed evidence of TBT accumulation in fish and mollusks.

It was during the 1960s that the chemical industry developed an effective antifouling paint using metallic compounds, in particular the organotin compound tributyltin (TBT). There was a breakthrough in the late 1960s with the development of the self-polishing paints, in which the organotin compounds are chemically bonded to the polymer base. The leaching rate is controlled because the biocide is released when seawater reacts with the surface layer of the paint.

In 1988, the problem was brought to the attention of IMO's Marine Environment Protection Committee (MEPC). As a result, the IMO in 1990 adopted resolution MEPC 46 (30) recommending governments, to adopt measures to eliminate anti-fouling paints containing TBT. From 1990 onwards, the IMO was presented with TBT monitoring study results, which confirmed the toxicity of TBT compounds to marine organisms. At the same time, the IMO was also given information on existing alternative antifouling systems, including their effectiveness and the risks posed to the aquatic environment by these systems.

Today's antifouling paint systems are able to create a durable, efficient, and environment friendly coatings that satisfy hull efficiency and long docking intervals. These new coatings, which are applied with conventional spraying equipment, are free of all metals and biocides, and will not have to be removed to avoid encapsulation. Manufacturers of such coatings claim the antifouling paints now manufactured and available to the marine industry are applied to ships in fewer coats. Ships can be refloated in much shorter intervals after applying the final coat because the final curing will be continued under water. Also, since there is no evaporation, painting and dock time are not at the mercy of the weather, humidity is not a factor, and painting can continue in the rain.

Some antifouling paint suppliers have already stopped producing TBT coatings and are boosting output of non-TBT products. Depending on the ship's speed, the new TBT-free antifouling paints promise up to thirty-six months service for the vertical sides of the hull and up to sixty months service for the flat bottom.

An important consideration for some shipowners is the cost and worldwide restrictions on the removal, containment, and disposal of hazardous antifouling coatings now on their ships. Some repair yards provide high-speed auto-mated robotic water blasting of hull plates to remove the old paint, and this is becoming the desirable steel surface preparation method. The cost of this method is a great deal less than grit blasting and even less costly than the hand-held water-jetting.

Skin Friction and Antifouling Paints

Skin friction and wave-making in clam seas make-up the total hull resistance of a ship under way at sea. With the introduction of the all-welded hull during World War II, which eliminated shell plate riveting, efforts to reduce skin friction resistance were further directed toward obtaining coatings that would produce a smooth surface, when applied to a bare metal surface of the hull's steel plates.

Surface roughness increases however, not only with service, but also with further painting during subsequent dry-dockings. This was exacerbated by the fouling of the underwater part of the ship's hull. It was found that with conventional paints, bottom fouling starts to affect the ship's performance as early as 20 days after dry-docking.

Paint coatings used for a ship's hull constitute a class of materials of a highly complex nature. Not only are the paints used to reduce skin friction, they are also used as a barrier sheathings to protect the ship's hull from corrosion. Today's paint coating technology has changed from the multicoated thin film, to single or double coat thick-film technology to better prevent and control corrosion and marine growth.

Marine growth and corrosion increase the roughness of the underwater part of the ship's hull. This leads to a thickening of the boundary layer, pulling even more water forward with the moving ship. Not only does this increase the resistance of the ship, but it also reduces the inflow velocity to the propeller, which in turn affects the propeller revolutions and the engine speed. This could lead to an engine overload situation.

In any economic environment, the competitiveness of a ship is dictated by its service speed and fuel consumption. Control of the speed and fuel costs is therefore important, and it is necessary to ensure the ship is operating at its most efficient level.

Tanker Ballast Water Exchange and Its Effect on the Marine Ecosystem

The United Nations Convention on the Law of the Sea requires signatory nations to take all measures necessary to prevent, reduce, and control the unintentional or accidental introduction of species, alien or new, to any part of the marine environment, which may cause significant or harmful changes.

One of the greatest threats to the world's oceans is the introduction of invasive marine species into new environments by a ship's ballast water and attached to the ships hull.

Development of larger and faster ships completing their voyages in shorter time, combined with the rapid increase in world trade, means that the natural barriers to the dispersal of marine species across the oceans are being reduced. As a result, whole ecosystems are being changed in various parts of the globe, resulting in major ecological, economic, and human health impacts. In response to this threat, the United Nations Conference on Environment and Development, held in Rio de Janeiro in 1992, arranged with the International Maritime Organization (IMO) to take action to address the transfer of harmful organisms by ships.

The IMO arranged for a coordination unit—part of the Marine Protection Environment Committee—to tackle the problem, and the Global Ballast Water Management Program (GloBallast) came into being. It was an initiative to address the severe environmental, economic, and health threats posed by harmful organisms carried in ballast water. It represented a concerted effort to provide technical assistance to member countries to implement IMO Guide Lines and Conventions. As shipping is considered the most international industry, the only effective way to address shipping related issues is through a standardized international system, rather than unilateral responses by individual states.

IMO's member states developed voluntary guidelines for the control and management of ship's ballast water to minimize the transfer of harmful aquatic organisms and pathogens. The guidelines were adopted in 1997 by the IMO Assembly, Resolution A. 868 (20), replacing the earlier, less comprehensive voluntary guidelines adopted in 1993, Resolution A774 (18).

The approaches recommended under the IMO guidelines are, however, subject to limitations. Reballasting at sea provides the best available risk minimization measure but is subject to serious ship safety limits. Even when a ship is able to fully implement this technique, it has been found to be less than 100 percent effective in removing organisms from ballast water.

A great deal of research and development work has been carried out to develop a more complete solution to this problem, and options considered included the following:

- Physical treatment methods such as filtration, separation, and sterilization using ozone, ultra violet light, electric currents, and heat treatment;

- Chemical treatment methods such as adding biocides to ballast water to kill organisms;

- Biological treatment methods such as adding predatory or parasitic organisms to ballast water to kill any other organisms it might contain.

For any of the above measures to be adopted, they must be safe, environmentally acceptable, cost efficient, and effective.

The shipping industry recognizes the problem and that it must be addressed. But their response to the IMO was that any measures must be safe, cost effective, and practical. In March 2002, the U.S. Coast Guard placed a notice in the *U.S. Federal Register* (vol. 67, NO. 42, March 4, 2002) requesting that comments on three options for "Goals" and four options for "Standards" for ballast water treatment be submitted no later than June 3, 2002.

How serious is the problem of ballast water transfer by ship to public health? When a ship arrives in port and discharges its ballast water, the possibility of contaminating the local waters with foreign bacteria is initiated. This starts a cycle of pathogen transport that continues as ships enter and leave the port taking on and discharging their ballast water, which is a potential source for the dissemination of pathogens as well as microorganisms.

An example of how serious the problem is can be seen in a review by Dr. Gloria Casale of the U.S. Health Resources and Services Administration. She reported that more than 10,000 people presumably died in South America in the early 1990s from an apparently ballast-water-mediated cholera epidemic. The threat to human disease dissemination via ballast water is greatly increased in developing countries. Any lack of sanitation and inadequate treatment of domestic drinking water supplies leave populations highly vulnerable to epidemic diseases that are carried to their harbors and estuaries in ballast water.

The transfer of invasive aquatic species has proven to threaten human health by introducing species that compete with, prey upon, interbreed with, or simply destroy endemic species or ecosystems. They also interfere with legitimate human use of coastal and marine areas, potentially causing significant socio-economic impacts, including impacts on fisheries, tourism, coastal and aquatic industries, even extending into fresh water sources. All IMO member states participating in the working group—forty-two countries and observers from twelve organizations—unanimously agreed that "ballast water serves as a significant mechanism for the transfer of aquatic organisms from ecosystems to which they are adopted, to those in which they can be harmful and invasive."

The IMO decided that the basic mechanism of implementation would be to create a "Ballast Water Management Plan" for each vessel, including programs for certification and record keeping practices such as pumping, treatment, and sediment minimization. The planning requirement enables each vessel to adopt procedures that are most appropriate to its configuration, operations, and other factors. Adoption of the convention, which has taken four years to prepare, by the Diplomatic Conference at IMO in London in February 2004, is regarded a major and historic breakthrough in addressing this serious issue.

The purpose of the Ballast Water Programme is to minimize the discharge of ballast water in port or coastal waters for reasons outlined earlier. Tanker hull designers have not taken into consideration the Ballast Water Programme requirements in the past, simply because, it is only recently that discussions on the program's importance have taken place. Existing tankers were designed with little or no consideration to the effects of ballast exchange while underway at sea.

Ballast water exchange sequences can be complex, and a wide range of issues including transverse stability, structural strength, slamming, resonant sloshing, and propeller immersion must be taken into consideration. The tanker industry must consider carefully how the new IMO Convention will affect the operation of existing tankers, because the complexity of ballast water exchange sequences will present safety concerns. The risk of human error and equipment failure could endanger the tanker as well. Also, crew training is absolutely essential to ensure the Ballast Water Programme will affect the tanker's performance especially when certain sea conditions are encountered during ballasting and deballasting while underway at sea.

As regards new tanker designs, ballast water management, and the process chosen to achieve it, should be considered as a basic component of a tanker's design. Ballast tank design should facilitate all aspects of ballast water management. Where ballast water exchange while under way at sea is the chosen method, the overall design, strength, and transverse stability, should be sufficient to permit its execution on all ballast voyages, and in all except the most severe weather conditions. For the guidance of the ship's Captain, the maximum sea state and swell conditions should be identified by the tanker builder, in which ballast water exchange can safely be carried out, and should be recorded in a Ballast Water Management Plan, which should be created for the tanker.

The Global Ballast Water Management Programme

The introduction of harmful aquatic organisms that cause diseases to new environments via any ship's ballast water is considered one of the greatest environmental challenges facing the international shipping industry today. The Global Ballast Water Management Programme, as it is now known, aims at preventing the spread of unwanted alien organisms and pathogens in a ship's ballast water and sediments. The program's aim is to develop mandatory regulations to address the problem of invasive species via ships' ballast water and sediments.

Early considerations to solve the problem were to treat the ballast water carried, using high temperature, ultrasound, filters, and biocides

Such measures did have merit, but all have drawbacks, such as measures of retrofit hardware on board a tanker. All were likely to need extensive research to confirm their effectiveness and feasibility for shipboard application. The studies concluded that an effective way to minimize the problem was to exchange the ballast water taken in continental waters for water taken offshore, to be an effective measure, since offshore species taken aboard in the exchange, are not likely to find favorable conditions for survival and propagation at the tanker's destination.

To reduce taking on board a tanker full of unwanted pathogens, the tanker should do the following:

- Limit the amount of ballast water taken on board
- Minimize the intake of port and coastal sediment
- Ballasting should be avoided in shallow waters; in stagnant areas; and in the vicinity of sewage outflows, and dredging operations. These are areas where marine organisms that can cause diseases are present.
- Whenever practicable, ballasting should be delayed until the tanker is in deep, open, ocean waters.

Ballast water exchange is considered the single most practical method for ballast water management. Such an operation can be accomplished by either the "empty-refill" method or the "overflow" method. Both of these methods have proven to be as much as 90 percent effective in eliminating unwanted aquatic organisms.

The "empty-refill" or "sequential" method of ballasting requires considerable planning to ensure that the tanker will remain within acceptable safety criteria. Using the flow-through method, will not normally affect the tanker's condition, it is important however to ensure that piping and overflow arrangements on the tanker perform well, so that the ballasting tank will not be over-pressurized. Two such considerations are venting and overflowing arrangements of the tank.

The "empty-refill" or "flow-through" methods have the added merit of requiring no retrofitting of hardware, it being simply an operational step using hardware for existing procedures. Consequently the ballast water exchange is being adapted as an immediate and ultimate control measure. The system, however, is not without its operational impacts and hazards. It requires that individual ballast tanks be emptied before refilling, and consequent changes in draft, trim, stability, and hull girder shear and bending stresses. In rough seas, such an operation could create bow slamming, and propeller emergence, that can create speed and torque transients in the propulsion machinery. Ballasting and deballasting must therefore be done carefully by properly trained ship's personnel.

A new International Convention for the Control and Management of Ship's Ballast Water and Sediments is well underway at IMO now. Their goal is to reduce impacts from aquatic bioinvasions, through improved control and management of ship's ballast water transfers. The IMO Convention provides a uniform, global regime for the control of harmful species transferred by ship's ballast water. It has created an institutional basis by establishing an "Office for Ballast Water Management" to act as secretariat to the new convention. Under IMO's Integrated Technical Cooperation Program, they will ensure the necessary sustainability after the adoption of the convention. It is hoped, adoption of the convention by the international maritime community will take the necessary steps towards sustainable management of marine and coastal resources.

Tanker hull designers have not taken into consideration the program's requirements simply because it is only recently that discussions on the program's importance have taken place. Existing tankers were designed with little or no consideration to the effects of ballast water exchange while the tanker is underway at sea.

The tanker industry must now consider carefully how the new IMO Convention will affect the operation of the existing design of tankers, because of the complexity of the ballast water exchange sequences will present safety concerns, and risk of human error and equipment failure could endanger the tanker. Also, crew training is absolutely essential to ensure the ballast water program will not affect the tanker's performance, especially when certain sea conditions are encountered during ballasting de-ballasting while under way at sea.

For new tanker designs, ballast water management and the process chosen to achieve it should be considered as a basic component of a tanker's design. Furthermore, ballast tank design should be such as to facilitate all aspects of ballast water management. When ballast water exchange while underway at sea is the chosen method, the overall design, strength, and transverse stability should be sufficient to permit its execution on all and in all ballast voyages, except severe weather conditions. The maximum sea state and swell conditions should be identified by the tanker designer in which ballast water exchange can be carried out safely, and should be recorded in a Ballast Water Management Plan.

Unless special ballast tanks are arranged on the tanker dedicated to clean ballast water only, it may be necessary to use some of the cargo tanks to ballast the tanker. Using correctly administered crude oil washing (COW) for the cargo tanks, the crude-oil-washed tanks can be used for clean ballast because cargo tank cleaning using the COW process is of a higher standard than can be obtained by water washing alone. It is necessary, however, to have good quality inert gas arrangements used during discharging or crude oil washing operations. Such operation must be carried out by competent tanker personnel.

The American Bureau of Shipping issued in October 1999 the *Advisory Notes on Ballast Water Exchange Procedures,* based upon studies and analyses focusing on fourteen typical tankers. The study cautions that the findings should be viewed as typical representative findings, and that they are highly dependent on an individual's tanker design and its structure, and which may vary greatly from one design to another. Conclusions however can also be drawn with respect to desirable features for new construction or designs.

The question may be asked, "Why Now?" Studies in various parts of the world are showing that the incidence of aquatic bioinvasions, including those introduced by shipping, is continuing to increase. This highlights the urgent need for a concerted management response, including the adoption and effective implementation of the *International Convention for the Control and Management of Ships' Ballast Water and Sediments.*

Ballast Water Management

On February 13, 2004, at the Diplomatic Conference at IMO in London, IMO member states adopted the *International Convention for the Control and Management of ship's Ballast Water and Sediments* by consensus.

The conference was attended by representatives of seventy-four member states, and the convention will enter into force twelve months after ratification by thirty states, representing thirty-five percent of the world merchant shipping tonnage. Under this convention, ships will be required to do the following:

- Implement ballast water management plans

- Maintain reliable records of ballast water operations

- Carry out ballast water management procedures to given standards

Parties to the Convention are given the option to take additional measures, consistent with international law and in observance of guidelines yet to be developed by IMO.

For many years, the introduction of harmful aquatic organisms and pathogens to new environments has been a major threat. Protection of the marine environment is beyond the scope of one maritime country and has global benefits. The new convention is beneficial for all maritime nations, and the international maritime industry will benefit from a uniform global regime. The negative impact on the marine environment will be reduced.

Parties to the convention are given the right to take, individually or jointly with other parties, more stringent measures with respect to the prevention, reduction, or elimination of the transfer of harmful aquatic organisms and pathogens through ship's ballast water and sediments. The specific requirements for ballast water management are contained in Regulation B-3, "Ballast Water Management for Ships."

With regard to IMO's Assembly Resolution A.868 (20), which in 1997 adopted the IMO "Guidelines for the Control and Management of Ship's Ballast Water" to minimize the transfer of harmful aquatic organisms and pathogens, the resolution guidelines have often been referred to as voluntary. However, they do have certain legal status under international law, having been adopted by consensus as a Resolution of the Assembly of IMO.

From a legal point of view, the status of Resolution A.868 (20) is not affected by the adoption of the new Convention. There is nothing in the new Convention that explicitly states that the Convention supersedes Resolution A.868 (20). In fact the new convention is based largely on A.868 (20) in terms of practical measures. Anything done to implement the resolution and guidelines will not preempt the convention.

At the time of writing, there is no formal international evaluation framework for ballast water management and treatment. A formal evaluation program has been proposed, and an informed debate has been arranged to stimulate awareness of the consequences of ship's ballast water discharge in coastal ecosystems vulnerable to alien invasion. Such debate can assist in risk assessments, recognizing the need for specific care or measures for standards required for the discharge of ballast water. Such standards will be a very important tool in proper ballast water management.

It is estimated that the amount of ballast water discharged globally each year by ships ranges from three to twelve billion tons. One of the options that has been proposed for the treatment of ballast water is the use of chemical biocides. One should be keep in mind that, in efforts to develop policies for the banning of harmful antifouling paints for ships, innovative industries rapidly responded to the challenge by developing less harmful antifouling systems. They also created a context for effective implementation of a ban on organotins from antifouling systems for ships. Several industries now appear to have accepted the challenge to develop ship's ballast water treatment methods.

There is agreement in the tanker industry that the long term answer to oil pollution and to an effective water ballast exchange program by the oil tanker is the inclusion of a segregated ballast tank in new tanker designs.

Using Buoyancy Reduction instead of Adding Weight to Adjust Ship's Drafts:

A recent report from the United States mentions the laboratory-bench idea for a ballast-free ship, designed to provide better protection of the marine ecosystem from the introduction of non-indigenous aquatic species through ballast water transfer. The concept uses the principle of buoyancy reduction rather than the addition of weight using ballast water to adjust the drafts for a ballast voyage.

The aim of the design is to eliminate the ballast water required in the light ship condition to ensure transverse stability and to provide bow and propeller immersion for the required maneuverability during a ballast voyage. The proposed arrangement could significantly reduce the transfer of aquatic species compared to the conventional practice of ballasting enclosed tanks that have to be cleaned with treatment process both during and at the end of the ballast voyage.

The system may not eliminate the transoceanic transport of ballast water at the end of the voyage, but could provide better protection from further introduction of nonindigenous aquatic species through ballast water at the end of the voyage.

Inert Gas

In December 1969, the oil tanker industry was rocked by huge explosions on board three very large crude oil carriers (both 207,000 dwt), the *Marpesa* and the "*Mactra,* both of Shell Oil Company, and the *Kong Haakon VII* of Norway. The explosions occurred off the South African Coast while the tankers were in ballast and the cargo tanks were being cleaned. All three survived the explosions, despite the heavy damage to the hull structure.

Some years later, (1975–1976) two more 207,000 dwt VLCCs, the *Bergeistra* and the *Berge Vanga,* also suffered explosions and quickly sank. In the case of these two crude oil carriers, the most likely cause of the explosion was in the double bottom pipe tunnel.

In the case of the *Marpesa*, the explosion occurred in the cargo tanks on December 12, 1969, with the loss of two lives. The vessel became a total loss. The *Mactra* explosion occurred in the cargo tanks on December 29, 1969, during tank cleaning. Two lives were lost. The tanker survived the explosion. The *Kong Haakon VII*, a 219,000 dwt VLCC, explosion occurred on December 19, 1969, during tank cleaning. No lives were lost, and the tanker survived the explosion.

The occurrence of these explosions initiated a wave of investigation and research activities in order to identify the cause of the explosions. Shell Oil, in their research, found that during the cleaning of the cargo tanks, the powerful water jets used to wash tanks created a mist with sufficient electrical charge to ignite the mixtures of air and oil vapors in the empty cargo tanks, thus causing the explosion. The same comments apply for the explosion that damaged the *Kong Haakon VII*. The investigations conducted by Shell Oil in New York, the U.K., and by the Norwegian authorities. over a two year period, concluded, the safest method to prevent explosions on board a tanker is to prevent the occurrence of a flammable gas mixture inside the tanks. The three elements that contribute to an explosion are fuel, oxygen, and an ignition source. This became known as the "Fire Triangle." Enclosed in a container, an explosion will occur. This is where the tanker industry made the mistaken assumption that the explosions that occurred at the time had something to do with very large tankers, when actually the size of the tank is irrelevant.

To avoid an explosion within a cargo tank, it is necessary to eliminate or remove at least one of the three factors that contribute to the explosion, namely, the source of ignition, oxygen (in the correct proportion to support combustion), and hydrocarbon gases.

A mixture of hydrocarbon gas and air cannot ignite unless its composition lies within the "flammable range" of gas in air concentrations. In the case of a crude oil carrier, on completion of discharge of the cargo and during the ballast voyage, mixtures of hydrocarbon gases and air will, under normal circumstances, exist in the cargo tanks. The actual hydrocarbon gas in any mixture depends on the volatility of the cargo, the ambient temperature, and the amount of cargo residues. To avoid the risk of an explosion, it is necessary to replace a flammable tank atmosphere with inert gas, the purpose of which is to remove the oxygen side of the triangle by keeping the oxygen content in the tank atmosphere well below the limit when an explosion may occur, even in the presence of an ignition source and hydrocarbon gases.

There are three operations that involve replacement of gas in cargo tanks of crude oil carriers: inerting, purging, and gas freeing. Inerting means the introduction of inert gas into a tank with the objective reducing the oxygen content within the tank to eight percent or less by volume. Inert gas has been defined as a gas or mixture of gases such as flue gas containing insufficient oxygen to support the combustion of hydrocarbons. For complete gas replacement it is important that the entry velocity of the incoming gas is high enough for the jet to reach the bottom of the tank.

Both the International Maritime Organization and the International Chamber of Shipping have published guidelines on the subject of inert gas safety. The objective of these manuals is to provide information conducive to safe practices for tanker personnel.

Crude Oil Washing of Cargo Tanks of Crude Oil Carriers

The idea of crude oil washing (COW) was researched and developed by B.P. Oil Company in 1972, using two of the company's crude oil carriers as "prototypes" for the process. During the research period, it was found that ballast water could be put into a tank that had been crude oil washed only, without water washing, causing only a minor discoloration of the ballast washing.

The procedure involves cleaning crude oil carrying tanks by washing the structure with crude oil itself. This is done while the oil cargo is being discharged. When sprayed onto the sediments clinging to the cargo tank structure, the oil simply dissolves the sediments, turning them back into useable oil, which is pumped ashore with the rest of the cargo. Using the COW process to clean the cargo tanks, which leaves virtually no oil wastes in the tanks, makes it possible to eliminate the provision of slop tanks in the cargo tank configuration.

By 1977, COW was widely adopted by the tanker industry as a means of sediment control and was considered an alternative to segregated ballast tanks (SBT). In February 1978, COW was introduced into IMO's MARPOL 73/78 Protocol as part of the 1978 Protocol, where the International Conference on Tanker Safety and Pollution Prevention, recognized COW as an important antipollution measure, and set a target date for entry into force of June 1981.

During the early stages of development of the crude oil washing process, it was found that for an existing tanker, the following were true:

- Provided the tanker's pumping system and shore facilities were compatible with the process, cargo tanks could be crude oil washed while the tanker is discharging its cargo without any undue loss of time,

- The results of cargo tank cleaning using this process are of a higher standard than can be obtained by water washing alone.

- Water washing of tanks is not necessary for sediment control.

- Good quality inert gas is essential during discharge and simultaneous crude oil washing.

- The time required for subsequent tank cleaning at sea is reduced considerably.

Because of the changes necessary to meet IMO's standards, the owner of an existing crude oil carrier over 40,000 dwt had the option of a segregated or converted ballast tank arrangement, or COW with the IG system. Because the converted ballast tanks of the crude oil carrier were originally used to carry cargo, converting them to SBT or CBT would reduce the tanker's cargo carrying capacity, thus reducing the earning capacity of the tanker. In the case of a

VLCC, the loss could be as much as thirty percent. Retrofitting VLCCs and ULCCs with COW and an IG system was the sensible choice.

Shipowners are required to *only use properly qualified personnel to carry out crude oil washing.*

The Load on Top System (LOT)

The load on top system (LOT) was introduced and developed in an effort to reduce pollution of the seas by the oil on board crude oil carriers.

Transporting crude oil is always done in one direction. The return voyage is done in ballast which necessitates ballasting the tanker to ensure good sea-keeping ability, propeller immersion, and maneuverability. Unless special ballast tanks are arranged on the tanker dedicated to clean ballast water only, it is necessary to use some of the cargo tanks for ballasting the tanker.

Shipowners have discovered that the amount of oil residue in the cargo tanks of a VLCC amounts to around 1,000 tons. For some crude oils, the residue can be as much as 2,000 tons because of heavy waxy deposits that are difficult to separate during washing of the tanks. A few decades ago, the general practice was that when cargo tank washing was carried out, the crew would simply strip off the washings and dump them into the sea. As crude oil movement around the world increased, the amount of oil discharged to the seas increased proportionally. Public opinion hardened, and shipowners recognized that a change in the practice of dumping oil residues into the seas was required.

Various alternatives were considered by the oil industry in Europe, and the one accepted and adopted was the load on top (LOT) practice. This involves retaining the highly concentrated oily water mixture on board that results from the cargo tank washing and making it part of the subsequent loading operation, that is, load the new cargo of oil on top of the residues collected from the previous voyage. To make it effective, the concept of LOT required that only oil that remains in the cargo pipelines or as clingage on the cargo tank structure would be collected and transferred to a common reception tank. Using good practices, almost all of the oil previously dumped into the seas could be retained on board.

The explosions on the three VLCCs in 1969 mentioned earlier drew attention to the possibility that the increased complexity of the LOT practice could increase the possibility of an explosion in the cargo tanks. It was also recognized that the LOT practice, although simple, was not easy to operate. Correct operation requires a sound understanding of the process of oil and water mixture and separation. In response to these feelings, a *Load on Top Guidance Manual* was published in 1973 by the International Chamber of Shipping, London, and the Oil Companies International Marine Forum. The guidelines set out to show people how to operate the system within the legal parameters.

There is no doubt the LOT process correctly applied contributes greatly to the reduction of oil pollution of the seas.

At a Symposium on Marine Pollution in London in 1973, the representative of the United States of America pointed out that in practice, the LOT procedure represents only "a useful quantum jump in oil pollution mitigation and unfortunately, is not the elusive panacea that we all seek in minimizing international oil discharges to the seas." The U.S. representative indicated, "the solution to the problem is the concept of 'segregated ballast,' and mentioned the study conducted in America by a joint industry/government group that was submitted to the IMO's Sub-committees on Marine Pollution and Ship Design and Equipment in June 1972, and February 1973. There was agreement in the industry that the long term answer to oil pollution by the crude oil carrier is the segregated ballast tank arrangement (SBTA).

OIL TANKERS AND THE ENVIRONMENT

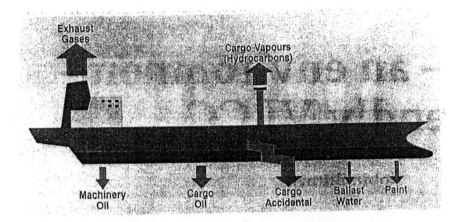

Exhaust Gases

Cargo Vapours (Hydrocarbons)

Machinery Oil

Cargo Oil

Cargo Accidental

Ballast Water

Paint

MAJOR POLLUTION SOURCES FROM OIL TANKERS.

Among the more serious atmospheric pollutants from ships are, the exhaust gases, Nitrogen Oxide (NOx), and Sulphur Oxide (SO_2), from the Main and Auxiliary Machinery, on board the tankers.

Estimated	SO_2	NOx	CO	HC	CO_2
Global emissions from ships (mill. tons)	4.58	5.09	0.12	0.22	272
Percentage of total global emissions	4.0	6.9	0.06	0.38	1.39

Based on CO$_2$ measurements, it has been
established the total emissions from ocean
shipping were 400 million tonnes each year.
This was derived from world transport
patterns, vessel type and fuel consumed.

THE VLCC "KONG HAAKON VII"
DAMAGED AFTER TANK EXPLOSION

THE SHELL TANKER "MACTRA"

SEVEN

The Double-Hull Saga and Hull Design Alternatives

The year 1992 will be remembered by the oil tanker industry as the end of an era, because on December 23, the U.S. Government, through their London Embassy, filed a declaration with IMO stating that the express approval of the U.S. will be necessary before the double-hull amendments to MARPOL 73/78 may enter into force for the United States.

By such action, the United States has reaffirmed OPA '90 as the standard for all tankers entering U.S. waters until such time as the U.S. Government expressly approves the entry into force of the 1992 double-hull amendments to MARPOL. This in effect means the end of the single-hull tanker.

The Oil Pollution Act of 1990 (OPA '90) is an act of the federal government of the United States, and applies to U.S. as well as foreign oil tankers entering U.S. territorial waters. The act provides, among other things, environmental safeguards in oil transportation. In conflict with OPA '90, the MARPOL amendments include the mid-deck tankers as an alternative to the double-hull design and a differing schedule for the retirement of single-hull tankers. OPA '90 does not permit alternatives to the double-hull requirement.

Carrying oil in bulk by tankers is a service that has been in existence for more than a century, and despite comprehensive international regulations, oil pollution of the seas by oil tankers continues to be a significant international problem. It is extremely difficult, however, if not impossible to legislate the risk of marine oil pollution out of existence. As there are no acceptable energy substitutes for oil in the foreseeable future, and transportation of the oil can only be done by oil tankers, accidents must be expected just as they do in other industries—commercial aviation, coal mining, the nuclear industry, and so forth.

Pollution of the Seas by Oil

It was in 1954 that the International Convention on the Prevention of Oil Pollution of the seas was concluded in London. The convention, known as "OILPOL 54," entered into force in 1958 and prohibited the intentional discharge of oil and oily water mixtures into the marine environment, and became enforceable by the flag state.

Following the formation of the Intergovernmental Maritime Consultative Organization (IMCO) in 1958 (now the International Maritime Organization IMO), another International Conference, held in Copenhagen in 1959, wherein the participants discussed the subject of oil pollution and recommended extending the effectiveness of the 1954 Convention.

The three major causes of accidental pollution from tankers are collision, grounding, and structural failure. The way in which ballast and cargo spaces are arranged in a tanker has a strong influence on the likelihood to structural failure and on the quantity of oil that may be released in the event of collision or grounding.

The March 1967 grounding of the *Torrey Canyon,* created the international regulation in 1973 for segregated ballast tanks (SBT) as one means of enhancing the pollution prevention capabilities of new tankers. (To compensate for the loss of cargo-carrying capacity, naval architects increased the depth of the tankers).

The 1973 IMO Convention became known as MARPOL 73. The Convention drafted a strong document that offers the prospect of significant reduction of pollution from accidental releases and operational discharges of oil. The aim was, and emphasis was placed on, the design of oil tankers from the point of view of minimizing accidental oil pollution of the seas.

Optimizing the location of SBTs as defensive space can provide significant improvement toward reducing accidental pollution. Some argued that design flexibility in the location of segregated ballast tanks is much to be preferred over specifying particular location, such as double bottom. The important point was that designers would be required to distribute segregated ballast spaces to provide effective protection against accidental releases, giving due regard to other parameters that must be satisfied such as longitudinal bending strength, tank size limitations, and survival injury in the event of an accident.

A number of serious accidents between 1974 and 1978 resulted in the MARPOL 1978 Protocol. Within weeks of this Protocol being enacted, the VLCC *Amoco Cadiz* ran aground off the Northern Coast of France causing serious oil pollution in the area. Oil shipping operations continued under the auspices of MARPOL 1973 and the MARPOL 1978 Protocol until the grounding of the VLCC *Exxon Valdez* in 1989 in Alaska. The grounding of this tanker, which caused serious damage to the environment, resulted in the passage of the Oil Pollution Act of 1990 by the U.S. Congress. The act is intended to provide environmental safeguards in oil transportation and addresses wide ranging changes associated with preventing, responding to, and assigning liability associated with oil spills at sea.

The historical record shows that oil spills from accidental groundings or collisions have been the dominant cause of oil pollution. The spills of the *Torrey Canyon* in England, *Amoco Cadiz* in France, *Metulla* in Chile, *Exxon Valdez* in Alaska, the *Aegean Sea* in Spain, and the *Braer* in Northern Scotland were all significant milestones in the quest for safer ships and cleaner oceans. Traditionally, naval architects have not designed tankers at the detail level to withstand collisions and groundings. There has never been comprehensive research and development, with the necessary effort and impartiality to develop a spill resistant tanker hull design which, in the event of a collision/grounding accident, the least oil spill would occur.

There is an endemic lack of data and knowledge that would result in placing decisions more nearly on a factual basis rather than on the basis of informed opinion that the major classification societies themselves are questioning publicly whether current strength criteria are adequate. The introduction of OPA '90 legislation was at first vigorously opposed by some international oil companies, some independent tanker owners, and some shipyards. The tanker industry was told that the U.S. Secretary of Transportation was charged with conducting a study to determine whether there were effective alternatives to a double-hull, and to base his determination on recommendations of the U.S. National Academy of Sciences and other organizations, and to present them to the U.S. Congress for legislative action.

Improved tanker design is one way to reduce the risk of oil pollution but the risk cannot be eliminated entirely. The *Executive Summary* of the U.S. National Research Council in March 1991 states, "The state of knowledge regarding the precise circumstances and structural effects of actual tank vessel accidents is so inadequate that any assessment of design alternatives will produce results that are dependent on the chosen assumptions and accident scenarios—artificial rather than actual criteria. This is true even of this study."

Design criteria tend to fix technology at a point in time, thus inhibiting innovation and removing the incentive to advance ship technology and design. Performance standards are preferable, in that they tend to promote new development in terms of structural and operational innovations that would result in meeting or surpassing the standards. However, to achieve that goal, such standards need to include: an integrated micro-understanding of the dynamics of ship structural failure and related factors; long-range research in failure theory; protocols leading to mandatory engineering documentation of casualties; and computational models resulting in outflow predictions.

Major research programs directed to design a spill-free tanker are being mounted in Japan, where a seven year study on alternative designs is underway. Norway plans a five-year study on tanker design, operations, and oil spill cleanup. The U.S. federal government, industry, and academia should cooperate in a coordinated, substantive research effort directed to complete the following:

- Perform a comprehensive risk-assessment study that would lead to the establishment of future risk-based design goals for tank vessels with attendant compliance guidance

- Accomplish the basic research needs noted

- Test and evaluate design concepts (including theoretical analysis, model tests, and field trials)

- Advance the capability to assess and value natural resource damages (better understanding of the environmental effects of oil spills, the feasibility and cost of restoration, and the development of accepted methodology for valuing environmental benefits would permit more reliable cost-benefit analysis of vessel design alternatives and other means of pollution control)

- Achieve optimal pollution control by integrating use of design alternatives with operational considerations

OPA '90 authorizes such a research program. The program should be coordinated with foreign research centers, notably in Norway and Japan, and the efforts of the IMO. Comprehensive research is essential if important, far-reaching decisions concerning the future of oil transportation by tanker are to be made on the basis of fact, as contrasted with informed opinion."

The Double-Hull versus the Mid-Deck

There was intense debate at IMO about the design of new oil tankers. Participants acknowledged that any new regulations should not inhibit the introduction of improved oil tanker designs. In particular, the mid-deck design promoted by the Japanese delegation and a European shipbuilding consortium, supported by some administrations, resulting in an industry proposal to IMO that a comparative study should be undertaken of the relative merits of the mid-deck and double-hull designs.

An IMO steering committee was set up to conduct the study, with an oil and tanker industry funded budget. The study concluded that the mid-deck design could be regarded as equivalent to the double-hull in terms of protection against accidental pollution resulting from collisions and groundings.

Detailed provisions covering both designs were included in the Regulation 13F of Annex I of the MARPOL Convention, adopted by the IMO's Marine Environment Protection Committee (MEPC) in March 1992. The Regulation became effective in July 1993, and requires all new oil tankers above 5,000 dwt to be of double-hull or equivalent design, and all oil tankers between 600 and 5,000 dwt to be fitted with at least a double bottom.

Regulation 13G, which covers existing tankers, was also debated at IMO in November 1991, where the general feeling was to develop an upgrading and phase out program. It was realized during this debate that if serious disruption of the trade were to be avoided, a method should be developed whereby the tanker operator would be given flexibility to decide which measures, equivalent in standard, would be appropriate to his fleet.

During the March 1992 meeting of the MEPC, members decided more stringent survey requirements should be applied with limited upgrading of older tankers to take effect two years after the entry into force of the amendments. Those involved in the decision making for the amendments should keep their fingers crossed, and hope to see the aging tanker fleet maintained in a safe and seaworthy condition.

Life for Pre-MARPOL Single-Hull Tankers after Twenty-Five Years

The main barrier to further trading for tankers built prior to 1980, also known as pre-MARPOL tankers, is the requirement to satisfy Regulation 13G when they reach the age of twenty-five years. This regulation, which covers existing single-hull crude oil tankers over 20,000 dwt, and products tankers over 30,000 dwt requires that pre-MARPOL tankers must have protective location covering thirty percent of the total cargo tank length at the ship's side or bottom.

Regulation 13G sets out a series of alternative arrangements for meeting these requirements. It offers four options for extending the life of these tankers from twenty-five to thirty years, including three which meet the thirty percent protective location requirement.

1. designating a certain portion of cargo tanks as non-cargo carrying spaces (keep empty);

2. converting cargo tanks to segregated ballast tanks (SBT), or dedicated clean ballast tanks (DCBT);

3. installation of longitudinal bulkheads to provide a double side or fit a double bottom. The bulkheads must be at least two meters in width, or in case of double bottom must be either two meters deep or about seven percent of the tanker's breadth;

4. adopt hydrostatically balanced loading patterns.

When considering the fourth option, the loading patterns make use of the difference in density between the oil carried and seawater so that in the event of a collision/grounding accident when the shell plating is breached, seawater enters the tank rather than oil escaping and polluting. It is important to keep in mind, if this alternative is adopted, hydrostatically balanced loading must provide the equivalent level of protection as the thirty percent requirement for protection. Using this alternative, however, there is the risk of structural damage due to the sloshing effects of the cargo in partially filled cargo tanks. With this alternative, no structural alternatives are necessary, and no changes to cargo pumping or piping should be necessary.

The table at the end of this Chapter, compares the four designs based on a pre-MARPOL built VLCC of 260,000 dwt. This alternative may be considered as the preferred option, from the point of view cargo carrying loss with no structural or other alterations to the structure or cargo handling.

New Global Timetable to Phase Out Single-Hull Oil Tankers

This accelerated phase out of tankers is one of range of post-*Erika* measures. At the Forty-Sixth Session of Marine Environment Protection Committee (MEPC), held in London April 23–27, 2002, a revised chapter 13G of the MARPOL convention was agreed upon by delegates from IMO's 158 member states, requiring all new oil tankers built since 1996 are required to have double-hulls.

The new regulations entered into force in September 2002, the new phase out time table sets 2015 as the principal cut off date for single-hull tankers. In the years leading up to that date, tankers will be withdrawn from service according to their year of delivery and the category to which they belong. (See OPA '90 Chapter for single-hull phase out in United States and E.U.)

Alternative Designs to Double-Hull

The mid-deck design is not a new development. The earliest record available where an oil tanker was actually constructed using the horizontal bulkhead concept was the steam tanker *Gluckauf*. The tanker, built in England in 1886, was the first ship to have the essential features of the modern tanker. It operated satisfactorily for several years until it wrecked on the south shore of Long Island, NY on March 4, 1893.

The idea of the horizontal bulkhead or intermediate oil tight deck (IOTD) was revived in the late 1970s when an American, C.S. Conway, took out a U.S. patent in December 1980. Also, Nils Polviander patented his design based on this principle in Finland about this time. A. Bjorkman of Sweden modified the concept in 1989 and named it "Coulombi Egg," while at the same time the Mitsubishi design became known as the "mid-deck tanker."

Both designs, submitted to the National Academy of Sciences Committee for evaluation, utilize the hydrostatic pressure principle in conjunction with IOTD. In order to be effective, they require that the IOTD must be below the waterline at all times when carrying cargo. One design provides side ballast tanks down to the IOTD level but are much wider, approximately B/5, ("B" is the vessel's beam). A third proposed design, known as the "POLMIS" concept, was submitted to IMO through the legal representative of the designer from Hamburg, Germany, on October 23, 1992.

The guiding principle in assessing any alternative design is the need to illustrate that it will be no less effective but hopefully more so than the double-hull tanker in preventing the outflow of oil following damage to the hull within the cargo tank area. The idea of the double-hull is to provide the tanker with an energy absorbing structure in a collision or grounding.

A fourth concept with a dry double-hull-MARPOL design was put forward in early 1994 by NKK Corporation of Japan. This design combines single-hull merits in double-hull design. In this concept, all double-hull spaces are void and dry. Ballast water will be carried in two pairs of permanent wing ballast tanks and the fore and after peak tanks.

Merits of the NKK design include the following:

- Inspections of the void dry spaces are much easier and safer

- A lower risk of pollution due to collision

- Much easier cargo valve maintenance

- The still water bending moments are smaller than the conventional double-hull design so that the hull girder bending stresses are less during the

•

operational life of the design; this is due to the suitable allocation of ballast water tanks in cargo oil space;

- , no increase in the corrosion margin should be necessary because of the fact that no corrosion of the steel in the double-hull spaces is expected; combined with the reduced bending moments, the proper use of higher tensile steel will be reasonable and justified; and

- the length of the PL/SB tanks is approximately forty percent of the cargo tank length. MARPOL 73/78 requires a minimum thirty percent of cargo tank length for the protectively located, segregated ballast tanks.

In June 1994, a presentation of the concept was made to representatives of the U.S. Coast Guard in Washington, D.C. by representatives of the NKK Corporation.

In September 1990, a work group of the "Tanker Structure Cooperative Forum" published the results of their efforts. They state in their summary, "The arguments surrounding double bottoms, double-sides, and double-hulls along with other alternative pollution preventive/mitigative methods are not clear cut. There are no easy solutions and there are valid arguments both for, and against, the various structural designs."

In their assessment of the various design concepts that could be used to help prevent oil spills, the National Research Council Committee said that "No single design is superior for all accident scenarios." The committee acknowledged that "too little is known about past accident conditions or the structural response of tankers. The paucity of the data, the gaps in knowledge, and the uncertainties make any conclusions, subject to conditional scenarios, assumptions, and judgments." The National Research Council is the principal operating agency of the National Academies of Sciences and Engineering in the United States.

A joint study for VLCCs only was carried out in Norway under the auspices of the Norwegian Maritime Directorate and published in Oslo in May 1990 states that:

> The study is based on available statistical information on damage, location, and extent. Additional oil spill caused by a grounding tanker, possibly breaking in parts, has not been considered in the study as this would necessitate a rather detailed analysis on the ultimate strength margins in damaged condition.

Class N.K., Classification Society of Japan, who coordinated a comparative study on double-hull and mid-deck tankers in order to assist IMO's MEPC Steering Committee mentioned in the *Class NK's Technical Bulletin* of 1992 that:

There is no sufficient data obtained from the model tests carried out by Tsukuba Institute in order to establish more reasonable modified assumption regarding the effect of rupture width.

The best effort, in my view, to share the knowledge and experience in order to gain a better technical understanding of the performance of tanker structures in service, was made by the work group of Tanker Structure Cooperative Forum. Members of the forum are major oil companies, some of the major classification societies and a few independent tanker owners.

In the summary published in September 1990, the Forum's work group stated that:

The arguments surrounding Double-Bottoms, Double-Sides and Double-Hulls, along with other alternatives pollution preventive/mitigative methods are not clear cut. There are no easy solutions and there are valid arguments both for and against the various structural designs. Because of the validity of the various view points that have been expressed, no attempt has been made to resolve differences in opinion.

It has become clear that none of the above studies could obtain a consensus of opinion as to the most effective design because of insufficient data. The studies were a hastily arranged reaction to the U.S. initiative, inspired by the grounding of the EXXON VALDEZ in March 1989 that resulted in the formulation of OPA '90.

It should be noted, it is the IMO that provides the mechanism for consideration for the value of a tanker design in terms of both safety and protection of the marine environment. The OPA '90 Legislation had the last word for the adoption of the double-hull, which is now universally accepted as the only design that protects the seas from an oil spill by a tanker.

In April 1997, the MEPC subcommittee of IMO found that the Coulombi Egg cargo tank design meets the outflow requirements of MEPC 66 (37), and therefore provides protection equivalent to the double-hull. The IMO, by consensus, adopted two alternative designs to the double-hull, the mid-deck and the Coulombi Egg, but neither of these designs can operate in U.S. waters.

The maritime industry has now learned to live and adapt with the most pervasive, sweeping, and costly unilateral legislation ever enacted by a port state, to regulate tankers in international and domestic trade. A school of thought exists in some maritime circles that despite its obvious flaws and pending problems, OPA '90 has served to upgrade the quality of oil tanker transportation in U.S. waters, and has served as a catalyst internationally to spark the IMO on matters such as improved tanker design and upgrading standards for existing tankers, and to draw the attention of flag states, port states, classification societies, underwriters, and tanker owners and operators to improve and expand their standards, inspections, and surveys of tankers.

The indisputable fact remains that accidental oil spills from tankers can result from collisions, groundings, structural or machinery failures, as well as fires and explosions. The threat of oil pollution therefore exists wherever oil tankers travel. It has taken a number of major failures, and in some instances, major disasters to force the adoption of design changes through legislation such as that of OPA '90, which resulted in development of a comparatively new generation of oil tankers, even though there was relatively little in-service data available on the performance of the hull structure. The only other similar type of double-hull structure in service today is the LNG carrier, which has been in service for many years.

We live in a changing world with technology often offering radically new opportunities or novel solutions to old problems, and that is set against a background of changing social standards where personal safety, human life, and protection of the environment are given increasing emphasis.

It is worth noting that in 1975, the largest double-hull tanker was the 121,000 dwt *S/T Prince William Sound*, built by the Sun Shipyard in the United States, followed by several more double-hull tankers of lesser deadweight over the years. The companies who owned and operated these tankers for more than fifteen years expressed no major problems during the life time of these vessels.

Acceptance of the double-hull by the tanker industry as the only design rendered the entire world fleet of ocean going crude oil carriers and other tankers obsolete. Once this was realized, shipyards in Japan, South Korea, and Europe, began an intense price competition for the building of the double-hull tanker, with emphasis on the lowest cost rather than developing a design incorporating features which will minimize environmental risks. The only exception has been the development of the "E3" design, which was the combined effort of a consortium of five European shipyards. The "E3" design is described in this book under a separate chapter.

In the United States, an attempt was made to introduce the "Mar C Guardian" tanker concept in the early 1990s. The project contemplated developing two deadweights for the carriage of crude oil. One of 348,000 tons and a smaller one of 125,000 tons. The smaller design was considered suitable for Alaska–U.S. West Coast trade.

The "Mar C Guardian" design utilizes a system of ship construction which is a departure from the conventional use of stiffened flat plate for shell and inner hull plating. The novel features of the Mar C Guardian technology were validated by a five year research effort, while the design concept had been under development since 1990, and the curved plate technology was developed into a highly producible double-hull mid-body concept. The fore and aft shaped ends of the hull would be transitioned into more traditional flat plate construction.

Subject to the ability to achieve MARPOL 73/78 minimum ballast draft requirements, a two-meter spacing between inner and outer hull satisfies regulatory requirements for all such tankers exceeding Panamax Beam.

By using slightly curved plating, for the inner and outer hull, which is inherent to the proprietary Mar C Guardian concept, it is possible to standardize the 2 meter hull spacing, 2.5 meter longitudinal girder spacing, and 15.25 meter spacing of transverse structure. This enabled the designers to use a mid-body construction method considered to be internationally competitive in both cost and construction quality. It was felt at the time that the need for tanker replacement was so great, that even a modest penetration of the market would result in a significant new construction program for the U.S. shipbuilding industry, and that the concept would present a significant opportunity to compete internationally. This and the fact that the Mar C Guardian project was considered to qualify for the maximum U.S. Government Title XI financing support of 87.5 percent of the ship's cost with up to twenty-five years, the design could also be used to secure construction financing.

The concept was the product of a long-term cooperation between U.S. tanker operators, shipbuilders, and experienced executives in the international tanker market. The project was considered at the time an interesting novelty with revolutionary commercial potential. It would appear ABS's involvement in the analysis of the proposed structure of the design was very extensive, using direct load analysis that resulted in significant refinements to the design. It was pointed out at the time, "Considerable professional judgment is required to produce a design which meets all the criteria of producibility, maintainability, and reliability, and all predictive formulae must be verified by extensive finite-element analysis under dynamic loads."

With regard to propulsion; tests were carried out at the Model Basin, and designers concluded that the twin screw performed better than single screw. This was mainly due to the shorter engine room that resulted in a shorter LBP for the same deadweight. Engineers calculated an improvement of 6.5 percent in fuel consumption for the same speed with the twin screw propulsion arrangement.

Those involved in this project who showed creative thinking deserve credit, but the industry has not appreciated their efforts. No Mar C Guardian tankers have been built so far.

The European Double-Hull VLCC "E3"

"E3" stands for Ecological, Economical, European, and is the result of efforts by a consortium of five leading European shipyards, from France, Germany, Italy, and Spain, to compete with the Far East shipyards.

The E3 is a 299,000 dwt VLCC, the design of which was based on the premise that, it will be ecologically sound, economically viable, and European in style. The design has the advantage of the experience of five European yards. The project was first discussed in June 1990 in anticipation of the introduction of international regulations, which were in the final stages at IMO and in the wake of the U.S. OPA '90 legislation. The six leading classification societies were closely involved from the outset.

The consortium examined three cargo tank configurations and adopted a two longitudinal and seven transverse bulkheads in the cargo spaces, providing twenty-four tanks of approximately thirty-two meters in length each. The objective was for a tank arrangement that will result in a very low outflow of oil in the event of damage, offers flexibility for parcel loading, and avoids the need to provide wash bulkheads if partial filling were a requirement.

The double bottom height of three meters is double that required by MARPOL rules for a ship of this size and allows a good height for inspection. The wing ballast tanks are four meters wide, twice the MARPOL requirement, with access ladders and partial longitudinal girders arranged as walkways. To comply with MARPOL requirements for segregated ballast tanks, the double bottom spaces must be properly cleaned and the cargo lines blanked off at the outset of the voyage if the vessel is to sail using them as ballast tanks.

Use of high tensile steel has been confined to the deck, top strakes of the side shell, and longitudinal bulkheads and the stiffeners on these panels, inner and outer bottom plating, and the transverse bulkheads amidships. In total, high tensile steel has been limited to approximately twenty-five percent of the steel weight.

An analysis of the collision strength and extent of damage in a wide range of situations, has determined, the energy absorption capability to be seven times that of a similar sized single-hull tanker.

The E3 principal particulars are:

Length Overall ....343.71 m
Length B.P. ....227.00 m
Breadth mld. ....56.40 m
Depth mld. ....40.40 m
Draft design ....19.80 m

Draft scantling ....21.55 m
Deadweight design ....269,480.00 tons
Deadweight scantling ....299,700.00 tons
Slow speed two stroke diesel ....32,000 BHP
RPM 84
Service Speed ....15.1 knots

The design is in full compliance with MARPOL 1973/1978 requirements including Regulation 13F, and U.S. Coast Guard Rules for foreign flag vessels.

The *Eleo Maersk* was the first E3 double-hull VLCC of 299,000 dwt, delivered in December 1992 to Maersk Tankers. By 1995, five more tankers of the same design and deadweight were delivered to the same owners. They are single screw, with transom stern, bulbous bow and semi-spade rudder.

The designers claim to have set new standards in cargo containment integrity, overall safety, operating economics, and quality of construction. The hull is designed to sustain a bottom raking damage well above the international requirement of sixty percent of the B.P. length. Cargo tank configuration will prevent any oil spillage, well above IMO standards, while segregated ballast capacity is thirty percent higher than required by IMO, and meets the requirements of OPA '90 for double-hull construction.

An interesting and important feature of the E3 is the ease of access for inspection and maintenance of the double-hull spaces, with fixed access arrangement in the side tanks and the double bottom.

Cargo tank configuration and cargo piping is arranged to handle three-way grade distributions of 20/30/50 percent and 10/40/50 percent.

The net steel weight of the structure is above the lwt/dwt factor of double-hull designs constructed by other shipyards.

The Double-Hull Design and Early Concerns

In the early 1990s, concern was expressed about the stability of the double-hull during cargo loading and discharging and during ballast water operations. Lolling incidents had been reported reaching angles of heel as high as ten degrees. The uncontrollable list of the tanker caused by inadequate transverse stability in the upright condition resulted in damage to piers and loading arms at oil terminals. This is caused by a combination of the large free surface effect generated during cargo transfer or ballast water operations when cargo and ballast tanks together are at intermediate levels and by the relatively higher center of gravity of the cargo due to the tanker's double bottom.

In July 1993, the lolling incidents were brought to the attention of the IMO by the Oil Companies International Marine Forum. The U.S. Coast Guard also issued a "Safety Alert" in early 1994, warning the industry of the potential loss of intact stability during cargo and ballast operations of double-hull tankers. The lolling event was unexpected because tankers have always been considered stable due to their more than adequate metacentric height. In the case of a double-hull design, lolling can occur after the cargo discharging commences. Operating procedures alone may not prevent the occurrence of lolling, and serious consideration was given to changes in the hull design that would lower the vertical center of gravity of the hull. Designers also considered introducing a center line bulkhead.

Other criticisms directed at the double-hull included the following:

- The evenly distributed cargo and ballast tanks create higher hull girder bending moments, whereas in a single-hull design, ballast tanks are positioned to minimize longitudinal bending and shear stresses.

- Inspection of ballast spaces between the inner and outer hull can be difficult, as can their gas freeing and ventilation, and yet it is imperative these spaces are well maintained.

- Coating areas are double those of a single-hull tanker.

In the early part of the 1990s, there was intense debate at the IMO about the design of new tankers where participants acknowledged that any new regulations should not inhibit the introduction of improved oil tanker designs. In particular, the mid-deck design promoted by the Japanese delegation and the European Shipbuilding Consortium sought to promote their unique designs. This resulted in an industry proposal to IMO that a comprehensive study should be undertaken of the relative merits of the mid-deck and the double-hull design.

An IMO Steering Committee was set up to conduct the study with a budget funded by the oil tanker industry. The intensive study concluded that the mid-deck design could be regarded as equivalent to the double-hull in terms of protection against accidental pollution resulting from collisions and groundings. This conclusion was detailed in the Regulation 13F of Annex I of the MARPOL Convention, adopted by the IMO Marine Environment Protection Committee (MEPC) in March 1992.

The regulation became effective in July 1993 and required all new oil tankers of more than 5,000 dwt to be of double-hull or equivalent design, and oil tankers of between 600 and 5,000 dwt to be fitted with at least a double bottom.

Perhaps without realizing it, the decision to settle on the double-hull or equivalent design was a sensible one because, for tanker owners who had decided to proceed with construction of a double-hull VLCC for instance, costing between US$70 to 100 million, and shortly afterwards being given the option to construct another VLCC design costing seventy to eighty percent that price, the expensive design would have to compete with the less expensive one for doing the same job.

It has been suggested recently that an effort be made by innovative minds to introduce improved tanker hull designs that can perform better than the present double-hull configuration. Naval architects must convince the tanker industry that the alternative design will perform much better than the double-hull now in service. Some problems have emerged with the present generation of double-hull tankers that are the result of hasty design, the aim of which was to build these tankers quickly and cheaply, incorporating a large percentage of higher strength steels into the hull structure, without regard to the long-term effects of this policy.

The tanker industry was also alerted to the dangers and consequences of fatigue cracking and the possibility of leakage of cargo oil or oil vapors into the double-hull space, which could create a gaseous atmosphere. The industry has been able to cope with some of the problems encountered with the present design of double-hull. Further improvements can be achieved, based on the experience gained during the past twelve years of operating double-hulls. To contemplate elimination of accidental oil spills from tankers is, in my opinion, an impossible goal.

A Safer, Maintenance Friendly Oil Tanker Design

A more maintenance friendly double-hull concept was developed by the Japanese shipbuilder, NKK, in the early 1990's—mentioned earlier in this Chapter—simplifies inspection of the hull structure and makes maintenance work easier.

The tanker industry's reaction to the concept was that in addition to the higher building costs that result from the increase in the amount of steel required, the concept had some drawbacks, such as:

- The width of the tanker would make it difficult for the Chicksan connections at some oil terminals, especially in Europe, because the arms of the shore installations are not long enough to reach the tanker's cargo manifold. Apparently, in Japan, and for the off-shore discharging system in the United States (the LOOP System), there should be no problem.

- The gross tonnage is approximately ten percent higher than that of a conventional double-hull of the same deadweight. This will affect port and dry-docking dues.

- Write-off of maintenance costs are difficult to quantify; some estimate it will require several years of the tanker's active life to write-off the additional initial construction cost.

- The lack of free-flow arrangement in the cargo tanks.

The following table compares the principal particulars of a conventional double-hull VLCC with NKK's concept with two alternative designs.

Principal particulars	Conventional Double-Hull VLCC	New Alternative 1 Double-Hull VLCC	New Alternative 2 Double-Hull VLCC
Length B.P. (m)	317.0	325.0	317.0
Breadth (m)	58.0	60.0	58.0
Depth (m)	31.4	34.0	32.9
Draft (m)	21.0	20.0	21.0
Gross Tonnage (tons)	161,000.0	185,000.0	167,000.0
Deadweight (tons)	280,000.0	280,000.0	280,000.0
Cargo Tank Capacity (cu. m)	350,000.0	350,000.0	350,000.0
Hull Steel Weight	100%	110%	103%
Coating Area of Ballast Water Tanks	100%	55%	75%

Alternative 2, costs less to construct, because less steel is required for the construction, where the double bottom spaces only are dry voids. The sides are used for water ballast, together with one pair of permanent wing ballast tanks along with the fore and after peak tanks. In this arrangement, the double side ballast spaces are easier to clean and inspect than the double bottom spaces. Also, since the double bottom is dry void space, it allows cargo valve compartments to be constructed and located in the area of the cargo valves. All cargo tank valves and hydraulic cylinders with the associated piping located in these compartments can be reached with relative ease, and if leakages from the hydraulic pipes occurred, these can be dealt with without having to degas and clean tanks to effect repairs. An important safety aspect of the proposed new design is that of the hull girder still water bending moment. The NKK designers have established that the new concept derives the same benefit as a single-hull post-MARPOL 73/78 single-hull VLCC, as regards hull girder hogging moment, because of the location and use of the permanent ballast tanks, while at the same time the concept is designated as a double-hull. This is important, especially when using the peak ballast tanks to adjust the tanker's trim and for propeller immersion.

The illustrations that follow, allow for an easy comparison of the concept with the pre-MARPOL, post-MARPOL 73/78 single-hull and conventional double-hull configurations.

The Double-Hull Tanker Structure

Once it was realized by the tanker industry that the double-hull configuration would be the universally accepted design, leading shipyards in the Far East and in Europe rushed to design a new hull structure. The switch to double-hull involved a fundamental change in hull dimensions resulting in a wider and deeper hull but reduced length for the same displacement. The change in dimensions allowed the shipbuilder to reduce main deck and bottom steel plate thickness, which was within classification rule requirements, so it cost less to build the double-hull tanker.

Building to minimum classification rules cannot and should not be relied upon to ensure a good design, no matter how good a classification society is considered to be. It is for this reason that active participation of the owner during the design stage is critical; he should be involved from the very beginning of the design. The owner/operator should demand tight tolerances of steel quality to be maintained.

Also of importance is the question of structural details, because a double-hull design requires a significantly greater number of components to distribute internal stresses efficiently. Particularly in the double-hull structure, factors that have caused concern are structural details and corrosion. Corrosion especially threatens to reduce the service life of the tanker. Corrosion is not confined solely to the ballast spaces; severe pitting has been found on both the cargo tank bottom and under the deck.

An interesting and important experimental test was carried out in the Netherlands early in 1998 on a one-third-scale and full-scale model of double-hull structure. The tests demonstrated the resistance of the structure was larger than expected and the structure suffered less damage than had been predicted by computer simulations.

From these tests, the Dutch discovered that rupture of the material did not occur. The external impact energy would be absorbed principally by plastic deformations. These were important double-hull collision tests, because engineers did not know the failure criteria used for predicting the rupture of tanker structures subjected to dynamic loads that produce large inelastic strains. The tests also demonstrated that, a small-scale structure or vessel could deform in a wholly ductile manner, while a full-scale structure or an actual tanker could suffer considerable damage due to rupture and tearing of the material.

EXISTING AND PROPOSED OIL TANKER DESIGNS
CARGO AND BALLAST TANK ARRANGEMENT.

■ BALLAST TANKS   □ CARGO TANKS

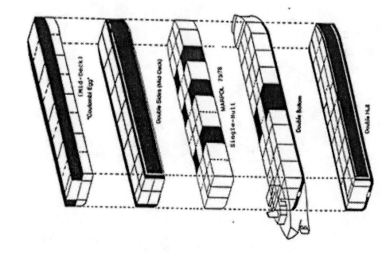

S/T "GLUCKAUF"

**3,100 TONS DWT., SINGLE SKIN OIL TANKER
BUILT IN THE U.K. IN 1886 WITH INTERMEDIATE
OIL TIGHT DECK (HORIZONTAL BULKHEAD)**

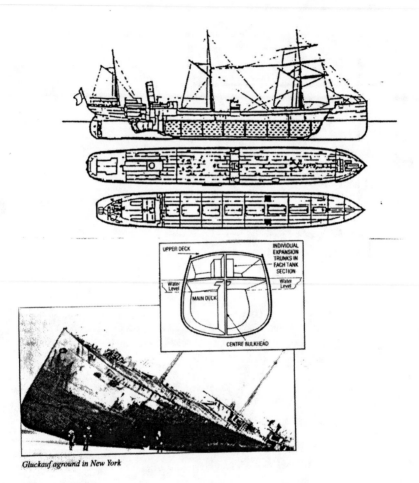

Gluckauf aground in New York

The "GLUCKAUF" was a typical design for the period. Each
oil tank had a separate expansion trunk extending up from
the main deck to the upper deck. A centre bulkhead split
each tank in to two, creating 12 to 20 individual tanks.
Sometimes the expansion trunks would be next to this
bulkhead, as is shown, or between this and the hull side
walls or even against the hull. The tween deck space was
normally used for reseve bunkers or case oil not bulk oil.

A DOUBLE-HULL VLCC UNDER CONSTRUCTION <u>CIRCA 1995</u>

EIGHT

The Quest for the Robust Tanker Hull Structure

The crude oil carrier was not invented; it has evolved over the years from practical experience. The growth in size of the tanker and innovative new developments have come out of the science of naval architecture. The naval architect's professional skill therefore, lies in the resolution of numerous conflicting problems, for he is fundamentally responsible for the crude oil carrier as a whole.

Naval architects alone do not produce ships. The shipbuilder, the scientist, the seaman, and the engineer all must be included in the design of the vessel. The naval architect is the originator and manager of a situation. The use of computers during the past few decades has significantly refined design work and accuracy. The speed at which design issues can be answered now has made the naval architect's life easier and more interesting.

An early contributor to the science of naval architecture was the Greek mathematician and inventor Archimedes (282–212, BC), who in 250 BC came upon the principle of buoyancy and shouted "Eureka" when he realized that "a body, partially or completely immersed in a fluid, is supported by a force equal to the weight of the fluid displaced." Archimedes also invented the Archimedean screw which even today has proven irreplaceable.

Another distinguished contributor to the science of naval architecture was Isaac Newton of England (1642–1727), who laid the foundation of many of the sciences, including naval architecture. Newton was a physical scientist and mathematician. He discovered differential and integral calculus, which is the most important single mathematical innovation since the time of the ancient Greeks. He also developed the method of calculating areas under curves and the volumes of solid figures.

During the seventeenth century, efforts to determine naval ship performance, both in Britain and in France, were concentrated on improving stability and steering capabilities of naval ships. Historians recognized at the time that "unless the fundamentals of naval construction were fully understood, design would continue to be a process of trial and error."

It was in April 1791 that the Society for the Improvement of Naval Architecture first met in London with the principal objective "to improve Naval Architecture in all its branches." Since then, naval architecture has come a long way in commercial ship design and construction, and the transportation of people and goods by sea is no longer a hazardous adventure.

A more recent contributor to the science of naval architecture was the English engineer and naval architect William Froude (1810–1879), who did pioneering work on hydrodynamics. He also introduced the model basin for the investigation of the laws governing the extrapolation from model to full scale, where he found that the chief components of resistance to motion were skin friction and wave formation and showed how the total resistance of a ship could be extrapolated from the results of ship model experiments. In all probability, Froude's methods inspired pioneers in aerodynamics to adopt model testing, which contributed to the rapid development of aircraft design.

Another distinguished personality inspired by Froude's work, was David Watson Taylor, who did a great job in ship hydrodynamics in the United States of America. The best known book David Taylor, published in 1954, was titled *The Speed and Power of Ships.* The United States Navy named their research facility in Maryland the David W. Taylor Model Basin.

Longitudinal Framing of the Cargo Tank Body and the Tanker

On the structural side of naval architecture, the problem of longitudinal strength had been troubling the naval architects in the U.K. for many years. It was John Scott-Russel, an English shipbuilder and engineer, who raised the subject at a council meeting of the Institution of Naval Architects, now RINA, in 1867. During that meeting Scott-Russel discussed changes in the structural design of merchant ships, including the longitudinal system of framing, but, for various reasons those were not widely adopted in merchant ships. A combination known as the "longitudinal and bracket floor system" came into general use at the time, mainly in naval vessels.

According to Scott-Russel, the transverse system of ship construction "was a mere tradition from the shipbuilders of wood, to the shipbuilders in iron. Planks of wood would not hold together without other portions of wood laid across them, to bind them in place and keep them in shape." This may be a reasonable explanation about the origin of transverse framing.

It was early in the twentieth century that longitudinal framing for oil tankers was introduced by Sir Joseph Isherwood. This was an important structural improvement in the tanker design, and by 1925, the world's tanker fleet was constructed to this design.

Soon after the adoption of longitudinal framing, the center line bulkhead was replaced by two longitudinal bulkheads, effectively creating three cargo tanks across the tanker. These two improvements enabled the tanker hull designer to increase the size of the oil tanker enormously, creating a new generation of oil tankers.

Another change in the design that occurred in the late 1970s and early 1980s was the extensive use of higher tensile steels for the hull structure. This allowed the hull designer to increase the spacing of the stiffening members and to reduce plate thickness. The use of computers and extensive use of higher tensile steels enabled the designer to optimize the structural steel weight in a new design, thus reducing steel weight against classification rules. This in effect means, in the later designs, the safety margins built into the tanker structure to account for unknown quantities in a design were significantly reduced.

Tables I, II and III, illustrate the reduction in scantlings weight achieved when using higher tensile steels compared to the period when mild steel was used throughout the hull structure.

Reduction in scantlings led to problems such as buckling and fatigue cracking in areas of high stress concentration. The tanker industry realized that the transverse strength of the new generation of crude oil carriers was just as important as the longitudinal strength. No such problems were encountered in the tankers built during the 1950s and 1960s, when a more robust structure with scantlings that provided a good margin against corrosion.

The tables contain information on representative single-hull and double-hull and VLCCs/ULCCs built in Japan during the 1980s. The average increase in the net steel weight for the double-hull compared to the single-hull MARPOL 73/78 VLCC/ULCC of the same deadweight is around twenty percent, depending upon the extent of higher tensile steels incorporated in the design.

Table I

Period	Approximate Deadweight(dwt)	Approximate Lightweight(lwt)	LWT/DWT
1940s	16,800 (T-2)	6,000	0.36
1950s	50,000	12,000	0.24
1960s	100,000	27,000	0.27
1960s	200,000 (VLCC)	30,000	0.15
1970s	300,000	40,000	0.13
1970s	500,000 (ULCC)	65,000	0.13
1970s	1,000,000 (PROPOSED)	140,000	0.14

Table II
Typical Single-Hull VLCCS/ULCCS Constructed During 1980s

Total Deadweight (dwt)	270,600	315,700	336,300	399,500
Cargo Deadweight	263,800	308,550	328,750	390,950
Lightweight (LWT)	39,800	45,000	49,000	60,000
Steel Weight (NET)	33,500	38,600	42,300	53,000
LWT/dwt	0.147	0.142	0.145	0.150
Steel (NET)/dwt	0.124	0.122	0.126	0.133

Table III
Typical Double-Hull VLCCS/ULCCS Constructed During 1980s

Total Deadweight (dwt)	263,650	306,950	328,350	391,800
Cargo Deadweight	256,850	299,800	320,800	383,250
Lightweight (LWT)	46,150	53,750	56,950	68,400
Steel Weight (NET)	40,450	47,350	50,250	60,700
LWT/dwt	0.175	0.175	0.173	0.174
Steel (NET)/dwt	0.155	0.153	0.154	0.153
Increase in Steel Weight:				
Double-Hull Structure	6,950	8,750	7,950	7,700
Percent Increase	20.74	22.67	18.79	15.49

Hull Design and the Hull Designer

The design of a ship's hull structure is not like designing a land bridge, where the structural engineer, through analysis of every point of the bridge structure, can determine precisely what is needed to achieve the design objective. Engineering analysis of a ship is much more complex than a bridge, which is subject to predictable, well controlled loads. The ship is subject to complex motions and external as well as internal forces. A ship under way at sea pitches, rolls, and heaves, and to take an explicit engineering approach to its design means to account for stresses and moments affecting the vessel in each phase of its motion.

Ship hull design has been mainly an empirical practice where successes and failures are based on observations of what has gone before. Such observations made on many thousands of ships were put in engineering terms and eventually became the primary basis of the classification society's rules, which in effect are, a compendium of experience factors.

During the last fifty years, the dominant construction material for the construction of ships has been mild steel, and yielding was the dominant mode of failure for a ship. Design considerations were therefore directed toward preventing yield. Other failure modes such as buckling and fatigue could, for the most part, be ignored because the heavy construction required for a mild steel ship effectively prevented this type of structural failure. With the introduction and extensive use of higher strength steel to replace mild steel, ships are being built lighter, and buckling and fatigue failure of ship's structure became more common.

Depending upon the type of ship hull to be designed, whether it is a large and bulky crude oil carrier with a large block coefficient, or a finer form container ship to be built for speed, each has its own characteristics. Leading classification societies have now developed methodologies and analytical models that identify the problem areas in a design and provide assistance to the ship hull designer to solve structural problems.

What has also evolved during the past several years is the simplification of utilizing and consulting all class societies' books of rules, available on CD-ROM. This enables the hull designer to flip through the pages of the rule book electronically, expediting the design and review processes. In fact, the American Bureau of Shipping has recently introduced the "Safe Hull Express," the use of which reduces design work from weeks to few days.

The Safe Hull Express software can be easily integrated into a shipyard's existing computer system. It is considered simple, technically advanced, and a significant time saver for design evaluation, enabling the designer to process a new design in less than fourteen days. Previously it required several weeks for the initial scantlings design.

The class societies are now becoming aware of the great need for more careful technical evaluation at the concept and initial-design stage. Some of the class societies have developed and made available advanced technologies to carry out the required analysis of the hull structure, particularly the dominant failure modes of fatigue, yielding, and buckling. Development of the new computer software helps the hull structure designer make sure the design complies with classification rules. Such new technological advances result in a more accurate evaluation in much shorter time, resulting in a less expensive design that complies fully with class and other requirements.

Hull Stress Monitoring

The tanker industry's feeling today is that hull stress monitoring is a worthwhile investment because it enables those on board the tanker to augment their judgment during ballasting and deballasting operations. It is of particular importance now that the IMO's requirements for ballast water exchange.

The stress monitoring system greatly improves awareness of the effects of loading. The system is useful to the ship's master so that he can know the wave-induced dynamic stresses when underway at sea.

Today's systems are interfaced with the tanker's Loadicator—loading computer—and each machine carries its own set of calculations for its own dedicated task, but both can also display each other's data, providing the officer on watch with measurements and predicated values simultaneously on both computers.

The link with the Loadicator provides a further reference point that allows those on board to monitor how things have varied since leaving port and any deviations that may be caused by changes in the bunkers, ballast, or structural integrity.

Stress monitoring is of great value, because knowledge of in-service hull loading, and structural performance methods for future hull structural design and in-service performance is essential for stress management and future design improvements.

Extensive use of stress monitoring was arranged recently on board three double-hull Suez Max tankers. The strain gauges were located on selected longitudinal stiffeners and their end connections and at higher stress regions on selected primary transverse structures, to measure localized stresses and associated loads on those members.

This stress monitoring will provide information on global hull girder stress, low acceleration, and bow bottom pressure. The information retrieved from these measurements will enhance knowledge of the overall structural integrity of a double-hull tanker design, and improve knowledge of the performance of critical areas of the hull structure.

Using strain gauges to measure stress on ship structural members is not new. In 1947, I made a presentation before the Scottish Engineers Students' Association in Glasgow, Scotland, titled, "The Electrical Resistance Wire Strain Gauge—Its Use in Static and Dynamic Testing of Structures." The presentation was based on research work on ship structures I was conducting for the British Ship Research Association (BSRA) in Scotland.

Tanker Hull Design Engineering

Not long ago, the design of a tanker's hull structure was based on a semiempirical approach that was considered adequate by an overwhelming majority of hull design engineers. From global and detail configurations to local scantlings, answers were usually readily available from design text books or classification societies' rules.

In general, such an approach evolved from successful operating experience, and in fairness, it had surprisingly good track record, despite the simplicity of the methods. The approach included the so-called safety margins built into the structure to account for the unknown quantities of stress in the structure that result from fatigue, corrosion, or both.

Designers from other fields characterized ship design engineering as a science with a limited theoretical base. They have called ship design engineering evolutionary. What has been overlooked, however, is that a ship is not like a land bridge. The ship designer has to cope with numerous variations of hull configuration, types of cargo to be carried, materials to be used, proportions, and the operating environment, while at the same time, keeping a close watch on costs and profit of the design.

As the world shipping market became increasingly competitive, the hull designer was compelled to reduce the steel weight. To achieve that goal, there was the clear path of either reducing the scantlings, increasing the percentage usage of higher strength steels, or both. Table I compares a tanker's hull deadweight and its lightweight at different periods of construction.

Tanker hull design has changed markedly in recent years, especially now that the designer has access to faster and more powerful computers, on which he can experiment with small changes in a design that in turn may result in worthwhile improvements. In such designs, the problems in fatigue and buckling intensified, because fatigue resistance capacities of higher strength steels and weldments are known to be inferior to mild steels with the result that, such tanker structures are operating at higher levels of stress.

A more rational approach to the design of a tanker's hull structure has been developed through the use of scientific, rather than prescriptive criteria, where an accurate assessment of the cumulative effects of corrosion and fatigue can be made. This also provides a more accurate decision making process that considers the risk, to which a tanker's structure will be subjected over its service life.

As a result of concerns over the growing use of higher strength steels and structural optimization, together with the problems identified with regard to tankers in service, leading classification societies developed computer programs that deal with the general and fatigue strength of today's structurally complex hull.

Since the structural integrity of the tanker's hull must be evaluated under sailing conditions at the design stage, the designer uses integrated systems to analyze complex phenomena, employing wave load analysis and structural analysis techniques. Such analysis is aimed at providing a practical tool to the rational assessment of the tanker's structural strength, which takes into consideration actual environmental conditions. Designers use direct calculations of wave-induced loads as well as three dimensional structural analysis of an entire tanker structure.

Today's computing technology can process enormous amounts of data in a short time, making it possible to accurately assess complicated structures such as that of the modern double-hull. Because of this facility, it is not uncommon for structural members to be changed in configuration and scantlings before the final design is completed.

Not all the problems that have emerged in the performance of a tanker's structure, however, should be blamed in the use higher tensile steels. The problems, either individually or in combination with the use of higher tensile steels, are compounded and magnified from the use of such steels in a design. These include the overall detail in a design, construction of the structure, corrosion, maintenance and repairs, as well as the tanker's operation when underway at sea, and when loading or discharging cargoes.

In the past, fatigue damage of a tanker's structure, has not been given as much attention as other design considerations, such as the global hull girder and local yielding strengths. The introduction of higher tensile steels in a design, however, signified a new era in which the importance of fatigue has gained acceptance and has become an integral part of the ship design process. In fact it has become a critical component in the assessment of a tanker's hull structure. This means the appropriate loads are determined, and that response, is compared against known failure criteria, such as yielding, buckling, and fatigue.

Traditionally, classification checks of a design have been performed as a final part of the design process to ensure the design complies with class requirements. Today leading class societies provide the designer with the means that give greater confidence that classification aspects of a design are right the first time or may only require the minimum of changes. The class societies have in recent years developed systems that determine structural requirements for a new design, and which are of great assistance to the hull designer.

In particular, the American Bureau of Shipping developed recently what is known in the industry as the "Safe Hull Express" mentioned earlier in this Chapter. It is a new version of the proven ABS "Safe Hull" system, first introduced in 1993 for tankers, which determines structural requirements for a new design. This latest system was developed in close cooperation with shipyard designers with the explicit aim of helping shipyards develop designs more quickly and easily. The end result is a more robust hull structure based on engineering analysis, than a structure designed using prescriptive rules.

Some of the benefits of the Safe Hull Express include the following:

- Its use as an initial design tool
- The ability to rapidly model a ship
- Initial scantling requirements and finite element analysis evaluation come from the same three-dimensional model
- The ability to confirm conformance to ABS requirements as the design progresses
- The significant time savings in the design and evaluation cycle

The new system is of enormous help in the turn around time of the structural plan approval process. ABS was able to achieve this with the cooperation of shipyard designers to accommodate the designers' needs. It also provides an automated report generator to help the designer ensure that his design is in compliance with ABS rules.

The other leading classification societies will without doubt, follow ABS's efforts, to assist the hull structure designer in his work.

Tanker Hull Structure

With the growth of tanker size into the range beyond 300,000 dwt, the problem of establishing criteria of longitudinal strength became urgent, because prior to this time, classification societies' rules had been applicable only to vessels below this size.

Shortly after the end of World War II, the size of tankers increased so rapidly, that in the absence of practical experience with regard to the structural performance of the larger tankers, the attention of the hull designer was focused upon the analytical evaluation of the various factors that influence longitudinal strength.

Selection of a section modulus requires that the magnitude of the expected bending moment must be determined and an allowable stress level chosen. Determination of the stress level, assuming the bending moment is determined, or at least conservatively estimated, is dependent upon the strength of materials used and past experience.

The various methods used to estimate the bending moments experienced by a tanker can be placed in one or more of the following categories:

- Empirical approach
- Standard analysis
- Model testing
- Observations on board existing ships at sea

Empirical approach and standard analysis were design tools at the time. Model testing was considered a useful contribution to the estimation of bending moments and stresses.

Regarding observations on board existing ships at sea, this was achieved using strain gauges suitably located on the ship's hull, where mass measurement of strains is made possible for either static, oscillatory, or transient strains.

Empirical Approach

Historically, classification societies' rules are a reflection of satisfactory experience. In the early 1950s, what were then considered large tankers were built to requirements not based on traditional experience, but on the best estimates that could be projected from experience with smaller tankers and the known factors affecting the probable stresses in ships at sea. During this period, classification societies had been using rules for the smaller machinery-aft tankers that approximated the load line section modulus plus twenty percent.

The design of a hull structure was therefore primarily, an empirical practice based on observations of success and failures of many previous ship designs. Such observations were put in engineering terms to become the primary basis for a class society's rules for tanker hull structures.

Today, the design of such a structure is developed according to "first principles," that is, a process through which loads are determined, load effects analyzed, and specific criteria are applied to judge the fitness of the design. This in effect means, the hull designer has access to a thorough quantification of the stresses which may exist in a hull structure, and he is placed in a position to know the fatigue, yielding, and buckling demands to be resisted by the hull structure. Because of this, the required scantlings will be used more efficiently and in a manner consistent with the loads and failure modes considered to be dominant during the design's lifetime.

For a reliable design, exhaustive attention must be given to structural strength and reliability, state-of-the-art finite element modeling, the incorporation of significant margins in the scantlings. The final step would be the adoption of a highly compartmentalized hull configuration to meet international rules in order to complement the application of the full redundancy principle of the propulsion and associated systems. This is necessary if a tanker is expected to endure the harsh weather and treacherous sea conditions. Such designs are adopted to conform to long-term risk management.

The Cost and the Risk

Today's' very large crude oil carriers represent the most complex mobile steel structures man has developed, where many of the strength requirements are rather uniquely important to ship hull design.

Tanker hull design practice is generally conservative due to the influence of two primary factors driving the design of a tanker's hull structure: the cost and the risk. Because of the high cost per ship, it is impractical to build prototypes to gain experience. Therefore the risk associated with a particular design may be high unless its performance can be confidently predicted through interpolation from closely related designs within the historical database. If empirical relations are used for the interpolation, the risk increases with increasing departure from proven designs.

Paramount in a design is the aspect of safety and reliability. This is most important even when designing for production, similar to the motor car industry. The quality of a ship however, is dependent greatly on the quality of its designer. Concept of detail in a design is greatly dependent upon the practical experience of the hull designer.

Investigations have pinpointed the causes that negatively influence a tanker's structural condition including the following:

- Improper design and poor workmanship during construction
- Imprudent use of higher tensile steels designed into the hull structure
- Lack of good quality protective coatings and their application
- Owner maintenance policies
- Quality of surveys and periodic inspections
- Operating routes
- Tight scheduling with resultant excess speeds that contribute to wear and other structural problems
- The age of the ship

Absolute safety at sea, assuming it could be justified economically, is another tanker industry's utopian goal. The challenge to the ship design engineer is to continuously strike a balance between safety and cost.

Higher tensile strength steels came into use together with improved methods for reliability predicting loads and structural response of hull structures. Hence, the so-called "safety margins" built into tanker structures to account for unknown quantities in the design have been significantly reduced as unknowns have been eliminated. An example of the effect that these changes have had on the construction of tankers can be seen in the following table.

Year	Deadweight (dwt)	Lightweight (lwt)	lwt/dwt
Figures are approximate			
1940s	16,500 T-2	6,000	.36
1950s	50,000	12,000	.24
1960s	100,000	27,000	.27
1960s	200,000 (VLCC)	30,000	.15
1970s	300,000 (VLCC)	40,000	.13
1970s	500,000 (ULCC)	65,000	.13

TABLE I

Tanker Hull Strength and the U.S. Ship Structure Committee

In October 1991, the U.S. Ship Structure Committee (SSC), an Interagency Advisory Committee, completed its report on a procedure for the development of a Marine Structural Integrity Program for commercial ships, with particular focus given to oil tankers. The committee recommended a sequence of actions to be performed in the life cycle of tankers in order to ensure better integrity of a tanker's structure during its useful lifetime.

The MSIP is based on developments from the U.S. Air Force and the Federal Aviation Administration Airframe Structural Integrity Programs, as well as recent experience of the maritime industry. Attempts were made in the development of the program to make appropriate and practical applications, recognizing that present ship and airframe structures and their associated integrity management programs differ in several important aspects.

The study, sponsored by the SSC and its member agencies, addressed developments of advanced Marine Structural Integrity Programs for VLCCs and ULCCs. In response to the many political and environmental concerns relative to oil tankers, the committee suggested a sequence of actions to be carried out by the various parties involved in the life cycle of oil tankers in order to ensure better integrity of the tanker structure during their useful lifetimes.

Technology transfer from aerospace to the maritime industry was considered to be timely and relevant in view of many common design, operation, performance, and maintenance operations of the airframes and ships. An international group of ship owners and operators, shipbuilders, researchers, government agencies, and classification societies participated in several meetings that covered such topics as preservation of aging marine structures and marine structural inspection and maintenance.

Aided by powerful computers the tanker hull structure designer has today, a clearer understanding of the characteristics of the ultimate strength of the hull girder, subjected to a combination of the three load components, namely the vertical bending moment, horizontal bending moment, and shearing forces. Such understanding provides a more precise assessment of ship structural safety margins and helps to evaluate the reserve and residual strength of intact and damaged structures.

In addition, a good knowledge of Reliability Technology and its application is essential when designing new generation hull structures where fatigue failures are expected to occur at welded joints and other points in the structures where there is severe stress concentration. Present experience indicates that the primary structure-related problems with the current generation of oil tankers are the result of steel corrosion and fatigue-corrosion cracking. Also, the majority of corrosion problems can be traced to a complete lack of coatings in ballast tanks and poor design of coatings and cathodic protection systems.

The Tanker Hull Structure Designer

The challenges the tanker hull structure designer has been facing is the fact that, until recently, all classification rules were prescriptive in nature, developed in a measured, repetitive process that generally kept pace with the historically slow evolution of ship designs, characterized by simplicity of format and application.

The rules had limitations because of their semistatistical nature and heavy reliance on operational experience to derive the empirical formulations. Prescriptive rules therefore had to be treated with caution when applied to structural designs of new generation tankers that are markedly larger and significantly structurally different from those of previous generations.

The question arises, have fundamentals of ship design really changed over the years? The use of computers during the past few decades has significantly refined ship design engineering. The speed and accuracy of computers have made the ship designer's life easier and the task more interesting.

This, together with the fact that the large number of tankers built during the last four decades, particularly VLCCs and ULCCs, created a vast amount of design data available to the tanker designer.

It was recognized that ship structural integrity programs have been in existence for as long as there have been ships. There was a general feeling, however, that such programs can be and must be improved. It was also recognized that the vast majority of ship casualties are not primarily related to structural causes, only ten percent of major ship casualties could be traced directly to structural integrity problems. Human and organizational related problems account for the majority of major casualties.

It is worth noting that the SSC had its origins in a board that was convened to investigate steel ship breakage after the T-2 tanker *Schenectady* broke in two in calm waters at her fitting out berth on January 16, 1943.

Upon the board's recommendation for continued study, the U.S. Coast Guard was directed by the U.S. Government to initiate a committee that would continue studying causes of welded-ship hull failures, and the Ship Structure Committee was born.

As the results of World War II research were digested, the committee began to recognize the new directions needed for research. Through the 1950s and 1960s, research was centered on mechanical metallurgy, chemical and physical metallurgy, transition temperatures, effect of edge preparations, and geometry of structural members.

Recommended improvements included the type of steel to be used and its treatment, as well as welding practices to avoid cracking, and structural design to avoid stress concentrations.

In the 1980s, fatigue failures in tankers with a large percentage of high tensile steel renewed concerns for oil pollution prevention, created interest in failure mechanism, and spurred research to arrest the problems. Several proactive projects attempted to predict problem areas and prevent failures in double-hull tanker designs. The committee realized that, even after sixty years, there is need for continued research in methodology to analyze human and organizational errors, cooperating with European and Asian maritime committees to develop reliability-based methods of ship hull design.

The Tanker Hull Structure

A tanker's light weight is the weight of the steel in the structure; plus forgings and castings' plus the weight of propulsion machinery and the weight of the accommodation, and is known as the "Light Ship." (The steel weight of a tanker's hull structure is around 85 percent of the tanker's light weight).

The primary tanker hull structure is modeled as a beam, and the load effects are determined by integration of the loads along the tanker's length.

Still-water loads are the forces that result from the action of the tanker's weight, the cargo carried, and the buoyancy. Cargo and buoyancy exert horizontal pressure on the hull sides. These horizontal pressures are resisted by the transverse structure of the hull, which is a secondary component. The primary component of the hull structure resists the vertical effects of the ship's weight, the cargo carried, and the buoyancy. The corresponding load effects are the vertical shear force and bending moment.

The variation of still-water loads depends on the cargo carried, because the hull weight is more or less constant throughout the tanker's life. The force of buoyancy is equal to the sum of the other two loads. Fuel consumption does make a small and gradual variation, and the significance of this effect increases with the duration of the voyage. This is more noticeable in long tankers where fuel is carried at the fore and after end of the hull.

Besides these small and gradual variations, large changes in load effects occur in a voyage during redistribution of cargo as a result of tank cleaning and changes of ballast. Engineers have found that tanker structures are predominantly subjected to sagging moments.

Tanker hull design has evolved over the years along with advancing technology, and as already mentioned, problems relating to the design of a tanker's structure differ from those of a stationary structure such as a land bridge. A tanker is a floating structure that is itself in motion; the system of support continually varies as the ship moves through the water.

Weather intensity and probable sea conditions encountered will have a bearing on the structural strength needed, and like any other engineering structure, tankers are designed for the work they have to do.

Existing traditional criteria to determine a tanker's hull scantlings that are established by classification societies are contained in the society's rules. The criteria, which incorporates nominal loadings, standard engineering design equations, and satisfactory service experience, are applied in order to obtain class acceptance. Whether the criteria are employed to determine overall strength or strength of local structural components, consider a combination of factors, the common element being expected loads and permissible stresses. Today's modern methods, aided by computer-based analytical tools, determine tanker hull scantlings using a more explicit engineering approach in order to determine the expected dynamic loads and permissible stresses.

The American Bureau of Shipping developed early in the 1990s what is now known as the "dynamic loading approach" (DLA), and was offered to the maritime industry as an optional class notation for tankers. The key to DLA is that it allows no decreases in scantlings below those obtained from direct application of the rule equations found in the society's Steel Rules. This is a particularly important benefit to the tanker hull designer intending to make extensive use of higher strength steels in the design, and who must ensure that care is taken to preclude failure modes, such as buckling and fatigue-induced cracking. The approach ensures realistic dynamic load distribution on the tanker hull structure, and increases scantlings where needed in the local structure.

Since the introduction of the DLA, other leading classification societies have developed procedures, such as these by:

- Lloyd's register   Ship Right or Safe Ship
- Norske Veritas   Nauticus
- Bureau Veritas   Veri Star
- Class N K   Ship Right
- Germanischer Lloyd   Poseidon
- Registro Italiano   Prime Ship

Hull Structure and Critical Waves

A tanker's structure is subjected to several loads that may occur simultaneously. In the design process, such loads must be taken into consideration for the possibility of their simultaneous occurrence. To meet classification rules, the effects of the two loads that must be accounted for are the still-water and wave-induced loads. Still-water loads are the forces that result from the action of the hull weight, the cargo carried, and the buoyancy.

In general terms, the design of structural members based on classification rules consists of optimum scantlings determination through a coherent, systematic series of steps. These steps range from estimating internal and external loads expected to act on the structure, assigning suitable scantlings, and evaluating the resultant structural strength based on the calculation of the physical characteristics under which the hull is expected to operate safely. This includes the calculation of ship motion, as well as detailed stress analysis within a dynamic wave environment.

The maximum wave hogging moment occurs with the maximum wave crest amidships in a wave with same length as the tanker. The maximum wave sagging moment occurs when the same wave has its trough amidships. Recent studies indicate the probability of occurrence of critical waves, that is the wave length is equal to the ship's length, depends upon the area a ship is operating, and upon the ship's length. Studies have also concluded that the occurrence of critical waves is much more frequent for short than for long waves.

The question is, in a tanker's 25-year operating life, how often will the tanker encounter "critical" waves? Here is the importance of wave statics, which operational oceanography can determine.

Hull Structural Failure

All steel structures when overloaded will fail, most commonly by fatigue. Fatigue is a fracture-mechanism, not a failure mechanism, and the use of higher strength steels in a tanker's hull structure offers no life improvement to the structure. Fatigue damage is a cumulative process and occurs under cyclic loading only. Static loads do not contribute to such damage.

As the design of a tanker's hull structure is dominated by wave loads encountered over the tanker's life, an estimate of the damage over the service life of the tanker is needed for a design check. Such damage is influenced both by the stress ranges, and the effective number of stress cycles. An analysis involves proper determination of long-term operational conditions when the tanker is in service.

The OPA '90 legislation resulted in a comparatively new generation of oil tankers for which there is relatively little in-service data available on the performance of the tanker hull structure. The only other similar type of double-hull structure has been that of the LNG carrier. Efforts have been underway for some time to obtain knowledge of in-service hull loading and structural performance, essential for improving the current theoretical prediction methods and future double-hull structure design. This is accomplished by using dedicated measurement systems installed onboard double-hull tankers in service for the collection of in-service structural loadings and hull stress data essential for cumulative damage approach analysis to determine long-term fatigue damage to the hull structure.

Using strain gauges, located on selected hull areas will provide information on global as well as localized hull girder stresses and associated loads on structural members, with a view to improve the design, construction, and maintenance procedures of double-hull tankers.

Major structural failures are preceded by failures in secondary or peripheral areas that are, nevertheless, vital to the integrity of the adjacent major structure. The designer must ensure there is adequate redundancy in a design, both in the primary and the secondary hull structure.

Construction method greatly influences the quality of the finished hull structure and although the tanker building industry has available today the technical background to do what is required to achieve durable and reliable tanker structures, the primary problem comes about when the available technology is not applied prudently.

Computer analysis of the hull structure, results in a variety of steel thickness and sizes of structural members in order to achieve an optimum design.

This may lead to faulty workmanship because of the complicated arrangement of structural members. For the double-hull design or any similarly complicated structure, because of the multitude of individual pieces that have to be joined together in a production oriented environment, alignment of the parts that make up the hull structure is critical. Unless correct alignment is achieved during assembly of the parts, fatigue cracks will soon develop, especially at the part of the hull structure where extensive use of higher tensile steels has been made, particularly in the region of three to five meters above and below the load water line. Equally important is the selection of stiffening members, such as side and bottom longitudinals, because there is considerable stress increase if there is asymmetry in the sections used.

Another major problem is that of corrosion, which becomes more acute in tankers of light scantlings designs, because extensive use of higher tensile steels makes such structures more vulnerable to this problem. Other structural failures are due to faulty workmanship. In a modern shipyard, where extensive use of automatic welding is made, the effect of faulty workmanship due to human error has been reduced considerably.

The Practical Aspect in the Design of Tanker Structure

Today's computer aided design (CAD) for a tanker's hull structure has attained a high level of development, and has become a very important design tool. There is however, another aspect that should be taken into consideration when designing such structures, namely, the practical aspect. The practical aspect is nothing more than the use of common sense and feedback information from in-service tanker experience expertly applied to a design.

Especially today, with the introduction of more complex double-hull structures, using common sense and the experience gained from observations of past structural failures and applying such experience to a design, the tanker hull designer can achieve a more robust structure without increase in steel weight. Such practice does produce surprisingly good results, by making changes in the details in the design that will minimize buckling and fractures in the structure, and reduce vibration problems.

Dynamic Loading and Strength

In the past, classification rules have been the mainstay of tanker design criteria. The rules are primarily semiempirical in nature and have been calibrated to, and proven by, successful operational experience. They provide valuable guidelines on how to treat first order design issues, such as primary loads and structural global strength. The semiempirical approach to tanker design has its advantages, primarily owing to its simplicity and the fact that through the years, it has absorbed the benefit of calibration with experience by way of fine tuning. In essence, it offers some degree of assurance that the primary strength of a tanker would be adequate to resist most adverse effects in its intended life span. The main disadvantage of the semiempirical approach lies in its inability to extrapolate to new technology and new designs.

Design of a tanker hull structure by direct calculation, if executed properly, may represent a positive step in the right direction. This approach is built around the belief that, if the loads induced by the wave environment and the strength of the structure, both global and local are estimated, based on scientific rationale, there should be a corresponding gain in confidence of the ship's safety measure.

In other parallel engineering disciplines, such as civil engineering, semiempirical designs are less evident, but heavy reliance on criteria given in design codes is quite similar to the ship design practice. The difference is that a tanker under way at sea is a moving object, very often in very hostile environment.

In general, the semiempirical approach is primarily effective only when dealing with global strengths and can be fine tuned with the operational experience that can further improve with analytical load computation.

Even so, the semiempirical approach has been found to be inadequate when dealing with failure modes of buckling, fatigue, and fracture. These considerations are becoming evermore essential in modern design practice and more complicated tanker hull structures. On the other hand, structural analysis by way of finite element (FE) methods is better developed and its results can be viewed with greater confidence. The FE method, however, should not be extended to buckling and fatigue. The structural behavior of these phenomena is less predictable, and it must be closely scrutinized. Fatigue, which is a principal mode of failure where higher tensile steels are used in the hull structure, should especially be monitored.

Japanese shipbuilders have in the past performed as a matter of routine such detailed structural analyses for the double-hull of liquefied natural gas carriers. In recent years the same procedure was utilized by one of the major

Japanese yards for one of their double-hull VLCCs, in cooperation with the American Bureau of Shipping, which is the first classification society to develop the Dynamic Loading Approach concept. Since then, ABS has institutionalized such practices by offering the tanker owner a new optional class notation. The new approach for VLCCs and ULCCs uses explicitly determined dynamic loads, and the results of the structural analyses are used as the basis to increase scantlings where indicated. However, this approach does not allow any decreases in scantlings from those obtained from the direct application by the ABS rules scantling equations.

The VLCC Energy Concentration

Can the back of a properly designed and built tanker be broken? If left in incompetent hands, yes!

The 216,269 dwt crude oil carrier *Energy Concentration*, originally named *Golar Betty*, was built by Kawasaki Heavy Industries at their Sakaide yard in Japan, was classed by Det Norske Veritas, and entered service in March 1970. In 1977, the tanker was changed to Bureau Veritas classification.

In July 1980, while discharging her part cargo at Rotterdam in Holland, the tanker broke its back. From the subsequent enquiry that followed the incident, it transpired that, the sequence of discharging the cargo at Rotterdam was such as to increase substantially the hogging moment above the already high value, as a result of cargo transfer at the previous port of Antifer in France. The eventual distribution of weight and buoyancy induced a hogging bending moment that exceeded the ultimate longitudinal strength of the tanker.

It took several years to complete the investigation, it was however a rare opportunity to compare the measured ultimate strength of a tanker of this size, with the predicted strength using theoretical methods.

Closing Remarks on Tanker Hull Strength

Technology alone to improve the design of the tanker structure does not hold all the answers to preventing oil pollution of the seas. At the end of the day, it is the old problem of the human factor. A tanker is as good as the men who sail on her. A classic example is the grounding of the *Exxon Valdez* in Alaska in 1989, ushering a new era in tanker design and redundancy, which is now the key word in the tanker industry.

Abnormal Sea Conditions

A ship, when under way at sea, is subjected to the effects of various sea conditions and ocean phenomena that affect the hull structure, particularly by wave-induced dynamic forces.

There are six degrees of motion in a tanker hull when underway at sea. Three are linear: surge, heave, and sway; three are rotational: pitch, roll, and yaw. Each of these motions has associated values of amplitude, velocity, and acceleration. To a hull designer, the accelerations are the key value, because they translate into forces on the hull structure.

The energy input for these motions comes from the waves, and each distinct wave has a height, the distance between trough and crest, and a period, the time between succeeding crests. The three primary motions of concern when designing a hull structure are roll, pitch and heave. Surge and sway are ignored, since their magnitude is usually small compared to the other motions. Yaw may be countered by the steering forces of the rudder. In extreme sea conditions, two other characteristics come into play. These are deck-wetness, the presence of green water on deck, and slamming, when the bow area is struck or comes down on a wave and creates zones of high pressure on the hull, followed by shaking of the hull girder. Slamming is clearly the more serious of these two characteristics.

The hull designer must also give consideration to the effects of the high dynamic loads and high impact sloshing pressures on the hull structure. Especially during a ballast voyage, when tanks may be partially filled, the sloshing effects can really challenge the strength of the structure.

Sloshing occurs when pitching and rolling of the tanker causes resonance of cargo motion in partially filled tanks. If the natural period for any filling level is within twenty percent of the roll or pitch period of the vessel, then sloshing is possible. With today's computer aid, it is possible to determine when sloshing is likely to occur by comparing the natural period of the liquid motion in both longitudinal and transverse directions, with the pitch and roll periods of the tanker.

If sloshing is deemed possible, computers will calculate the resulting pressures on bulkheads. A comparison will then be made between the sloshing pressures and the pressure from the standardized load cases in order to determine the required scantlings for tank bulkhead plating and stiffeners. Regulatory agency rules usually state that special provisions must be made to insure that, dynamic loads that result from liquid sloshing are taken into account. In many cases, the use of partially filled tanks is specifically prohibited.

To understand better such wave forces, including those relating to slamming, extensive research has been carried out in recent years by leading classification societies. They have obtained unmanned measurements of transient responses to high-wave impact and when slamming and shipping of green-seas or deck-wetness occur. (Deck-wetness refers to the presence of green water on deck, not just spray.)

Based upon the data obtained from these measurements, and the results from model experiments and theoretical methods using computers, accurate evaluation of wave induced and other forces acting on a tanker's hull are determined.

From the foregoing it is clear that when designing a tanker hull, sea-keeping is an important characteristic, because it refers to motions of a vessel in waves. Motion, energy, and design play key roles in determining the sea-keeping qualities of a design. In recent years, some of the major ship operators have recognized the virtues of continuous hull stress monitoring and have installed stress monitoring systems that identify the actual longitudinal stresses impacting on the structure from massive hammering of the hull from the environment. The concept can make a significant contribution to ensuring the safety and integrity of the hull under all operating conditions, whether at sea or in dock. The aim is to provide an instant and visible means of summarizing the condition of the ship's structure, where the monitors display the stress levels.

The question however is, what are the correct courses of action when stresses arise above acceptable levels? At this stage of development, a stress monitoring system is of value, because it alerts the ship's personnel to the stresses to which the hull is being subjected during a given period. Some operators, however, see more to the concept than purely the safety aspect. They consider such an installation as helping to improve the owner's image as part of the overall commitment to the quality of the ship. Leading classification societies do incorporate into their operational notations such installations under various guises.

Sea-Keeping and Hull Motions

Sea-keeping refers to the motion of the tanker in waves. Motion, energy, and design play important roles in the sea-keeping quality of a tanker. The energy input for motions comes from waves, and each distinct wave has a height and a period. Because of the varying nature of winds, operating areas, and seasons of the year, it is necessary to use statistics. Such statistics use the Beaufort scale, which matches wind velocity to wave conditions, adopted to define design conditions for tankers.

The Beaufort scale was arranged by Admiral Sir Francis Beaufort in 1806. It is a twelve-point numeric scale used to designate the force of the wind, from calm (force 0) to hurricane (force 12)—"that which no canvas could withstand."

The British Admiralty accepted the scale for the open sea in 1838. It was adopted by the International Meteorological Committee (IMC) for international use in 1874. The scale, as originally drawn up, made no reference to the speed of the wind, but attempts were made later to correlate wind force and wind speed. This was arranged by the IMC in June 1939 in Berlin, Germany. The Beaufort force numbers 13 to 17 were added in 1955 by the U.S. Weather Bureau.

Abnormal Sea Waves

What are "abnormal" "freak" or "rogue" waves, and how is wave height determined?

A presentation at the Royal Institution of Naval Architects in London by Professor D. Faulkner, in April 1996 it is mentioned, "such waves form under particular weather conditions, mostly at certain times of the year, they can travel great distances in the Atlantic, Indian, and Pacific Oceans.

The probability of the occurrence of abnormal waves can, in principle, be estimated by the statistics of rare events."

For a ship hull designer, is there an alternative to statistics and the probability of occurrence to determine sea conditions globally? Today, the answer is yes, and the source of information is operational oceanography, a relatively new activity, even though its beginnings can be traced to classical time of Aristotle, who was commissioned in 323 BC to explain the current in the Euripus Straits in Evia, Greece.

Until very recently, accurate prediction of the sea-state, that is, the ensemble of all sea characteristics, both physical and dynamic, on multiple space-time scales, was extremely difficult to predict, because of the gap between ocean observations and their analysis.

A remaining problem of ocean forecasting is the scarcity of oceanographic observations in time and space. Moreover, contrary to methodology, there is no coherent synoptic monitoring technology for the oceans since, even with the latest technological developments, a significant part of the oceans is not monitored.

Real time data for ocean forecasting purposes are still scarce, and they are essential because they form the necessary input to numerical models in order to achieve reliable ocean predictions. It is such data and their subsequent use that operational oceanography provides in its forecast model outputs as products to the end user. The claim by some organizations with monitoring equipment mounted on sea-buoys and located in certain areas of the ocean to record winds and waves appear primitive compared to today's advances by operational oceanography, the two components of which include the following:

- Technological; that is, the efficient, reliable, and low cost methods and devices for the collection, transmission, analysis and distribution of oceanographic data to the end users, and the satellite ocean remote sensing.

- Scientific; which is the theoretical understanding of oceanic processes and phenomena, and advanced numerical modeling and assimilation schemes for operational forecasts.

It is therefore correct to say, operational oceanography is dependent upon the progress of ocean sciences, advanced technology developments, user demands, and some urgent environmental priorities.

Today, the two maritime nations technologically and scientifically ready to apply reliable ocean prediction models on an operational basis are the United States of America and Japan.

The European Global Ocean Observing System (EuroGOOS) was founded in 1994 with the specific target to develop a common structure at European and national levels for the quality control and management of oceanographic data to improve operational oceanography and forecasting skills.

Globalizing oceanic services, by using global ocean monitoring systems and global numerical models, is a significant trend of operational oceanography that will provide precise and detailed descriptions of the prevailing sea-state in a given geographical area, as well as continuous and reliable forecasts of the sea-state at local, regional, and global levels. Such advances are particularly important and timely, especially since the International Panel on Climate Change (IPCC) has warned, in their latest authoritative study, about the impact of global warming. They are projecting disaster for areas vital to international shipping.

IPCC is a group of scientists assembled by the United Nations, to advise governments on climate policy. They have indicated that global warming affecting the oceans and the atmosphere has created a series of weather disasters at sea and along the coasts. The study points out that hurricanes may well grow stronger and more frequent due to the increased energy generated by the interaction between the warming sea surface and the atmosphere. It will be prudent for the international shipping industry to seriously consider the long-term effects of climate change, and how it will affect the design for a safer ship.

Global Wave Statistics

In December 1986, with the full authority of the British Maritime Technology Limited, a book titled *Global Waves Statistics* was published in the U.K. This is the first single volume directory to contain wave data for a global selection of 104 sea areas. It covers a selection from some fifty-five million sets of wind and wave data from all over the world, recorded over a period of 130 years through 1984.

The book replaces its forerunner, *Ocean Wave Statistics*, published in 1967, which was then considered a first class reference source, despite the exclusion of the Pacific Ocean. The new book contains statistics of wave heights, periods, and directions, based on observations from all over the world.

Definitions

Pitch
: the rotation of the ship about its transverse axis, that is, how much the bow and stern rise and fall due to the wave motion on the sea. The period of pitch is expressed in units/time (seconds) to complete one cycle.

Roll
: the rotation of the ship about its longitudinal axis, that is, how much the boat rocks side to side due to the wave motion. The period of roll is expressed in units of time (seconds) to complete one cycle.

Sway
: the horizontal translation of the ship's center of gravity perpendicular to the center line of the ship. A primary cause of sway would be the port to starboard sloshing of liquid cargo and how that affects the ship's center of gravity.

Surge
: the horizontal translation of the ship's center of gravity in a fore and aft direction. A primary cause of surge would be the fore to aft sloshing of liquid cargo and how that affects the ship's center of gravity.

Heave
: the motion of the ship along its vertical axis without any rotation, that is, how much the center of gravity of the ship rises and falls.

Yaw
: the horizontal rotation of the ship about its vertical axis, that is, the degree to which forces acting on a ship move the bow port or starboard.

Heel or List
: the angle of static transverse (port or starboard) inclination of the ship, that is, the tilt or degree to which the internal forces acting on a ship cause it to lean left or right, most evident in calm waters.

Trim
: Defines the longitudinal static inclination of the ship. It is expressed as the difference in drafts at the bow and the stern, that is, the tilt or degree to which the internal forces acting on a ship cause the bow to rise or fall, most evident in calm waters.

Sloshing
: The liquid cargo movement in a slack tank that contributes to any of the dynamic movements described above.

A TANKER
IN ROUGH SEAS

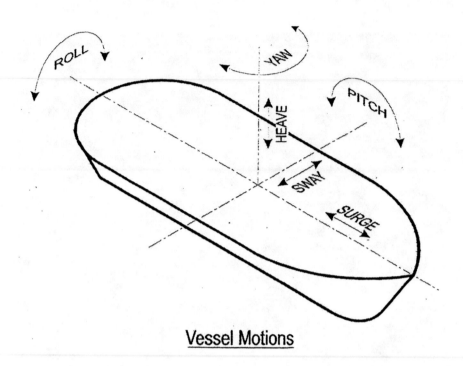

Vessel Motions

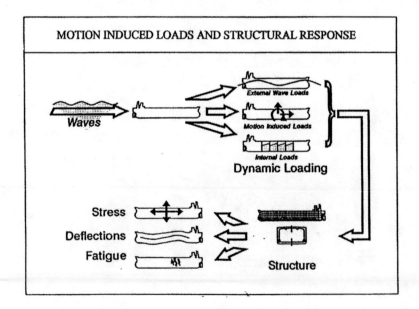

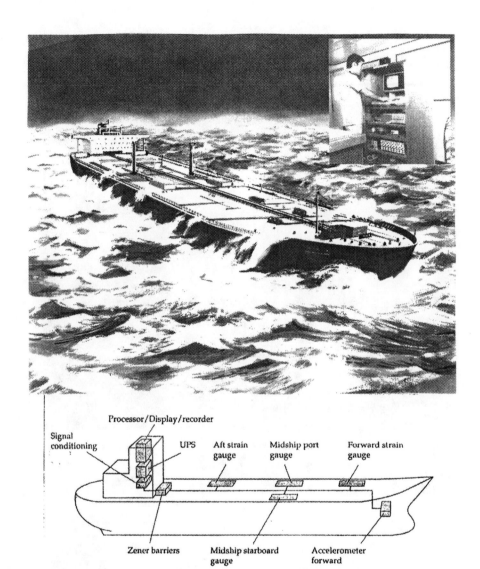

Processor/Display/recorder

Signal conditioning

UPS

Aft strain gauge

Midship port gauge

Forward strain gauge

Zener barriers

Midship starboard gauge

Accelerometer forward

TANKER HULL STRESS MONITORING

The VLCC "ENERGY CONCENTRATION" originally named "GOLAR BETTY" was completed in March 1970 by Kawasaki Heavy Industries Ltd. at Sakaide in Japan. The tanker had the following principal particulars:

Length overall	326.75 m
Length B.P.	313.00 m
Breadth	48.19 m
Depth	25.20 m
Draught	19.59 m
Gross tonnage	98,894 tons
Deadweight	216,269 tons
Machinery	Steam Turbines

Originally classed by D.N.V., in 1977 changed to B.V. class. The tanker broke its back, while discharging at Rotterdam in Holland in July 1980. From the subsequent enquiry that followed the incident, it transpired that the sequence of discharging the cargo at Rotterdam was such as to increase substantially the hogging moment above the already high value as a result of cargo transfer at the previous port of Antifer. The eventual distribution of weight and buoyancy induced a hogging bending moment which exceeded the ultimate longitudinal strength of the tanker.

It took several years to complete the investigation, however, it was a rare opportunity to compare the "measured" ultimate strength of a tanker of this size with that predicated using purely theoretical methods.

NINE

QUEST FOR THE ENERGY EFFICIENT OIL TANKER

Today's advanced technologies are contributing a great deal towards the development of an energy efficient tanker design. The parameters to be considered include the following:

- The fuel consumed by the main propulsion unit creating the thrust that moves the hull through the water; the hull's frictional and wave-making resistance is negatively affected if the hull is fouled or rough, however, and potential speed is lost

- The fuel necessary to produce electricity for the operation of the auxiliary machinery and other equipment on board

- The fuel necessary for various heating functions such as heating of the fuel oil, lubricating oil, and for hotel services

The major portion of the fuel used is for the propulsion system, which is around sixty percent of the total fuel used. The propulsive efficiency of the system is therefore important and is defined as the ratio of the main engine output that can effectively be used for the propulsion of the tanker to the total main engine output. That is the ratio of effective horse power (EHP) necessary to overcome hull resistance—both frictional and wave making—to the delivered horse power (DHP) that is transmitted from the main engine to the propeller.

The Underwater Hull Form

Developing the underwater hull form for a hydrodynamically efficient tanker requires a series of calculations that are necessary to determine the principal dimensions and block coefficient, which in turn provide the optimum performance within the dimensional constraints of the design. These include the following:

- Restrictions in the overall length
- Restrictions in the deadweight
- Restrictions in the loaded draft
- Restrictions of face of berth-fender for the parallel mid-body
- Restrictions in manifold height, for the cargo loading arm
- Restrictions in the air draft to ensure adequate bridge clearance

In addition to the efforts to obtain an efficient hull form, careful attention is required to achieve the following:

- Good sea-keeping qualities of the tanker
- An efficient propulsion system
- A robust hull structure, adequately protected against corrosion
- An optimized navigation system

In developing the hull form, attention must be paid to the fore end of the hull lines for the development of a suitable hull at the bow, and to the after-end hull lines to ensure good water flow to the propeller.

Adopting a low-revolution, large diameter propeller, will improve the propulsive efficiency. Further improvement in performance can be achieved by the addition of stern appendages that will gain from the water flow to the propeller and from the propeller wake. It is necessary however, to investigate carefully such additions from the perspective of the following:

- Performance results
- Maneuverability
- Subsequent maintenance
- Cost effectiveness

It should be kept in mind that a well designed underwater hull form should not require propulsion improving devices to save energy.

With regard to the propulsion plant and system, the thermal efficiency of today's main diesel engine is around sixty percent. The tanker hull designer can do nothing to change that. The remaining percentage of energy used is in the form of waste-heat, and a great deal can be done to recover some of that heat through to exhaust gas economizer.

Electricity Generation to Meet the Tanker's Requirements

A third and equally important source for energy conservation is the use of electrical energy to meet the needs for the propulsion plant, navigational equipment, and hotel services.

In a modern propulsion installation on a VLCC, there are normally three types of electricity generating units:

- Steam driven turbogenerator
- Main-shaft driven generator
- Diesel generator

Proper design of the electricity generating system can save energy and includes:

- Using a scoop for the turbogenerator condenser instead of an electrically driven circulating water pump
- Making use of natural ventilation of certain spaces
- Voltage and frequency control of pump motors using a variable voltage/frequency control to regulate motor speed for pump operation at optimum capacity

Consideration should also be given to the installation of a modern weather routing system that provides information to the tanker on weather and seastate via satellites. Having such a system on board is of immense value to the personnel on board so that they can optimize their navigation planning and adjust the draft and trim of the tanker during the ballast voyage. Reducing the fuel consumption of a tanker also reduces atmospheric pollution.

An important contributor to enhancing the propulsive efficiency of a tanker is the propeller. Today, the large diameter fixed pitch propeller, designed to absorb high shaft horse power is in constant demand by the tanker hull designer. Transmission of high power, however, increases the significance of propeller-related vibration characteristics in comparison with the requirement for high-propulsive efficiency.

Vibration characteristics are a function of the action of the propeller in the nonuniform wake. Such characteristics are of particular importance in a tanker where the crew accommodation and navigational equipment are located directly above the propeller, and where problems arise from propeller- or wake-related excitation forces. It is necessary therefore to give careful consideration to the requirements for a successful propeller design such as:

- High-propulsive efficiency
- Eliminating the undesirable effects of cavitation
- Imposing torque loading within the engine builder's recommended range throughout the tanker's life
- Good quality propeller material with good reparability

Selection of the number of propeller blades is made by the tanker hull designer, because the designer is in possession of the hull structure, machinery, and propeller shafting vibration characteristics. The propeller designer's contribution is in the form of guidance information.

Success in prediction of vibrations depends greatly on the feedback from full-scale measurements on board ships. It is also necessary when calculations are made at the design stage to make assumptions and simplifications for both the excitation forces and the modeling of the hull structure.

If harmonic or resonant vibration occurs, changing the number of propeller blades may solve a serious vibration problem. For instance, the boundary layer effect is the mass of water which is dragged along with the ship's hull as it moves through the water. Depending upon the size of the tanker, the thickness of the boundary layer varies from half-meter to more than two meters. This boundary layer movement causes severe inflow irregularity when the propeller blade tips penetrate the layer to a large percentage of its thickness. As each propeller blade moves from the high velocity region to a lower velocity region, it experiences a change in the angle of attack resulting in an imbalance of the thrust. This change in thrust on each blade produces an oscillating bending movement in the propeller shaft. Both an oscillating torque and thrust result in the shaft bearing and through the shaft respectively.

Fuel/Energy-Saving Devices

In a modern tanker hull design, fuel economy is recognized as a very important design factor. The most efficient form of propulsion today is the single screw propeller, powered by a long-stroke, low-speed cross-head diesel engine, burning heavy marine fuel oil. Any improvements to the basic philosophy mentioned here are always of interest to an owner/operator, where modifications or additions may improve hull propulsion performance.

It is a well-known fact that the biggest gains are those obtained by using low propeller revolutions and large diameter propellers. Ducted propellers were recognized in the 1960s and 1970s as having some advantage in improving propulsion performance. In the past years, however, there has been a decline in the number of new designs for which ducts were specified, because efficiency is improved by lower revolution, larger diameter propellers. In cases where there is limitation to the propeller diameter, for example, because of draft limitation, ducts continue to be used. Nozzles, reaction fins, and other devices, installed forward of the propeller do improve water flow to the propeller, and help reduce propeller-excited vibration forces, while improving propulsive efficiency. In order to gain maximum effect however, the devices must be optimized by tank testing.

The Contra Rotating Propeller (CRP)

The origin of the contra rotating propeller system is attributed to J. Ericsson, who patented the idea in the U.K. in 1836. An experimental unit was installed on the Italian training ship *Cristoforo Colombo* in 1934. The system has been employed in torpedoes, and was also installed in the U.S. nuclear submarine *Jack* in March 1967 with a view to obtain information on noise.

In a contra rotating propeller system, two propellers in tandem, rotate in opposite direction, eliminating the swirl effect of the wake, that is, the rotational energy in the slipstream of the forward propeller is recovered by the aft propeller, effectively generating thrust in the forward direction only.

In the case of the conventional propellers, swirling flow energy is wasted in the slip stream. In the CRP system, swirling flow energy produced by the forward propeller is recovered by the aft propeller thus saving energy. Also, the load on the two propellers is reduced because the total generated thrust is shared by the two propellers.

Two CRP systems have been developed, the synchronous (SCRP), where the dual concentric shafts rotate in opposite direction at the same speed, and the asynchronous (ACRP), where the concentric dual shafts rotate at different speeds. The ACRP system can achieve higher energy saving than the SCRP system by lowering the speed of the forward propeller.

This system has been refined in Japan during the past decade, where two of the leading Japanese shipyards have installed it on several commercial ships, including the VLCC *Okinoshima Maru*, in 1993. This is a 258,000 dwt crude oil carrier, and during sea trials, engineers established that the ship had an energy savings of fourteen percent. It is a costly installation, and there have been problems in the course of its development. This obliged tanker owners to adopt a wait-and-see attitude.

A simpler variation of the contra rotating propeller is the Grim vane wheel propeller system. It is a German design that has a free-running propeller on the shaft in the slipstream of the powered propeller. Engineers report from tests carried out at the Hamburg Ship Model Basin an improvement in the propulsive efficiency similar to the contra rotating propeller with far less complex mechanics.

The Off-Center Propeller (NOPS)

An interesting energy saving arrangement, also developed in Japan in the late 1990s, is known commercially as the NKK off-center propeller arrangement. Engineers established that by locating the propeller off-center, there is an important gain in propeller efficiency known as NOPS. The arrangement is the same as that for a conventional single screw in a symmetric stern, except for the positioning of the propeller.

In the NOPS arrangement, the propeller shaft is shifted from the center line to starboard side of the hull, for a clockwise (right hand) turning propeller, and vice-versa if a left hand turning propeller is selected. Shifting the propeller position results in an increase in the flow velocity to the propeller in the opposite direction of the propeller rotation, thereby gaining an increase in propeller efficiency.

Especially in a hull with large block coefficient, such as tankers and bulk carriers, bilge vortices produce a nonuniform wake that increases viscous resistance, which in turn reduces propeller efficiency. When designers placed the propeller and the rudder slightly off the hull's center line, it was found the propeller efficiency improved by making effective use of bilge vortices.

The NOPS arrangement performed well in both tank tests and at sea trials of commercial vessels. The actual sea trials produced a gain in propulsive efficiency of approximately six percent, and together with other passive energy devices installed on the vessels, the builders claimed a total gain of fourteen percent in fuel economy, compared with vessels of the same deadweight and speed without the NOPS arrangement.

No other alterations in the hull design are necessary to accommodate the NOPS arrangement. Only minimal modifications to the engine room layout and propeller shaft design are required.

Because of the repositioning of the propeller, wake distribution within the propeller disc is asymmetric, resulting in different forces acting on the propeller bearing compared to those of a conventional design. Propeller shafting, bearings and lubrication arrangement has to be modified accordingly to take care of the forces resulting from the relocation of the propeller to one side.

Location of the main engine, auxiliary machinery, including pumps on the lower engine room floor, differs slightly from the conventional arrangement floor. Also, relocating the rudder requires rearranging the after structure to support the rudder horn. The propeller bossing must also be redesigned because of the asymmetry created by the relocation of the propeller to one side.

During sea trials of the 230,000 dwt ore carrier *Onoe Maru* with the NOPS arrangement, no significant differences were noted, in the directional stability, or during maneuvering of this ore carrier when compared with ships of similar size and speed with conventionally located propellers. The NOPS arrangement has been incorporated in several commercial ships built in Japan, and are operating satisfactorily.

Designing the Fuel-Efficient Tanker Hull

The most important aspect in the design of a fuel efficient tanker lies in the choice of a hull form that will minimize resistance and maximize propulsive performance. The hull designer directs his efforts toward reducing frictional and wave-making resistance either by the complete hull profile or adaptations to it.

The challenge facing the designer is to obtain a design that will carry its cargo and crew in safety and relative comfort economically. However, there will always be a trade off between speed, power required, and fuel consumption. Considerable progress has been made in recent years in hull design, because sophisticated computer programs can predict flow around the hull in both two and three dimensions.

For a tanker that operates half its life at one draft and the other half at another draft, model tank tests, even though costly, are essential to refine the underwater hull form. As the ship's draft and trim have an important effect on fuel consumption, it is worthwhile during the model tests to carry out trials at a range of drafts and range of trim conditions at each draft in order to determine the optimum conditions in service.

In any design, the bow and stern sections, along with the propeller, produce the largest savings in resistance. These are of particular importance for a tanker because of the two draft operations, loaded and ballast, during the ship's service life. Today's computers enable the hull designer to exploit thoroughly the theory of hull form and to predict the water flow distribution on the hull surface with greater accuracy than in the past, because now the viscous resistance can also be computed.

Viscous resistance is reduced by redistributing the displacement, that is, by making the lower part of the stern section finer, so that the displacement is shifted upward as far as practicable. The aim is to obtain a set of underwater hull lines that will give optimum propulsive performance, that is, a hull with the minimum possible resistance. This will reflect on the fuel consumption throughout the ship's service life.

For a given design the propulsive performance is considered in two broad aspects. One relates to the performance of the hull and the other to the propeller. The designer endeavors to optimize these two aspects separately. A third aspect is that of the hull-propeller interference. Despite many years of designing ship's hull with screw propellers, the difficult science of ensuring perfect flow around the after end of the hull, through propeller blades, and past the rudder has still not completely been mastered, in spite the enormous amount of research work and the advent of powerful computing systems.

The use of screw propellers as thrusters for ships was introduced more than 200 years ago and gradually replaced the paddle wheels. Despite the technological advances in propulsion equipment and devices to reduce fuel consumption, especially in the last half century, no substitute has been found for Archimedes' screw, (Archemides's rotating propeller)

Viscous Resistance

Viscous, or frictional, resistance is the primary resistance especially in a full hull form such as that of today's VLCCs and ULCCs. Frictional drag reduction has been a goal of the naval architect for a very long time. Programs are currently underway in the United States, Holland, and Germany, known as Frictional Drag Reduction Advance Technology Programs, that allow researchers to find techniques that will obtain optimal results. The objective is to look at air lubrication of water repellant coatings. This is a first-ever, first-principles modeling of bubbles in turbulent flow, that indicated that small spherical bubbles can produce drag reduction even at low void fractions. The idea is to discover the properties of optimal additives that may not be polymers or microbubbles.

Naval architects have known for many years that adding polymers or microbubbles to the flow of water around flat plates can reduce friction drag considerably. Despite the fact that such techniques have shown considerable promise at laboratory models, such techniques have never been tested at full scale.

The Bulb at the Bow and Stern

The bulbous bow has been introduced to reduce wave-making resistance by setting up "anti-phased" waves to cancel out those created by the ship's bow. Engineers have discovered that the bulb is more important for ships of higher speeds than the average tanker's speed. Wave making resistance can comprise as much as 50 percent of the total resistance. In such cases, a bulbous bow could reduce the resistance substantially. For a tanker, the reduction is a smaller proportion of the total resistance, probably ten to fifteen percent, but is still significant.

Working on the same philosophy, one of the leading Japanese shipyards developed a stern-end bulb, which is claimed to produce fuel saving of around five percent. The stern-end bulb is designed to counteract the wave resistance generated by the stern of the vessel. Such improvements in overcoming the hull resistance at the bow and stern enable the designer to use a larger block coefficient, which in turn allows extra cargo carrying potential in a given design. This, together with determination of the optimum trim conditions, will result in fuel saving.

Recently, one of the leading Japanese yards has developed the optimum bow shape for medium-speed vessels that reduces significantly the bow wave-resistance drag. The name given to the new bow design is SEA Arrow (sharp entrance angle bow as an Arrow). The design retains the effect of the bulbous bow, while eliminating the protrusion from the bow. Designers claim the new bow produces a fuel savings of around six percent.

Another of the Japanese leading yards has designed and already installed what is commercially known as the "Ax-Bow." The design is particularly suited to vessels of full hull form such as oil tankers, and is claimed to be superior to conventional bows.

The Quest for Greater Propulsive Efficiency

In recent years, in addition to the efforts to refine a ship's underwater hull lines in order to improve the hydrodynamic efficiency and reduce propeller interference with the rotational flow of water, several active as well as passive energy saving devices have been developed in Japan and in Europe, and have been installed on new and existing ships.

Passive devices include the following:

- Wake equalizing ducts (WED)
- Additional thrust fins (A.T. Fins)
- Nozzles installed in front of the propeller
- Fins mounted on the ship's hull at the stern
- Propeller ducts with symmetric or asymmetric nozzles
- The Mitsubishi Reaction Fin
- Asymmetric stern or skeg
- Grothnes Vortex-Spoiling Fins
- Rudder bulb system with fins (RBS-F)
- Nomura's Flow Control Fins (NCF)
- Mitsubishi Stator Fins
- Mitsui Ducted Propeller
- Schneekluthe Wake-Equalizing Duct

Passive devices are mainly guide vanes arranged either in front of or behind the propeller. The vanes arranged in front, are intended to introduce a momentum to the water flow entering the propeller disc. The vanes arranged behind the propeller, are intended to extract form the slipstream the momentum generated by the propeller that does not contribute to the propulsion and convert it into additional thrust.

Active devices for the improvement of propulsive efficiency include the following:

- Large diameter—low RPM propellers (Designers found that increasing the propeller diameter and lowering of RPM improves the ship/power relationship, resulting in fuel consumption reduction.)
- Contra-Rotating propellers
- Tip Loaded propellers with end plates

- Grim vane wheel
- Propeller Boss Cap Fins (PBCF)

The concept for propulsion-improving devices in the region of the ship's aftbody and the propeller, were under consideration early in the twentieth century. The flow conditions at the propeller, however, were not as well understood as they are today. Fundamentally, the energy saving devices mentioned in this chapter can be combined with each other. Such combinations have already been done with satisfactory results. The savings in energy from the combined arrangement, however, did not produce the sum of the gains attainable with each single device.

With the exception of the large diameter, low RPM propeller and the contra-rotating-propeller system, all other energy saving devices, both passive and active, have produced a savings of three to five percent. The dilemma an owner has to face is whether an energy saving device is necessary for his ship. Do installation and subsequent maintenance costs justify the installation?

Hydrodynamic aspects play an important role in the quality of a ship. Dominant criteria in hull form design are the resistance and powering performance. Detailed knowledge of the flow around the after part of a hull therefore is crucial, because flow separation may occur with important consequences for the resistance and power. The flow field experienced by the propeller is also affected. Unfavorable characteristics of this flow field may result in noise and vibration stemming from the operation of a propeller in the disturbed flow field behind a hull. The classical approach to predicting the flow around the hull of a ship and the flow to the propeller is to perform measurements on a scale model in a towing tank. Another method would be to do as we did during model testing of the first 100,000 dwt tanker built in United States: use a circulating water tunnel.

Such measurements need to be translated into full scale, which is usually done using semiempirical methods or experience. This arrangement introduces inaccuracies, particularly in the propeller inflow field. Until now, validation of full-scale ship viscous flow predictions has been insufficient mainly due to the absence of suitable full-scale wake field data.

Efforts are underway to develop methods to refine and validate computational fluid dynamics (CFD) predictions for the viscous flow around the ship's hull at full scale, and to introduce such predictions into practical underwater hull and propeller design. CFD is used in the early stages of developing the underwater form in a design, as a complement to experimental investigations. It is a worthwhile effort and expense, as it can give an early warning of difficulties, especially in designs with full form such as those of VLCCs or ULCCs.

This method of analysis is now considered a practical analysis tool by the ship-building industry, and has been integrated into fully automated optimization procedures during the design stage by the hull designer.

Computational Fluid Dynamics (CFD)

Computational fluid dynamics is a recently developed state-of-the-art three-dimensional computational method for ship hydrodynamic design, and has emerged as an advanced tool for the computation of the flow past ship hull form in both calm waters and in waves. CFD is an analysis and a design method, used to evaluate calm water performance, sea-keeping, wave-induced structural loads, and added resistance for all types of commercial, naval, and recreational vessels. It has been recognized as a reliable, versatile, and inexpensive hull design tool that may be used along side the traditional model towing basin.

Especially today with the emergence of high speed commercial vessels, the CFD method enables the naval architect to better understand the issues involved in the design of a more efficient hull operating in severe seas. In the past, the use of two-dimensional methods, such as strip theory, had limitations in their application, especially to high-frequency encounters. To overcome these limitations, the three dimensional theories have been developed, which are valid across the range of frequencies, speeds, and wave headings, particularly for hulls of simpler geometry, such as those of commercial ships. For sailing yachts of multihull design, the analysis is more complicated.

The three dimensional method has produced satisfactory answers to the problem of evaluating the hydrodynamic performance of such ships, particularly high speed commercial ships, naval vessels, and sailing yachts, where such evaluation is of great importance to the naval architect in estimating power requirements. A typical design study, to produce results of acceptable accuracy, such as the SWAN method used at MIT, may require up to one hour of computer time to execute a completed solution of the sea-keeping problem. Especially in designs with full forms such as those of VLCCs or ULCCs, using CFD in the early stages of developing the underwater hull form is a worthwhile effort and expense as a complement to experimental investigations because of its ability to give early warning for difficulties.

Propulsion Machinery for Oil Tankers

For the past 150 years, the primary sources of energy for the propulsion of commercial ships have been coal, and fuels derived from crude oil. Coal is available in great abundance but difficult to extract from the ground and difficult to handle on board ships compared to oil. Nuclear energy, while a viable source for commercial ship propulsion, will only become attractive in the future if present environmental, political, and economic obstacles can be removed.

The conversion of the energy source into power for ship propulsion is accomplished by the use of external combustion process such as a boiler, which produces steam to drive a reciprocating steam engine or steam turbine; gas to drive a gas turbine, or by the internal combustion engine, such as the low speed, medium or high speed diesel engine. The external combustion process has the advantage of using coal or low quality oil fuels, but it has a poor specific fuel consumption compared to the internal combustion process.

Post-World War II demand for increase in tanker size ran parallel with the demand for power increase in the steam turbine. The period from 1944 to 1948 was the era of the supertanker having a deadweight of 25,000 to 28,000 tons, 12,500 shaft horsepower, and steam turbines. From 1949 to 1955, the tanker size increased to 30,000–40,000 dwt with an average propulsion of 20,000 shaft horsepower. From 1956 to 1958 the tanker deadweight increased to 50,000–60,000 tons, and the propulsion power to 25,000 shaft horse power.

After the two closures of the Suez Canal, (1956 and 1967) the tanker size increased to 150,000 and 300,000 dwt. These were the Very Large Crude Carrier requiring 30,000–40,000 horsepower for the propulsion machinery, followed soon after, by the Ultra Large Crude Carrier of 400,000–500,000 dwt requiring propulsion machinery of 50,000 horsepower, or two 25,000 horsepower engines.

During the period from 1946 to 1962, there was no marked change in the steam conditions, that is, steam pressure of 40 kg/cm^2 and temperature 450º C was used to drive the steam turbines The fuel consumption rate was 235 gm/SHP/h. An increase, in the steam pressure to 60 kg/cm^2 improved the fuel consumption rate to 210 gm/SHP/h. After 1965, the steam reheat cycle was developed, reaching a steam pressure of 100 kg/cm^2 and temperature of 510º C, which improved the fuel rate to 178–185 gm/SHP/h.

During the period 1960 to 1962, tanker owners adopted machinery automation with the consequent reduction in engine room personnel, and it was decided to adopt steam conditions of 60 kg/cm^2 and steam temperature of 510º C. The fuel consumption rate under these conditions was 210 gm/SHP/h. It should be noted that the World War II, T-2 tanker of 16,800 dwt had turboelectric propulsion of 6,600 SHP; steam conditions 425 psi pressure; temperature of 725° F, and the fuel rate was 0.662 lbs/SHP/h (300 gm/SHP/h). Further automation of the propulsion plant enabled the tanker owners to operate the plant without human supervision once steady sea conditions were attained after leaving port. This was the beginning of the unmanned engine room, designated as U.M.S. by the classification societies.

Many developments in all areas of marine design and operation have enhanced the efficiency of marine propulsion systems over the years. Perhaps one of the most impressive is the development of the marine diesel engine to its current high efficiency level, achieving in some cases, thermal efficiencies in excess of fifty percent.

The most competent early study of the thermodynamic aspects of the internal combustion engine was that of the French scientist N. L. S. Carnot, who in 1824 presented his work titled "Reflection on the Motive Power of Heat," in which he discussed the possibility of igniting fuel by compressing air to one fourteenth (1/14) of its original volume. In an internal combustion engine, a fuel-air mixture is burned in such a manner that the hot gaseous products of combustion exert a force on moving parts of the engine thereby generating power.

The internal combustion engine (ICE) cannot be attributed to any one particular inventor. The internal combustion engine followed the steam engine. The latter was developed by James Watt in the mid-eighteenth century. The internal combustion engine was an improvement in the thermal efficiency over the steam engine.

Steam turbine propulsion for commercial ships progressively surrendered its traditional territory to the diesel engine in the last century on all types of ships: general cargo, passenger, container, LNG carriers, and tankers. As the size of the tanker increased, requiring greater propulsion power, diesel engine builders increased the power and sophistication of the low-speed, two-stroke engine by introducing models with more cylinders and extended the potential power limit to 103 MW per engine. Additionally, there are operational benefits by the introduction of the so called intelligent, low-speed engine with higher operational flexibility, enhanced fuel economy, and lower emissions.

Diesel engine builders, having the advantage of a more thermally efficient engine, pushed hard to increase the per cylinder output in horsepower while still operating on heavy fuel of 3500 SEC Redwood No. 1, achieving a fuel rate of approximately 159 gm/BHP/h., against a modern steam turbine plant of approximately 200 gr/BHP/h.

The lubricating oil consumption of a diesel plant is higher than that of the steam turbine, and maintenance is also higher in the diesel plant, but the diesel is still competitive.

In the early 1950s, steam powered ships with either reciprocating or turbine machinery outnumbered diesel driven ships in the world commercial fleet by a three to one margin. By 1965, the dominance had been reversed in favor of the diesel engines by a nine to one margin. The oil crisis and the search to reduce oil consumption were the reason for reversing the trend in the mode of ship propulsion. The diesel engine eventually ousted steam turbine installations from VLCCs, container, and cruise ships. The steam turbine's last bastion has been the LNG carrier, where the steam boilers are able to operate on fuel oil and the gas from the cargo boil-off.

Even in the LNG carrier sector of the shipping industry, diesel engine builders have introduced the dual-fuel, low- and medium-speed diesels, as an alternative to the traditional steam turbine plant. The attractiveness of the dual-fuel diesel for LNG carriers is the adoption of high pressure gas injection where the engine can deliver the same power output on gas as the straight diesel, and with the same high levels of thermal efficiency.

Diesel-Electric Propulsion

Today, diesel-electric propulsion, the merits of which are appreciated by the large cruise ship operators, made a breakthrough in the North Sea shuttle tankers. This indicates penetration of the tanker market. For today's crude oil carrier, diesel-electric propulsion is an attractive option. The concept opens up interesting possibilities in the machinery room layout where, for such an installation, medium speed diesel engines could provide power for AC motors through frequency converters and "assignment switching." The advantages of diesel-electric propulsion are the result of the combination of two concepts; the power plant concept and the variable speed electric transmission concept. These include the following:

- Operation of diesel engines at optimum load
- Easier automation
- Full redundancy
- Simplicity in operation
- Simpler machinery room
- More efficient use of space

An Integrated Approach to Energy Saving on Board Crude Oil Carriers

1. Bulbous bow designed for optimum performance in both loaded as well as ballast voyages, bearing in mind a crude oil carrier splits its service life equally sailing either in a loaded or ballast draft condition;

2. self polishing antifouling paints;

3. bulbous stern;

4. super long stroke, two-cycle, cross-head slow speed main engine;

5. large diameter, low RPM propeller

6. main shaft driven generator

7. two to three stage pressure type exhaust gas economizer system

8. superstructure to be designed for low wind resistance

9. optimization of navigation system—that is, a computer-aided automatic navigation system normally consisting of four sub-systems

    a. position fixing

    b. navigation planning

    c. automatic maneuvering

    d. data recording

Under the control of such systems, the vessel will navigate, exactly according to the planned optimum route, and the navigation distance is the shortest possible under normal weather conditions.

Nuclear Energy and Commercial Ships

Over the years, physicists and chemists discovered that all material things around us contain one or more of the basic 103 elements that make up matter. The smallest particle to which we can reduce the mass of an element forms an atom, which is the basic building block of matter. The atom, so named by the Greek physicist and philosopher Democritus in 450 BC,—has an internal structure consisting of a densely packed nucleus containing practically the entire mass of the atom, surrounded by electrons continuously moving about the nucleus. The nucleus consists of two kinds of infinitesimally small particles known as protons and neutrons tightly bound together. Each proton carries a single unit positive electrical charge, while the neutrons have no charge. This gives the nucleus a net positive charge.

It was the British physicist, Sir James Chadwick, who in 1932 discovered the neutron, a hitherto undetected constituent of the atom, electrically neutral and with a mass equal that of a proton. This provided a new weapon for atomic disintegration, since neutrons, being electrically uncharged, could penetrate undeflected to the atomic nucleus. The discovery of the neutron by Chadwick may be considered the key to nuclear energy.

In 1934, the Italian physicist Enrico Fermi demonstrated that nuclear transformation occurs in nearly every element subjected to neutron bombardment.

In January 1939, the German chemist Otto Hahn, working with physicists Lise Meitner and Fritz Strassman, reported the important discovery of splitting the heavy uranium atom, which released the energy locked in its structure, and suggested the term fission for this process.

The discovery of the fission process was found to release energy locked in the structure of the heavy atoms of uranium and was the basis for all methods to tap atomic energy, including the development of the atomic bomb.

Otto Hahn, worked as research assistant with Sir William Ramsay in London, and with Ernest Rutherford at McGill University in Montreal, Canada. In 1906, Hahn returned to Germany and set up the first radiochemical laboratory, which later became the Kaiser Wilhelm Institute near Berlin. In 1938, Lise Meitner, an Austrian citizen, was forced by Hitler to leave Germany. There are indications that Otto Hahn helped Meitner leave Germany unharmed.

Enrico Fermi, who moved to the United States from Italy to avoid Mussolini's decrees, showed how to fit the key into the lock to produce a chain reaction of fissioning (splitting) uranium and take the nucleus out of the laboratory for full scale energy release.

On December 2, 1942, Fermi directed the first controlled nuclear chain reaction. Fermi became aware of the fact that if the fission could be made into a self perpetuating chain reaction, enormous quantities of energy could be released. He and Hungarian physicist Leo Szilard realized the important military implications, and decided to demonstrate this to the U.S. Government. They asked Albert Einstein to appeal directly to President F.D. Roosevelt, pointing out the dangers if Hitler's Germany succeeded in developing a bomb based on these principles. Einstein's famous letter to President Roosevelt resulted in the *Manhattan Project*, which led to the development of the atomic bomb.

The fundamental equation on the subject of atomic energy is Einstein's theorem, which showed that the relationship between mass and energy is given by the equation: $E=MC^2$, where: E = energy in ergs, M = mass in grams, and C = speed of light, 3×10^{10} cm/second or 186,000 miles per second.

The British scientist Sir Oliver Joseph Lodge wrote in 1920, "The time will come when atomic energy will take the place of coal as a source of power. I hope that the human race will not discover how to use this energy until it has brains enough to use it properly."

The first atomic bomb to be used in warfare was dropped on a Japanese army base in Hiroshima at 0815 hours on August 8, 1945, and a second such bomb, was dropped on Nagasaki at 1102 hours on the of August 9, 1945. The detonation of the atomic bomb gave an awesome and terrifying demonstration of one practical application of this new source of energy. The war years were years of military priority, and there were valid reasons for this preoccupation.

The first nuclear electricity was generated in December 1951 at the experimental breeder reactor operating at the Idaho National Engineering Research Laboratory. The power generated was minimal but it anticipated the five MW from Russia's reactor at Obninsk by three years, and sixty-five MW from the first Calder Hall reactor in the U.K. by five years. Since the end of World War II, accelerated activity, especially by the United States, supported by the U.K. and Canada, enabled these countries to harness fissioning uranium in a controlled reaction to produce atomic energy for the generation of electricity. This required development of steam-generating equipment and fuel, which was entirely new to the electric utilities.

Today, in nuclear power installations in the Western world, all equipment is required to be constructed and maintained to levels of excellence which ensure that availability and reliability of the nuclear plant, is of the highest order commensurate with the sound safety principles and regulatory requirements.

The Fast (Breeder) Reactor

The U.K. authorities dealing with nuclear energy, and who recognized the importance of nuclear energy as means of generating electricity, were concerned over the future availability of uranium supplies, when the first thermal reactors were brought into service some fifty years ago. It was decided that the development of a fast reactor with the potential of releasing some 100 times more energy from the available uranium should be pursued with vigor. In parallel, design teams in France and Germany, were busy with their designs of commercial fast reactors.

In 1989, a formal agreement was signed bringing together, and rationalizing the separate European programs which became known as the European Fast Reactor Utilities Group, who defined a specification for the European fast reactor (EFR).

Contacts had always been maintained with the teams operating fast reactors in Russia, Kazakhstan, the United States, and particularly with Japan, who were busy with their fast reactor MONU. The Japanese joined the "operators club" in April 1994 and a great deal had been done to share experience to the benefit of future designs.

The MONU prototype fast reactor began to supply small amounts of electricity to the electricity grid at the end of August 1995. On December 8 1995, there was apparently a coolant leak, from the fast reactor, which had caused the Reactor to overheat and obliged the operators to switch it off, indefinitely.

The costs to develop the fast reactor, in order to produce cheap electricity proved much greater than had been envisaged, and France's Super-Phoenix and U.K.'s Dounray Fast Reactor had already been switched off. The fact that the shortages of uranium supply envisaged in the 1950's and 1960's did not develop, a need was not seen to introduce fast reactors on a commercial scale in the near term.

The question now is, how long will the traditional energy sources last? Decades, centuries, or longer? Oil and gas will probably only last a matter of decades. Coal should last a few hundred years, Uranium, the basis of nuclear energy, could quite conceivably last much longer than any other energy source, perhaps thousands of years.

For decades, scientists have been aiming to create a limitless supply of energy, with machines that mimic the nuclear fusion process that drive the furnace at the heart of the sun and stars. At the Geneva summit meeting between Mr. Gorbachev of Russia and Mr. Reagan of the United States, an agreement was signed "to develop fusion energy for the benefit of all mankind."

The idea has its origins 68 years ago, when the physicist Hans Bethe, of Cornell University, solved a century-old question for astronomers—where do the sun and other stars get their energy from? Bethe suggested that the energy came from the fusion of the lightest of all elements, hydrogen atoms. They were transformed into helium, but with 1% of the mass of the hydrogen converted into energy. The practical test that showed Bethe was right came with the hydrogen bomb, which was detonated on November 1st 1952, at Eniwetok.

The vindication will rest on the success of the international thermo-nuclear experimental reactor (ITER), a prototype of the power sources that could keep the national grids of the world supplied with energy during the second half of this century.

The aim is to achieve control of the reaction, thus creating a small sun-on-earth, with an almost limitless source of energy because of the abundance of hydrogen as fuel, with the ultimate goal as that achieved by burning coal, oil, gas or nuclear fuel, to generate steam which drives a power station's turbogenerators that produce electricity.

In December 2003, officials involved in the International Thermo-nuclear Experimental Reactor (ITER), met in Washington, D.C., to choose a host for the project, which is worth twelve billion U.S. dollars. The countries involved are, the United States; China; Russia; South Korea; the European Union, and Japan. As stated earlier, the goal of the ITER project is to create a sustained nuclear fusion reaction that will provide a safe and efficient source of pollution-free energy.

The purpose of the December 2003 gathering was to choose the site for the construction of the reactor. There were two proposals, the village of Rokkasho in Japan or Cadarache in France, near Marseille. Apart from the prestige, the economic stakes are high. The reactor's construction is expected to take a decade and provide two thousand jobs.

Early in July 2005 an international consortium chose France to be the host of the world's first nuclear fusion reactor that many scientists see as key to solving the world's future energy needs. Cadarache will be the site for the ITER and work on the reactor will begin during 2006. The Cadarache reactor is a development project intended to solve the various technical problems involved and prove that fusion can be harnessed as an economically viable energy source. A second reactor will be a prototype for power generation. There is growing recognition of fusion's potential as a solution to the world's looming energy crisis.

The question however still remains, "What if nuclear fusion is not a success?" Can there be a fast breeder reactor renaissance? The feeling in the industry is that, there will have to be. Several countries, notably India, Kazakhstan, and more, particularly Japan and Russia, are still busy in this area of endeavor.

What went wrong with the first attempts to establish FBR technology was mainly the capital cost for fast breeder reactor power stations, which was around fifty percent greater than conventional nuclear stations.

There was also a genuine proliferation consideration because, the plutonium bred in the FBR, unlike the mixture of plutonium isotopes bred within the fuel of most power reactors, can be very suitable for weapons production.

It is important to keep in mind that extracting more than 100 times more power from a given mass of uranium than can be done through thermal reactor systems, is an important consideration. Uranium 235 is the only readily fissionable isotope found in nature, constitutes only 0.7% of natural uranium, and only half of this is used by current reactors. The Japanese, in their persistent search for energy independence, are busy with the design of a plant to extract uranium and along with it, vanadium and other minerals. (Sea water contains about 3mg of uranium per cubic meter, extractable at a cost of about US$450 per kilogram).

Estimates of the world's uranium reserves vary from six to thirty million tons, depending on the maximum extraction price. Thirty million tons of uranium could provide the world's electrical energy, at the present level, for ten thousand years. Add to this the possibility of extracting a hundred times more power using the fast breeder reactor system, the period of generating nuclear electricity will be many more thousands of years. What is also important is the effect on the atmosphere.

Trends in Energy and Nuclear Power

World energy consumption over the past 30 years has risen by 3.3% per annum, and nuclear power has contributed approximately 17% to the world electricity production. In the United States of America, nuclear energy provides about 20% of total electricity, and in the European Union the average is 33%. In Japan and South Korea, the percentage is approximately 33% and 40% respectively.

The Supply of Nuclear Fuel

The demand for nuclear fuel is satisfied through primary production, or through the use of secondary sources. The secondary sources of supply include inventory reductions, recycling of fissile material delivered from the reprocessing of spent fuel, the re-enrichment of tails, and from military stockpiles.

The cumulative world production of natural uranium since 1945 to the year 2000 is estimated at two million tons from all regions. Combining all primary and secondary supply sources, it would appear that the nuclear fuel market will be adequately supplied for the next twenty years, for fuel to be used by civil power reactors for electricity generation.

The Nuclear Industry's Dilemma

In December 1992, the nuclear industry worldwide celebrated the fiftieth anniversary of the world's first artificially initiated self-sustained nuclear chain reaction in uranium in the United States. The demonstration of the controlled chain reaction was considered a necessary step toward a bomb, but it soon became clear that peaceful energy could also be produced. December 2, 1942 was the day it was demonstrated that the work through half a century by scientists around the world had come to fruition.

Nuclear technology even today is still confused by its heritage unclear whether to be proud that it rapidly responded to the political/society requirement to create the ultimate deterrent, or ashamed that it let the genie out of the bottle. The past cannot be changed; it has an influence on what we do now. A politician's role is to represent society and society's choices. Choosing nuclear power was the choice to provide cost effective and reliable supplies of electricity to the public. Although the immediate reason for the choice has been to reduce carbon dioxide emissions, the underlying motive is to diversify energy resources and reduce dependence on imported fossil fuels.

One of the many challenges facing the nuclear industry is achieving wide public and political acceptance, continuing to improve safety, and demonstrating the safe management of spent fuel and nuclear waste—fission products which are intensely dangerous—and the industry is struggling to find safe ways to dispose of the most hazardous and radiologically toxic forms of the material which are presently held in temporary storage facilities. In the meantime, accumulations of nuclear waste continue to grow.

The management of radioactive waste, including its disposal, has now become a matter of urgent consideration by the nuclear industry in Europe and North America, because it has been recognized that radioactive waste management at present is inadequate.

In spite of these concerns, the European Union Commission has endorsed the view that there is need to keep the nuclear option open, simply because it is the only major source of electricity production that does not produce any significant quantities of greenhouse gases. Also, it is one of the E.U.'s most secure energy resources—very diversified sources of supply—a fuel whose high energy makes it easy to stockpile and which results in an extremely low risk of supply interruption.

So far as the European Union is concerned, there exists a European Union Treaty known as the Euratom Treaty, which defines the frame work for the E.U.'s activities in the nuclear sector. The treaty does require the establishment of uniform safety standards to protect workers in the industry and the general public. It did not however, explicitly establish a EU Community responsibility for nuclear safety. There is a well developed European Safety perspective as a result of voluntary cooperation between the main nuclear industry participants. It is built upon fundamental common principles that form the basis of all European Union national nuclear safety regulations and is so stated in various internationally accepted documents.

The environment issue with the fear of global warming has been the trigger for the new debate on nuclear power. This coupled with the fact that the world population is increasing at an alarming rate—it is expected, world population will double in the next fifty years, and electricity demand will increase proportionally—it is forcing governments to keep the nuclear option open, because without nuclear power, there is no chance of meeting the needs for electricity and reducing carbon dioxide emissions. Also, the civil nuclear power is a key source of the energy needed to maintain material standards in developed countries.

As the environment becomes increasingly important, climate change is an issue that raises fundamental questions about the relationship between industry and society, and between one generation and the next, and of course about costs. To some, the costs of taking action could be enormous and threatens growth. On the other hand, the costs of doing nothing now could be far greater given the risk of what may become necessary to do in the future, if the evidence of climate change becomes overwhelming.

The incentives for developing and implementing civil nuclear power application may be summarized as follows:

- Economic advantages
- The need to conserve the non-replaceable hydrocarbon resources
- Environmental advantages as compared with fossil energy resources

The question also arises, is today's nuclear technology so advanced as to make it absolutely dependable and safe? One can say with some comfort that so far as the Western world is concerned, in competent hands, the present technology works well. Development engineering by its nature, must involve judging whether adequate precautions have been taken to allow for unavoidable uncertainties in innovation. The safety record of over 40 years of reactor development has been impressive. Because a serious accident in a nuclear plant could be disastrous, the design and construction of the nuclear plants have been the most thoroughly studied, engineered, constructed, and checked out plants in any industry. In the Western world, the atomic power industry believes that, because of these strict measures, the risk from nuclear plants is exceptionally low. On the other hand we must accept the fact that modern society cannot exist without the production and utilization of energy and there will necessarily be some hazards. For the present, and by Western world standards, these hazards appear to be acceptable, when balanced against the quite different hazards that a nuclear energy ban would bring.

Nuclear Energy and the Shipping Industry

In November 1973, during discussions in the United States in the House Merchant Marine and Fisheries Committee on the development of nuclear merchant ships, a spokesman for the Nixon administration admitted that an incentive support scheme—in effect a development loan—could not be recommended at this stage because of unresolved doubts as to economic feasibility, licensing and regulation, safety, financial responsibility, third party liability, indemnification limits, and international reaction.

At the same hearing, spokesmen for the Atomic Energy Commission and the U.S. Coast Guard, while admitting the administration's doubts were valid, expressed the view that safe nuclear-powered merchant ships could be built and operated. The Shipbuilders Council of America also expressed support for development along the lines of the incentive support scheme, which would thence be recoverable from the vessel's net earnings.

Prior to the start of this debate, the Energy Corporation of America revealed its plans for a series of twelve nuclear powered 414,000 dwt tankers. They were well advanced, and an application for a Construction Differential Subsidy had been filed. It was obvious at the time, however, that at least until some measure of international agreement was reached, over the question of safety, liability, and so forth, the Administration's lack of enthusiasm was likely to continue.

Also in November 1973, at a gathering sponsored by SNAME's Metropolitan Section and the Maritime Administration at Kings Point, New York, the subject of nuclear power for commercial ships was discussed extensively. The parties agreed on the new and difficult considerations in constructing nuclear ships and the need to get them licensed by the U.S. Atomic Energy Commission and foreign government agencies.

Putting a 120,000 hp reactor into a VLCC involved several new technical problems that go beyond the state-of-the-art. During this meeting, it was mentioned that there has never been a VLCC of the size and with so much power built before. Such a tanker can only be designed by extrapolation. As for the propulsion machinery, it was pointed out by the steam turbine manufacturers that, the nuclear engine room is similar to, yet somewhat different from, the conventional machinery plant. As a nuclear reactor produces steam of only a few degrees of superheat, moisture separators must be used, between the H-P and L-P turbines, and interstage moisture separation, within the L-P turbine casing. One of the objectives for the construction and operation of the *NS Savannah*—was to achieve a standardized nuclear propulsion plant applicable to a wide variety of ships that would permit an operator to obtain a nuclear plant, on a firm-price basis, with the same kind of performance guarantees he could obtain for conventional propulsion plants.

A nuclear powered tanker requires a higher capital investment than the alternative fossil-fueled conventional tanker. This higher capital investment, and the uncertainties surrounding the nuclear tanker's operational performance, raises the important question whether the nuclear tanker can earn an acceptable rate of return. For this reason, a tanker operator may not see fit to invest in nuclear powered tankers. In 1973, it was estimated to build in the United States a twin-screw VLCC of 414,000 dwt, with a speed of twenty-one knots would cost US$170 million. This was twice the price of a conventionally powered tanker of the same size, speed, and power.

The Nuclear Ship *Savannah*

In the United States of America, as in the U.K., France, and Russia, nuclear ship propulsion in naval ships was an existing fact. During President Eisenhower's presidency, the Administration conceived the "Atoms for Peace" program and built the first nuclear merchant ship to accomplish the following:

- To demonstrating technical feasibility of atomic energy for commercial ship application
- To obtain information for second generation nuclear ships
- To gain world acceptance of atomic energy for peaceful purposes

Those responsible for the program had reached the conclusion that the time was right to introduce this system of propulsion to commercial ships, and that it could compete with the conventionally powered ships on very long voyages at high speeds, and that, as time passes, the relative position of nuclear powered commercial ships will improve.

The contract to build the ship (except the nuclear reactor) was awarded to New York Shipbuilding in Camden, New Jersey, on November 16, 1957 and the contract to build the reactor was awarded by the Atomic Energy Commission to Babcock and Wilcox Co. on April 3, 1957.

- The keel of the ship was laid on May 22, 1958.
- The ship was launched on July 21, 1958.
- Fuel was loaded in November 1961.
- The reactor went critical in December 21, 1961.

- Sea trials were carried out in March and April 1962 and on May 1, 1962, the Maritime Administration handed the ship to States Marine Lines as general agents for further familiarization, tests, and for operation.

In 1962 and 1963, the *NS Savannah* visited eleven domestic ports, beginning with the City of Savannah. In May 1964, the American Export Lines took over the operation of the ship, during which time, the ship made her maiden Atlantic crossing. Four demonstration voyages were made between foreign and domestic ports. When the ship returned to Galveston, Texas, on March 10, 1965, she had visited a total of fifty-five ports, had been viewed by 1.5 million people, and had traveled, the equivalent of nearly four trips around the world, carrying cargo and passengers in domestic and foreign waters.

During her two years of demonstration operation, established an internationally accepted pattern of marine operations for commercial nuclear ships. In addition to impressions made on those who visited the ship, the *Savannah* influenced the acceptance of atomic energy for peaceful purposes.

On completion of the demonstration phase, the experimental commercial phase was initiated, conducted under bareboat to First Atomic Ship Transport, Inc., a wholly owned subsidiary of American Export Lines. The ship was operated in this manner from August 1965 until July 1970, when it was placed in lay-up because it was considered that, the intended purpose for the construction of this ship was accomplished.

During five years of experimental and commercial operations as a cargo liner, the *Savannah* had accomplished a great deal. Among the accomplishments, was the fact that the ship added to the prestige of the United States through demonstration of an advanced type ship and ship propulsion.

The *Savannah* traveled 332,405 nautical miles on its first nuclear core, after which four of the thirty-two fuel elements were replaced, and the remaining twenty-eight were relocated in the core matrix. After this shuffle refueling, the ship sailed an additional 122,270 nautical miles on seven voyages to the Mediterranean and one voyage to the Far East.

In over 450,000 nautical miles of operation without air pollution, the ship used only 163 pounds of enriched uranium fuel. By comparison, a conventionally powered ship traveling the same number of miles would require 28,800,000 gallons of fuel oil, and would have released some 340 tons of sulfur-bearing pollutants while in port.

Although fulfilling the mission for which this ship was designed and built, it was impossible for the *Savannah* to be an economic success. The experimental/commercial operation was completed on July 25th 1970, and the ship was decommissioned. On September 1973, the U.S. Secretary of Commerce authorized the transfer of the *Savannah*, to the City of Savannah, Georgia, without monetary consideration, to be used as a museum-ship, and for other public purposes, but not for transportation.

As a founding member of the Institution of Nuclear Engineers in London, I took a keen interest in the *Savannah*, from the inception of the design, during construction, and throughout her operational life, because in discussing with Mr. Onassis the application of nuclear power to merchant ships, Mr. Onassis, had accepted the possibility of building nuclear tankers in the United States for our fleet of tankers. Obtaining special permission from the authorities, I frequently visited the shipyard at Camden, NJ, while the *Savannah* was under construction.

The Nuclear Ship *Mutsu*

In February 1992, the Japanese Atomic Energy Research Institute, announced the completion of the experimental navigation of the oceanographic, nuclear powered ship *Mutsu*, named after the city of Mutsu in Aomori Prefecture.

The *NS Mutsu* covered a distance of 47,592 nautical miles over a period of 3,816 hours sailing, with the nuclear reactor at almost 100 percent output. This is equivalent to 81.09 million kWh. using approximately 4.2 kilograms of uranium-235.

The Japanese authorities reported very satisfactory performance of the propulsion plant which responded to all demands during maneuvering and during various sea conditions the vessel met during the voyages.

The *Mutsu* propulsion plant was dismantled and the reactor and its shield, were removed from the vessel in one piece, and together with the reactor room are stored in specially constructed storage building in the area of Sekinehama.

The Nuclear Reactor for commercial ships:

Marine nuclear power has been in use for many years by the navies of the United States, U.K., France, Russia, India, and China for surface war ships and for submarines. Merchant ship nuclear power experience however, is limited to the experience gained during experimental and commercial period of the *NS Savannah* in United States, the *Otto Hahn* in West Germany, and the *Mutsu* in Japan. (Technically, the first nuclear commercial ship can be claimed by the Russian icebreaker *Lenin*).

In all three installations, an enriched uranium-fueled, pressurized water coolant, neutron-moderated reactor was used to exploit what was considered at the time, the particular nuclear power advantage of containing an enduring energy source in a small volume. The pressurized water system (PWS) employs ordinary water, highly purified, to remove heat generated in the reactor fuel elements by the fission process and transports it to a steam generator. The steam generator is basically a shell-and-tube heat exchanger in which feed water is evaporated inside the tubes by heat transferred from the reactor-heated water surrounding them. The reactor core, which is the source of heat, is made up of bundles of rods, in which are the fuel elements. Simply put, a nuclear reactor is a source of heat, similar to the furnace of a boiler, with the notable exception that up to several years worth of fuel is contained in the reactor core.

Pressurized water reactors are robust and proven reactors for naval vessels. Their dominance in nuclear power generation for ship propulsion is a consequence of the early selection of water as a coolant, due to its moderating properties, heat transfer capacity, pumping versatility, availability, and cost. For merchant marine application, however, specific volume and weight PWRs are not the best choice.

It has now emerged, for commercial ship application, a derivative of the gas-cooled reactor (GCR), is a better choice. This type of reactor has been used extensively in the U.K. on land. For commercial marine application however, the system is now under development, and variants of the GCR, have been proposed recently, because such an installation would result in a lighter and simpler plant, and would be less sensitive to ship motion than a pressurized water reactor installation.

The advanced gas-cooled reactor is similar to an aeroderivative gas turbine, except for the existence of a nuclear reactor instead of fuel burners, and the choice of a closed helium cycle which results in a decrease in the compression ratio. Helium is heated by the nuclear reactor and expands across the turbine blades. The helium is recompressed and redelivered to the hot side of the engine. Helium gas is the best coolant, and its inertness, reduces radioactivity within the turbomachinery.

A helium-cooled reactor for installation on a VLCC is still very costly because of the reactor cost. The estimated cost for a power plant today is in excess of US$500 million. In addition, such an installation will have to overcome the problems of acceptance in foreign ports, as well as insurance liability.

For a nuclear tanker with GCR propulsion system, and assuming it has gained acceptance, there are accident categories that must be considered during construction of the hull and during operation of the propulsion plant such as collision, grounding, and sinking.

The above are potential events for any tanker. In the case of a nuclear tanker, however, the reactor must be shut down safely to minimize the probability of radioactive release.

On the propulsion side, loss of gas turbine blading could result from overspeeding or manufacturing defects.

The development of nuclear propulsion for commercial ships may be a distant reality. If ever such event does take place, there are certain principles that the individuals who will assume the responsibility of nuclear plant installation and operation must adopt and adhere to, the principles that have been defined by Admiral Hyman G. Rickover of the U.S. Navy (Rickover is considered the Father of the nuclear U.S. Navy).

The World Nuclear University (WNU)

This is not a new campus. It is a network of regional networks in the U.S.A., Europe and Asia, aiming to achieve massive worldwide transformation to clean energy, which will maintain/improve living standards and prevent damage to the environment. The University's network spans some thirty nations and is coordinated by its London headquarters. It includes highly regarded Universities and Research Centers with strong programs in Nuclear Science and Engineering. The aim is to encourage a broader application, particularly among students choosing careers that nuclear science and engineering offer in an expanding global industry that provides essential service to humanity. Also, to elevate the status of professions associated with peaceful uses of nuclear technology in sustainable development.

WNU was established in September 2003, and the U.S. Department of Energy provided leadership in launching the first WNU "Summer Institute" at Idaho Falls in July-August of 2005 where, 140 applicants from 45 countries and 63 organizations participated. The next "Summer Institute" is scheduled for 2006 and will be hosted by Sweden in Stockholm, with technical visits to French nuclear installations. The WNU's new chancellor is Dr. Hans Blix.

Admiral Rickover's advice to nuclear plant operators includes the following:

- Require rising standards of adequacy
- Be technically self-sufficient
- Face the facts
- Respect even small amounts of radiation
- Require adherence to the concept of the total responsibility
- Develop the capacity to learn by experience

On responsibility, Rickover mentions it is a unique concept that can only reside and inhere in a single individual. "You may share it with others but your portion is not diminished. If responsibility is rightfully yours, no evasion or ignorance, or passing the blame can shift the burden to someone else."

Electromagnetic Propulsion

Over the years, the only concept that has been considered to replace the propulsion of ships by propeller has been the electromagnetic system of propulsion (EMS). In 1961, there was a great deal of interest in the development of EMS, and a patent was taken out in the United States of America for using electromagnetic thrusters.

An electromagnetic thruster (EMT) is a type of linear motor used as a method of ship propulsion, based on the Fleming's left hand rule. The reaction between the magnetic field generator by the fixed super conducting magnets on board the ship, and electric current passing through the sea water, generates, what is known in the electrical science, a Lorentz's* force in the longitudinal axis of the ship, and thrust created, as a reaction of sea water jet, moving astern. (That is jet propulsion produced by the EM thrust). The electromagnetic thrust, transfers the electromagnetic energy directly into thrust without the need of intermediate moving parts, such as shafting and propeller.

The prime mechanical requirement for this type of propulsion would be for an electrical generation capacity to produce the required electric current for the propulsion system and its cooling requirements, together with the usual auxiliary services in a machinery room.

The basic principle of electromagnetic propulsion is that a fixed coil is placed inside the ship, and an electric current is passed through the sea water from electrodes at the bottom of the ship. For the concept to be successful, it needs to embrace the concept of zero resistance or superconductivity. The main problem has been that in order to maintain zero resistance, the superconducting coil has to be kept at the temperature of liquid helium, that is -269°C. To maintain this condition, high quality insulation is necessary.

Superconductivity is the conduction of electricity without loss to resistance, and to achieve this, the material must be cooled to absolute zero. Today superconductivity is no longer a laboratory-bench technology. The David W. Taylor Naval Ship Research and Development Center in Annapolis, MD, already has the world's first superconducting generator and motor, operating in a boat on the water. Some of the development work was carried out in the

---

*   Lorentz force is the electromagnetic force in a flip coil closely related to the mechanical forces exerted by the field when the coil carries current. When the coil moves, it takes its electrons along with it. The force is named after Hendrik Antoon Lorentz, (1853–1928), a Dutch physicist, for his work on the influence on electromagnetism.

United States in 1967, and there were discussions on the prospect for electro-magnetic propulsion of submarines.

The electromagnetic system provides a means of marine propulsion free of the normal hydrodynamic noise and vibration considerations experienced by a ship using propeller propulsion. Using the EMS for propulsion, the need for the propeller; a propulsion shafting; gear boxes and other mainshaft line rotat-ing components are eliminated.

In 1986, electromagnetic Propulsion received a big boost from the Muller and Bednozz work in Zurich Switzerland, who developed a ceramic material for thermal insulation. As a result, efforts were intensified in the United States, Japan, India, and China to develop further the phenomenon of superconduc-tivity. Significant progress has been made in basic research and application of this method, of ship propulsion. A great deal of work is still required however before EM propulsion becomes a reality.

Superconductivity, as a possibility for warship propulsion, was first dis-cussed in the United States in the early 1960s. At that time, it would have been necessary to incorporate enormous refrigeration plant to cool the coils of a generator/motor to almost absolute zero.

In the 1970s, model tests were carried out in Japan, where electromagnetic propulsion was taken up by the Japan Foundation for Shipbuilding Advancement (JAFSA). In 1985, a six year development program was initiated. JAFSA is now known as the Ship and Ocean Foundation.

The successful sea trial of *Yamato 1* in Japan was a historic event. In the summer of 1992, sea trials were completed using the Superconducting Electromagneto-Hydrodynamic Propulsion System (EM HD) installed on board this experimental craft. The *Yamato 1* has a length of 30 meters, a draft of 1.50 meters, and a displacement of 185 tons. During the trials the craft attained a speed of eight knots using two thrusters and an electric power through the sea water of 3600 KW.

The shipping industry is interested in this type of propulsion for commer-cial ship application, because the feeling is that there is great scope for this type of propulsion system, especially for high speed passenger and cargo ships, with superconducting electrical machinery. Although the standard theory of super-conductivity was created thirty-five years ago, a much fuller basic scientific understanding will have to be obtained before superconductivity becomes widely used.

Will this type of propulsion replace the Archimedean screw? Present day propellers cannot dispense with propeller cavitation problems, which limit its application to the almost forty knots speed range. With SC-EM propulsion, there is no reason not to break through this barrier.

Wind-Assisted Propulsion

There are five wind-assisted propulsion systems available for application, which include the following:

- Traditional soft sails

- Rigid or semi-rigid airfoils

- Magnus effect devices, such as the Antone Flettner Rotor

- Wind turbines

- Airborne sails or kites

The basic concept of all these systems is to develop aerodynamic forces by inducing a circulation of air around the rig in exactly the same way as an upended airplane wing. The forward component of these forces produces ahead motion of the ship.

In assessing the performance of the wind-assisted propulsion, it is essential to obtain prior knowledge of both the direction and strength of the wind. Today, such information may be obtained through efficient meteorology. The course of the vessel must therefore be constantly directed relative to the ever changing weather systems in order to optimize its speed towards the ship's destination.

Basically, the problem is one of seeking strong and advantageous winds and is exactly the reverse of what the already well established method of weather routing for power driven ships, seek to do. A commercially viable, wind assisted ship would have to make constant use of such weather information. Since power propulsion would also be available, the choice of the optimum route would pose a most interesting challenge to a ship's master.

During the late 1970's, the five basic systems mentioned above were studied in the U.K., Japan, West Germany, France, and the United States. The traditional soft sails were actively developed in Japan, where comprehensive research was started in 1977 to investigate various shapes of sails. The decision was made to build a two-masted coastal tanker using diesel propulsion as the primary and the sails as secondary means of propulsion. The results of eight months continuous operation of the installation on the *Shin Aitoku Maru,* and fuel savings were around ten percent.

Despite the relative optimism of those involved at the time in the field of wind-assisted propulsion, there was reluctance on the part of shipowners, including our company, to show serious interest.

The reason for the lack of interest is the fact that, in general terms, economy of operation lies in much larger ships than anything produced in even the last days of sail. Basic laws of physics of size dictate that, larger ships need stronger winds to drive them at the speed appropriate to their size, and one aspect which does not change in this concept is the amount of wind available.

The Development of the "Fuel Cell" and Its Application to Ship Propulsion

Sir William Grove (U.K. 1811–1896) is known as the father of the "fuel cell" (1853). He produced the first Fuel Cell in 1839, basing his experiments on the fact that sending an electric current through water splits the water into its component parts of hydrogen and oxygen. Grove tried reversing the reaction, combining hydrogen and oxygen, to produce electricity and water, which is the basis of a simple fuel cell. (The term fuel cell was coined in 1889 by Ludwig Mond and Charles Lauger.)

Grove's work was the first "gas battery," the usefulness of which was diminished, as the dawn of cheap fossil fuels became available. With the discovery of the steam engine by James Watt and the introduction of the internal combustion engine, today's society developed around the use of fossil fuels to produce electricity. Later, the use of nuclear power reduced our society's dependence on fossil fuels.

In the early 1960s, the National Aeronautics and Space Administration (NASA), was developing systems for the first prolonged, manned flight into space, that required a source of electricity to meet the needs of the space craft while in space. Batteries were ruled out because of size, weight, and toxicity (toxic gases produced by the battery). Photovoltaic cells at that time were not practical due to the size and weight of the solar panels. To solve the problem, NASA used fuel cells to provide power for extended missions to space. The earlier problems of cost and fuel that prevented the use of "fuel cells" became irrelevant as the spacecraft was already carrying liquid hydrogen and oxygen.

An additional benefit of "fuel cells" over other technology was that, those on board the space craft could use the water produced by the "fuel cells" in the process of electricity generation on board. Today, NASA's space craft, the Shuttle, relies on "fuel cells" to generate electricity and drinking water while in orbit. (Fuel cells furnished power for the Gemini and Apollo spacecrafts as well.)

In the past decade, the amount of interest in "fuel cells" has been tremendous, and billions of dollars has been spent already on research to commercialize "fuel cells". Grove's original fuel cell used dilute sulfuric acid and became the prototype for the phosphoric acid fuel cell (PAFC), which has had a longer development period than the other fuel cell technologies.

Sir Francis Thomas Bacon (1904–1992) built a fuel cell in 1939 that used gauze-electrodes and operated under very high pressure (3,000 psi). Bacon's fuel cells, though expensive, proved reliable enough to attract the attention of Pratt and Whitney, and were used for the Apollo Spacecraft.

The Principle of the "Fuel Cell"

A fuel cell is an electrochemical device that combines hydrogen fuel and oxygen to produce electricity, heat, and pure water. Oxygen is taken from the ambient air, while hydrogen is extracted from liquid fuels such as methanol or gasoline, using a reformer or processor.

Operation of the "Fuel Cell"

A fuel cell operates without combustion, so it is virtually pollution free. Since the fuel is converted directly to electricity, a fuel cell can operate at much higher efficiencies than internal combustion engines, extracting more electricity from the same amount of fuel. (A modern fuel cell is more than three times more efficient than today's internal combustion engine.) It has no moving parts, which makes it a quiet and reliable source of power.

Composition of the "Fuel Cell"

The fuel cell is composed of an anode, (a negative electrode that repels electrons), an electrolyte membrane in the center, and a cathode, (a positive electrode that attracts electrons). The fuel cell therefore is a sandwich of two electrodes—an anode and a cathode—with a polymer membrane serving as an electrolyte placed in the middle. The thickness of a modern fuel cell is as little as 0.1 inch (2.5 millimeters).

How the "Fuel Cell" Works

As hydrogen flows into the fuel cell anode, platinum coating on the anode helps to separate the gas into protons (hydrogen ions), and electrons. The electrolyte membrane in the center allows only protons to pass through the membrane to the cathode side of the fuel cell. The electrons cannot pass through this membrane and flow through an external circuit in the form of electric current thus producing electricity. In simple terms, the fuel cell combines hydrogen to oxygen to produce electricity while avoiding combustion and emissions except water and heat.

Like a standard battery, the fuel cell produces power from chemical reactions (electrochemistry rather than combustion). However, unlike batteries, as long as fuel is supplied to a fuel cell, it will continue to produce electricity.

The "Fuel Cell" Stack

Individual fuel cells can be combined into a fuel cell "stack," and the number of cells in the stack determines the total voltage, and the total area of each cell determines the total electric current. Multiplying the voltage by the current, yields the total electrical power generated.

Electricity Production by the "Fuel Cell"

More than 160 years after its invention, the fuel cell is now becoming a commercial reality. Its key features as an energy converter is the significant reduction in the emission of greenhouse gases and its ability to deliver highly efficient fuel economy. If hydrogen and oxygen are placed together in an electrolyte, they will combine to produce electricity, heat, and water. This process is the basis to the operation of the fuel cell.

Hydrogen

Hydrogen is the least complex, least massive element, and is the most abundant element in the universe. In my book titled *Energy and Ships*, published in London in 1988, I say the following in Chapter 4:

> Hydrogen, although a primary energy by itself, in the context of a hydrogen economy is not a primary energy source, it is a fuel. It is not like petroleum, natural gas, and coal, which exist freely in nature.
>
> Hydrogen is a secondary source of energy that has to be manufactured and can be made from any of the primary sources such as oil or natural gas in a complicated machinery known as converter or reformer. Such machinery will convert gasoline or any of the other candidate fuels to Fuel Cell grade hydrogen.

Characteristics of Hydrogen

Hydrogen has the smallest atomic structure of all elements and is the most abundant element in the universe, but rarely exists in its free state. It is normally found in combination with oxygen as water or with carbon as methane and other hydrocarbons. As a result it requires energy to free it for use.

To produce hydrogen, one approach is to strip it out of hydrocarbons or by electrolysis, which separates hydrogen from water using electricity. This is an energy intensive process. The preferred process for hydrogen generation from carbonaceous fuels is the catalytic steam reforming (CSR). This process has been found to provide the highest hydrogen yield per unit of feedstock as well as the highest fuel gas quality. In the CSR process, all hydrogen needed to oxidize carbon is provided by steam. This maximizes hydrogen production because both fuel and steam yield hydrogen to the product gas.

The most difficult of the hydrocarbons to process/reform to hydrogen is gasoline. However, gasoline is the most readily available source. The problem today is interfacing fuel cell power plants with the fuel's infrastructure and power plant costs, to produce and dispense the hydrogen fuel.

Hydrogen's Physical Properties

To understand more fully the safety implications of hydrogen, it is necessary to examine hydrogen's physical properties.

- Liquid hydrogen is a very cold material, -423° F (-252.8° C). Contact with human body tissue will result in severe burns, destroying tissue almost like the burn from a flame.

- Hydrogen as gas has a very low density and diffuses very quickly into the air, that is, it rises very quickly through the air.

- Hydrogen burns mixed with air over a much wider range than methane or gasoline. A mixture as low as 4 percent of hydrogen in air, and as high as 74 percent will burn. The corresponding ranges for methane are 5.3 to 15 percent, and for gasoline it is a very narrow range form 1.0 to 7.6 percent. Jet fuel's flammability range is even narrower, from 0.8 to 5.6 percent.

- When confined in a completely enclosed space such as a room, or a tank, hydrogen can be detonated, that is exploded, over a wide range of concentrations ranging from 18 to 59 percent (by volume) in air. Methane explodes only in concentrations ranging from 6.3 to 14 percent, and gasoline and jet fuel detonate in a range form 1.1 to 3.3 percent.

The Problems Facing the Use of Hydrogen

Hydrogen is the fuel of choice for developers. Even though it appears that it will be in commercial fleet vehicle use, in the near term it is not likely to be available as a retail fuel soon. One of the problems for wide application of the fuel cell is the fact that our today's world is not set up to deliver hydrogen on demand. It will take time and a great deal of money to build the necessary infrastructure to make hydrogen readily available.

The three problems that must be overcome are safety, storage, and supply.

Safety

On the question of safety, hydrogen is often perceived as dangerous. It is correct that hydrogen is flammable. On the other hand, hydrogen is a gas at room temperature and disperses rapidly, unlike gasoline or methanol. With a little education, hydrogen can be just as safe as today's other fuels.

Storage

The storage of hydrogen presents two problems. Because hydrogen atoms are so small, they can get through the crystal lattice of the material used to contain it. The leakage from the pressurized hydrogen tank could be significant.

The second problem is a consequence of the fact that, being so small, hydrogen is exceptionally light. In a typical gaseous storage system, it has only one tenth (1/10) of the volumetric energy density of gasoline. The answer to both these problems is to store hydrogen in containers made of material to prevent leakage, and the container to be made to withstand very high pressures.

There are companies in the United States now testing containers capable of storing hydrogen at 10,000 psi. One such company is Energy Conversion Devices (ECD) of Troy in Michigan.

Supply

As mentioned earlier, hydrogen is manufactured by stripping it from hydrocarbons. Some companies in the United States are manufacturing hydrogen from natural gas at centralized plants, and this is used to make ammonia fertilizers, and to lighten heavy grades of crude oil.

The production costs of hydrogen from such establishments could be competitive with that of gasoline. The problem however is that expensive pipeline or tanker systems would still be needed to make the hydrogen available to consumers.

The next few years will see a great deal more in the development of the fuel cell systems in the road and sea transportation.

Hydrogen and Economic Sense

Today's big question is even if the hurdles of safety, storage, and supply are overcome, can hydrogen be phased in over time? It would appear that explicit government support will still be needed, because the clearest advantage of fuel cells over the internal combustion engine is the zero or near zero emissions. For the public however, a more meaningful benefit will be the fuel cell's superior efficiency compared to that of the internal combustion engine, which converts only 15 percent of the heat content of gasoline into useful energy.

At present, the high cost of fuel cells has limited their use to specialized applications. A kilowatt of electricity produced by a fuel cell is about eight times more expensive than a kilowatt produced by utilities. Developers of fuel cells will have to achieve a number of design and manufacturing improvements to make it competitive in price, and together with its very desirable features it will become a very important factor in electricity production.

There are 85 organizations, including 48 in the United States, doing research work developing the fuel cell or PEM as it is known in the industry (proton exchange membrane). There are five main types of PEM in the U.S. market today, each named after the electrolyte used in the system:

- Phosphoric acid (PAFC);

- Molten carbonate (MCFC);
- Solid oxide (SOFC);
- Proton exchange membrane; and
- Alkaline

The phosphoric-acid (PAFC) cell is the most mature technology and is the only one today being offered commercially in capacities above 100 kW. The biggest challenge to this technology at present is how to produce and store the hydrogen fuel.

The "Fuel Cell" System for Commercial Ship Propulsion

Research and development has been underway in Japan since the early 1990s for the practical application of the fuel cells using phosphoric acid, which has shown very interesting potential for the propulsion of commercial ships because of the system's high thermal efficiency.

One of the leading Japanese shipyards, I.H.I., together with the Ship and Ocean Foundation of Japan, starting in 1990, has developed a "fuel cell" system (FCS), that converts molten carbonate into electrical energy, which is used to propel the ship through an AC motor. An LNG tanker, a large ferry boat, and an observation ship were selected for the installation of the FCS. Sea trials were carried out with satisfactory results, confirming that the system's prospects for commercial ship propulsion are very promising.

The FCS has important advantages over the conventional propulsion systems of today, which include the following:

- A much higher thermal efficiency than the Carnot cycle in the internal combustion engine

- Quiet operation and less vibration, which make a difference to the performance of the instrumentation of the machinery and the living conditions of those on board

- Easy maintenance because there are no moving parts

- Reduction of atmospheric pollution because of its very low content of nitrogen, sulfur oxides, and hydrocarbon particulate in the exhaust gases, because the maximum temperature is lower than in a boiler installation or internal combustion engine

- Easy automation

- Less space required in the machinery room and is ease of arrangement

- A smaller number of operating personnel are required on board the ship

- Less expensive to operate.

On the economics of the system, compared to conventional propulsion arrangement, for an LNG tanker it has been established, the FCS offers greater economy over the tanker's life compared to the equivalent conventional installation, including reduced crew—thirty-two crew members for the conventional against twenty-nine for the fuel cell propelled LNG tanker.

One of the problems encountered during the sea trials was responsiveness to load changes. This can be simplified or eliminated by proper handling of the propulsion equipment.

BOW DESIGN VARIATION TO
IMPROVE HULL PERFORMANCE

STERN DESIGN TO IMPROVE HULL PERFORMANCE

STERN DESIGN TO IMPROVE HULL PERFORMANCE

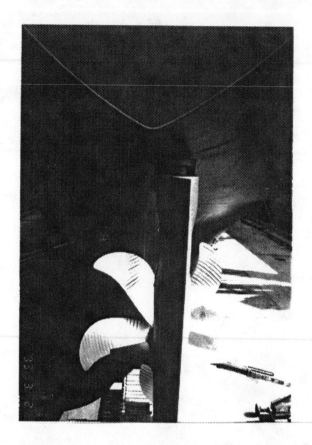

OFF-CENTER PROPELLING SYSTEM

It has been found, moving the propelling system off-center improves water flow to the propeller which improves propeller efficiency.

For a clockwise rotating propeller, shift to star-board side, and to port side for anticlockwise propeller rotation.

CONTRA-ROTATING PROPELLERS

KEY: 1. Aft Propeller 2. FWD Propeller 3. CR Seal 4. Outer Propeller Shaft 5. CR Gear 6. Highly Elastic Coupling 7. Plumber Block 8. Shaft Generator 9. Main Engine 10. Rudder

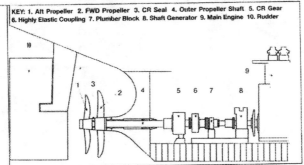

Typical arrangement of a CRP system for a VLCC. IHI has already installed one such unit on the 259,000dwt *Okinoshima Maru* in 1993.

CONTRA-ROTATING GEAR SYSTEM
(Star-Compound Type Epicyclic Gears)

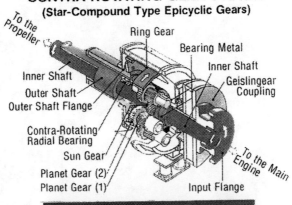

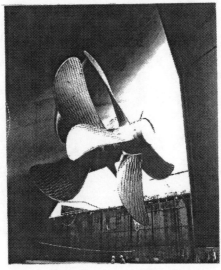

Nuclear Ship "SAVANNAH", 1962 to 1970

THE FUEL CELL

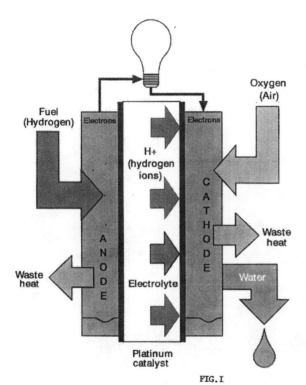

Fuel (Hydrogen)

Electrons

H+ (hydrogen ions)

A N O D E

Electrolyte

Platelet Platinum catalyst

Waste heat

Oxygen (Air)

Electrons

C A T H O D E

Waste heat

Water

FIG. I

- • A Fuel Cell Reacts Hydrogen and Oxygen To Produce Electricity and Pure Water

- • It Operates With Zero–Emissions and at High Efficiency

- • A Single Fuel Cell Produces 100 - 200 Watts at 0.6 - 1.0 Volts

FOR TRANSPORTATION APPLICATIONS
MANY SINGLE FUEL CELLS ARE ASSEMBLED INTO ONE "STACK"
TO PRODUCE HIGH VOLTAGE AND POWER

150 - 300 VOLTS
20 - 40 KILOWATTS

ELECTROMAGNETIC SHIP PROPULSION

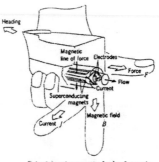

Principle of magneto-hydrodynamic propulsion

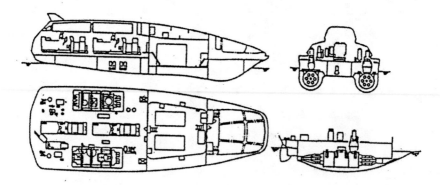

General Arrangement of Experimental Ship

"YAMATO 1" at sea

TEN

The Shipbuilding Industry

The Competitive Challenge for International Shipbuilding

Shipbuilding is a construction industry that uses a wide variety of manufactured components in addition to basic construction materials. The industry employs various skills or trades working within an established organizational structure at a specific location, known as shipyard, in which necessary facilities are available.

Shipyards contain several specific facilities laid out to facilitate the flow of material and assemblies and have grown according to the availability of land and waterfront as well as in response to production requirements.

A modern shipyard is arranged into six functions: administration, engineering, purchasing, production, project management (contract administration), and quality assurance.

The precise origin of shipbuilding in Britain is unclear. For the purpose of this book, it is fair to start with the tanker *Gluckauf*, which was the first ocean-going, purpose built oil tanker in 1886. Tanker building in Britain dominated the world market up until the 1920s. During World War II and for a short period afterwards, the United States of America was the dominant shipbuilding nation.

During the 1960s and 1970s, Europe controlled more than seventy percent of world shipbuilding output. In particular Kockums of Malmo, the Swedish commercial shipyards had emerged as the world's leading builder of VLCCs and ULCCs in the 1970s. Because of its unmatched productivity, and at its height in 1973–74, the yards had the biggest order backlog. At one point the yards were turning out a supertanker once every forty working days.

Then came the oil shock and a prolonged shipbuilding crisis. By February 1986, after years of alternating hope and despair, Kockums ended operations. This meant the end of the entire Swedish merchant shipbuilding industry, which was second only to Japan. Sweden had been recognized as Europe's premier shipbuilding nation, widely recognized as an innovative and efficient builder.

The European share of world shipbuilding has now shrunk to less than twenty percent. Critical to that shift was the period between 1975 and 1980, when world shipbuilding fell from thirty-four million to thirteen million gross registered tonnage per year, a sixty percent drop.

Over the same period, European shipbuilding output was reduced from thirteen million to less than three million gross registered tons per year, a seventy-five percent drop.

During the last forty-five years, the fundamental shift of the world's shipbuilding industry has been from American and European dominance to Asian dominance. (Some technologically advanced shipbuilders sold their technology for short term gain, making their customers their competitors.)

Year by year, as Europe's shipbuilding industry became more difficult to manage, European governments paid heavily for the cost of care and encouraged their shipyards to hold on in the hope of market recovery. The governments poured billions of dollars in subsidies into the industry, but by the late 1980s, the decision makers wondered whether it had all been worthwhile, because the industry's dominant share of the world market had been eroded first by Japan, then by South Korea, followed by China, who has been moving up close behind.

By the late 1980s, the European shipbuilding industry realized the crisis was not going to go away, and the question was then whether the industry could survive at all, because it could no longer be nursed back to real health. It was recognized that only a small modernized core of shipyards, equipped with ultramodern production equipment and processes as well as modern management and marketing techniques could make it.

A reconstructed shipbuilding industry in China has today the design and construction capacity large enough to build VLCCs. The new building dock, inaugurated in 1998, is committed to construct a series of five 300,000 dwt VLCCs for the National Iranian Tanker Company.

In the past twenty-five years, China's shipbuilding industry has grown rapidly, and is now the third largest shipbuilding country after Korea and Japan. This is a long way from its seventeenth place in the 1980s. The industry's long term aim is to dominate the world market within twenty to twenty-five years.

The shipbuilding industry also accepted the fact that the Asian shipbuilders were determined to stay ahead. The notion that these shipbuilders were focused on the labor intensive contracts such as large tankers and bulk carriers was incorrect. Another interesting development is that today, even though the Japanese shipbuilding industry excels over the South Korean in nonprice competitiveness, it was only a matter of time before the gap closed. The South Korean shipbuilder has worked hard to become more competitive than the Japanese in winning orders in the international market to the extent that Western as well as Japanese owners placed orders for new vessels with the South Korean shipyards. As of June 2002, the percentage share of the market was approximately forty-five for South Korea and forty for Japan, in compensated gross tonnage.

In shipbuilding, international competitiveness has three aspects: the shipbuilding cost, the technological advancements available on the ship, and the overall quality of the product.

Shipowners loyal to the Japanese shipbuilders, however, have remained their best customers, despite the price difference in a given contract, which could be as much as six to ten percent. Such owners were aware of the technology and product quality difference and preferred to pay the difference in price. The Japanese shipbuilders, despite the difficult and erratic existence of the mid-1970s, suffered because of their love for order, but they have done so constructively. They outsourced a large part of their component requirements and above all invested wisely in modern technology. This has made the Japanese shipyards the world's most efficient and productive and enables them to remain in control of quality shipbuilding.

The Japanese shipbuilders who have endured many economic fluctuations are fully aware that unless they are careful, they will lose the advantage in nonprice competitiveness, despite their formidable efficiency and productivity. To counter such possibility, the anticipated response by the Japanese shipbuilding industry will be another round of painful rationalization and more shipyard mergers.

It is worth noting that South Korea has established what is probably the world's largest shipbuilding company located in Ulsan. During its 30-year history, this yard has delivered 1,000 vessels equivalent to 77.5 million dwt. The yard currently accounts for fifteen percent of the world's shipbuilding market.

With regard to the Chinese shipbuilding, it must be recognized that the Chinese shipbuilder will not accept the argument that they can remain on the simple stuff for very long. With technical help from Europe and elsewhere, the Chinese shipyards are set to double their share of the world shipbuilding market, and they are moving to a new level of technical sophistication.

Another factor that has emerged lately and must not be overlooked is Russian commercial shipbuilding, which has now entered the international shipbuilding market. During the Soviet Union period, they had a formidable shipbuilding industry, which was geared primarily for naval ships of the most advanced designs. Since the break-up of the Soviet Union, the Russian shipbuilding industry has had to remold itself in order to meet the market-oriented commercial shipping needs of the twenty-first century. This will require updating design, construction facilities, and management techniques. It is understood that Russia's Central Government is currently helping the industry to restructure itself to become more commercially oriented. This will take time and will require cooperation with overseas companies if Russia is to become a major international player.

As for the European shipbuilding industry, it would appear no shipbuilding country in Continental Europe, except Germany and Poland, will bring any major change in the international shipbuilding market in the foreseeable future. Even these two countries face an uphill struggle and can succeed by increasing competitiveness while maintaining the quality of their products.

Shipbuilding in Continental Europe is kept alive because of the cruise and special purpose ships, where Italy, France, Germany, Finland, and the Scandinavian countries have the monopoly for the design and construction of cruise ships. Even a high level of specialization is not enough to overcome the difficulties facing the European shipbuilding industry.

The reasons for the decline in the U.K.'s shipbuilding industry have been different. Year by year, as the shipbuilding industry became more and more difficult to manage and less competitive, compared first to Japan, then South Korea, and now China, the U.K. government paid heavily for the cost of care in the hope of recovery. The question was then asked, could a policy of reconstructing help the industry, or in fact could shipbuilding in the U.K. survive at all? For example, in 1954, Scotland built twelve percent of the world's ships. By 1968 the figure was one percent. The yards in the U.K. were faced with a price gap of as much as thirty percent from the Asian shipbuilders. It has been suggested that shipbuilding in the U.K. has no other future than a basic strategic resource for the Royal Navy.

Commercial shipbuilding in the United States has not faired any better than in the U.K. Immediately after the end of World War II, the gigantic shipbuilding industry of the United States rapidly sunk back to its prewar size. Concentration on construction work for the Navy, the availability of construction deferential subsidies, and the requirements that commercial ships for the "Jones Act" built in U.S. shipyards, made the yards uncompetitive internationally. This affected the industry adversely to the point that existing ship designs and building techniques became outdated. For example, in 1947 only forty-five commercial ships were completed, and in 1948 only twenty-six commercial ships were delivered. By 1988, only a few commercial ships of more than 1,000 tons were being built in the United States.

Faced with the enormous challenge of reentering the commercial ship-building market, the U.S. shipyards adopted a two pronged approach in efforts to catch up. In short term, the best way to achieve rapid re-entry was to import foreign technology from Europe and Japan. In the long term context, it involved the U.S. shipyards looking at revolutionary developments that would place them ahead in technology, productivity, and product quality. These efforts were funded through Maritech's Advance Research Projects Agency (ARPA) to accelerate technology transfer and progress change. Early in the year 2003, the National Steel and Shipbuilding Co. (NASCO), delivered the first commercial dry cargo vessel to be built in ten years. This was the trailer ship *Midnight Sun,* built to carry 600 trailers.

Despite the U.S. government's efforts to eliminate subsidies of shipyards in all shipbuilding countries, prompted by considerations for the economic health of local communities, and therefore the national economics, such efforts would bear no material benefit to the shipbuilding industry of the United States or the U.K. without a major upgrading of the shipyards to make them competitive internationally. It is sustained in order to meet defense requirements.

Today's Asian shipbuilding industry, on the other hand is organized on a post-World War II basis with constantly improving techniques, equipment, facilities, modern management techniques, and quality control.

In general, world-class shipyards of today operate with ultramodern production equipment and processes that include direct numerical control for fully automated marking, cutting, feeding, and distribution of profiles and plates. They have several five-axis three-dimensional articulated welding robots. All manufacturing information for steel preparation is downloaded directly to the cutting machines where details include, marking, cutting, beveling, and printing.

Developments in heavy lifting and transport equipment have resulted in more efficient ship assembly methods ashore as well as in the building dock. This, together with the modular assembly approach, where much of the pipe work and auxiliary machinery is incorporated into the modules, further improves productivity and simplifies subsequent maintenance of the equipment by the ship's personnel. During the last decade, the Computer Integrated Manufacturing Systems (CIMS), developed by Japan, enabled the Japanese yards to integrate design, planning, and production data to improve productivity. Such systems reduced costs by as much as fifteen percent.

The graph at the end of this Chapter titled "Global Trends in Shipbuilding through the Twentieth Century" illustrates the progress made in shipbuilding during the past century. In the 1900s building time on the building berth was almost equal to the total construction time of the ship. Depending on the ship size, it varied between three and a half to four years. No prefabrication was attempted, and the productivity level constituted 450 to 500 man hours per ton of steel. By the end of the century, a modern shipyard's productivity had improved tremendously.

The essential elements for a modern shipyard to achieve international competitiveness include the following:

- Organizational excellence
- Total management and quality control
- Project and planning management
- Cost control
- Marketing techniques

Mechanization of steel prefabrication has reduced the production to a homogeneous process, resulting in improved dimensional accuracy. Welding technology, computer integration, and mechanization of steel prefabrication has resulted in better and more accurate block assembly, which in turn resulted in further improvements in yard productivity making shipyards more profitable.

Technological advances in shipbuilding have three principal and interdependent motivations:

(a) The need to continuously improve performance and reliability

(b) The desire to produce the items in a shorter time scale involving minimum human effort

(c) The need to produce these items at a lower cost

To satisfy (a), it is essential to reduce adjusting work of the parts to be assembled; (b), promote mechanization and robotization (c) stabilize production quality. The accuracy of joints to be welded during block assembly and erection must be within the respective tolerances for the applicable welding methods.

For more than twenty-five years, computer aided design (CAD) and computer aided manufacturing systems (CAM) have become a vital part of the shipbuilding industry and have evolved into highly capable tools. The change form two-dimensional to three-dimensional CAD has increased the use of the system dramatically and improved integration of the CAD and CAM data. Some shipyards, especially major yards, have developed and employ their own home grown systems. Other yards make use of software developed by consulting companies specializing in software systems for the marine industry on data management, productive engineering, and shipbuilding.

Paint Application to New Structures

In block assembly, after all welding has been completed, surface preparation for painting is done by robots. The robot arm is manipulated by numerical control with excellent results. The outer surface of the hull plating of the completed ship is also done using robots. In order to improve the working environment at the Japanese shipyards, and to compensate for the lack of skilled workers, The Ship and Ocean Foundation, together with leading shipyards and other organizations has developed a work robot for cleaning, derusting, and painting a ship's outer hull. The robot scaffolding boom has a reach of fifteen meters and a working radius of over thirteen meters. Though not intended for totally autonomous operation, it automatically achieves cleaning, derusting, and painting work according to the instructions of the operator.

The notion that automation and robotization will create unemployment in the shipbuilding industry is totally wrong. In fact the opposite is the case; lack of technology threatens closure of shipyards.

The European Shipbuilding Industry Today—The Struggle for Survival

At a special seminar during the North Shipping gathering in 1999 in Norway, a delegate who specializes in international economics and shipping presented a very gloomy report on "The Future of North European Shipbuilding." The report was clear in its examination of the issue and concluded that, "if the shipbuilding industry in this part of the world is to survive, competitiveness must be increased via improved productivity, and existing sources of competitive advantage must be exploited more fully." The report concludes. "Today's Western European shipbuilding industry, has several fundamental features that are unattractive, such as competition by cost, cyclicality, and looming overcapacity, and since the world's shipbuilding industry's characteristics will not improve, shipyards in Europe are left with the choice of adapt, or face the exit." The report makes important recommendations and points out that survival will be an uphill struggle, emphasizing that the Asian shipbuilders are determined to stay ahead.

As a River Clyde trained shipbuilder, I feel it is appropriate, proper, and worthy of special mention to talk about shipbuilding on the Clyde.

In a book titled *Iron Fighters, Outfitters and Bowler Hatters,* published in 1997 in the U.K., the author of the book, Geo. C. O'Hara, states, "the inability to shorten the period of time from riveting to welding techniques, prolonging demarcation arguments and general trade union tribalism, was the reason for the demise of an industry upon which so many Clydesiders depended." Glasgow, and in particular the River Clyde, was synonymous with marine engineering and shipbuilding excellence. when a ship was launched it was a highly social product and social event.

In the four decades since World War II, 1,901 ships were built by the thirty-one shipyards and engineering works on the River Clyde alone. The war took its toll in the U.K. and its shipbuilding industry, including the Scottish shipyards. This resulted in the move of talented and creative professionals from the River Clyde shipbuilding industry, a less forward-evolving industry, for a more promising one where they could find fulfillment.

My comments on the European shipbuilding industry must not be construed by the reader that European shipbuilding is a static, old fashioned industry that makes limited contribution to a country's economy. On the contrary, shipbuilding today is a modern, vital, and challenging industry that offers skilled employment to many people, including the subcontracted work in Europe. The industry needs young naval architects and engineers to take up the future challenges for the European shipbuilding industry.

Global Shipyard Capacity and Shipyard Output

The Compensated Gross Tonnage (CGT)

Global available shipbuilding capacity is substantially less than the potential capacity of shipyards, because the latter includes mothballed facilities that have the potential to be activated at comparatively short notice. To this one must add the potential further utilization of active facilities corresponding to the performance of not hired, but recruited expertise in design engineering, planning, and the recruitment of skilled workers as well.

Assessing how many ships can be produced on a global basis, therefore, is not a straightforward process. The starting point is to consider the physical size of the various shipyards worldwide and to consider the organization, the available equipment, manpower, and the extent of automation in each shipyard. The speed at which a ship is built, however, is not necessarily a reflection on the yard's efficiency, because building complex ships such as cruise ships or LNG carriers takes longer than building simpler designs, such as tankers or bulk carriers. Rather than simply counting the number of ships built or adding up the total deadweight produced, the comparison is made on the basis of what is known in the shipbuilding industry as the compensated gross tonnage (CGT). This method takes into consideration the amount of effort required to build a certain type of ship.

Another factor that enters into the end result equation is the technical possibility of highly automated production speeds output. On the other hand, some shipyards employ large number of subcontracted work for a specific project. Such practices vary from region to region, it is therefore essential to evaluate shipyard capacity on a yard by yard basis for the major shipbuilding countries, in order to assess the potential impact on the shipbuilding market.

During slack periods in the shipbuilding industry, some yards are able to reduce output by mothballing part of their facilities. During prolonged slack periods and on occasion, shipyards simply go out of business.

The Association of West European Shipbuilders (AWES) evaluates shipyard capacity using coefficient factors to determine the compensated gross tonnage, as shown in the Table at the end of this Chapter, also global shipbuilding capacity, between the years 1975 and 2000.

A word of caution to the owner's representative empowered to sign or approve technical specifications of a shipbuilding contract: keep in mind that ship design and construction is a constantly evolving science, and there are few, if any, absolutes. It is a constant learning process.

Precision in a contract specification and clarity of the specification's intent are essential to avoid creating or having to face future disputes. The owner's representative must be very careful to ensure clarification of any vague or imprecise terms offered by the shipbuilder for inclusion in the contract specification such as, "in accordance with shipyard's standards/practice," "shipbuilding standards/practice," "shipbuilder's standards/practice," "shipyard's experience," "best practice," or "best endeavor." Such inclusions provide latitude for error and create future disputes or problems.

A modern shipyard in Japan where production
facilities include highly computerized and
automated fabrication assembly lines.

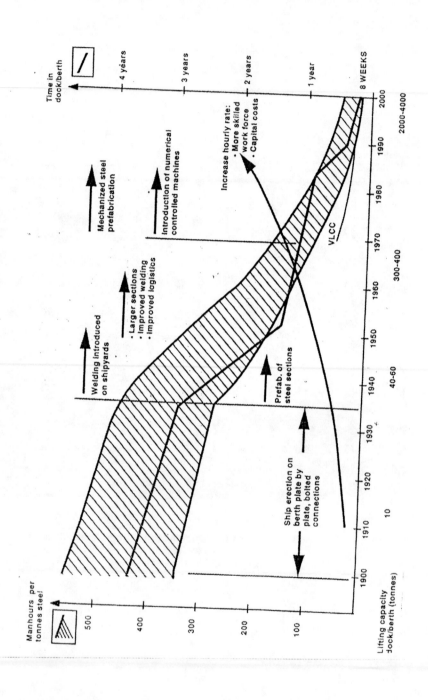

GLOBAL TRENDS IN SHIPBUILDING THROUGHOUT THE 20TH CENTURY

**Ship Riveting on the River Clyde, Scotland
(CIRCA 1940s)**

Coefficient factors for compensated gross tonnage (sample figures)

Ship type/size	Multiply gt by Coefficient	Ship type/size	Multiply gt by Coefficient	Ship type/size	Multiply gt by Coefficient
Crude oil tankers (single hull)		10,000 - 20,000 dwt	1.00	**Lng carriers**	
80,000 - 160,000 dwt	0.4	20,000 - 30,000 dwt	0.85	30,000 - 50,000 dwt	1.00
				Over 50,000 dwt	0.75
Crude oil tankers (double hull)		**Reefers**			
Under 4,000 dwt	1.85	Under 4,000 dwt	2.05	**Ferries**	
10,000 - 30,000 dwt	0.85	4,000 - 10,000 dwt	1.50	Under 1,000 gt	3.00
30,000 - 50,000 dwt	0.70	Over 10,000 dwt	1.25	1,000 - 3,000 gt	2.25
Over 80,000 dwt	0.45			3,000 - 10,000 gt	1.65
		Full container ships		10,000 - 20,000 gt	1.15
Product and chemical tankers		4,000 - 10,000 dwt	1.20	Over 20,000 gt	0.90
Under 4,000 dwt	2.30	10,000 - 20,000 dwt	0.90		
4,000 - 10,000 dwt	1.60	20,000 - 30,000 dwt	0.80	**Passenger ships**	
10,000 - 30,000 dwt	1.05	30,000 - 50,000 dwt	0.75	Under 1,000 gt	6.00
30,000 - 50,000 dwt	0.80	Over 50,000 dwt	0.65	1,000 - 3,000 gt	4.00
				10,000 - 20,000 gt	2.00
Bulk carriers		**Ro ro vessels**		20,000 - 40,000 gt	1.60
4,000 - 10,000 dwt	1.10	Under 4,000 dwt	1.50	40,000 - 60,000 gt	1.40
10,000 - 30,000 dwt	0.70	4,000 - 10,000 dwt	1.05	Over 60,000 gt	1.25
30,000 - 50,000 dwt	0.60	Over 10,000 dwt	0.80		
50,000 - 80,000 dwt	0.50			**Fishing vessels**	
80,000 - 160,000 dwt	0.40	**Car carriers**		Under 1,000 gt	1.00
Over 160,000 dwt	0.30	10,000 - 20,000 dwt	0.65	1,000 - 3,000 gt	3.00
		20,000 - 30,000 dwt	0.55	Over 3,000 gt	2.00
Combined carriers					
10,000 - 30,000 dwt	0.90	**Lpg carriers**		**Other non-cargo vessels**	
		Under 4,000 dwt	2.05	Under 1,000 gt	5.00
General cargo ships		4,000 - 10,000 dwt	1.60	1,000 - 3,000 gt	3.20
Under 4,000 dwt	1.85	10,000 - 20,000 dwt	1.15	3,000 - 10,000 gt	2.00
4,000 - 10,000 dwt	1.35	30,000 - 50,000 dwt	0.80	Over 10,000 gt	1.50

SOURCE: AWES

World merchant shipbuilding capacity

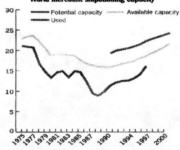

Potential capacity ·········· Available capacity
Used

AWES forecasts distinguish between used, available and potential capacity: **used** equals capacity utilised for construction of seagoing ships completed in an year; **available** includes in addition to used also merchant shipbuilding capacity utilised in activities similar to building of new ships i.e. inland waterway vessels, ship conversions which can be reconverted for merchant shipbuilding purposes when the possibility arises; **potential** capacity among others includes moth-balled facilities and further utilisation of active facilities corresponding to the performance of not hired, but recruitable expertise in design, engineering, planning and of skilled workers.
The global available capacity is expected to reach 20.8m cgt in year 2000 according to AWES. The potential capacity is, however substantially larger than the available, estimated at 24.5m cgt in 2000.
Actual global shipbuilding production in 1996 was 16.6m cgt according to Lloyd's Register.

SOURCE: AWES

ELEVEN

The Use of Steel in Shipbuilding

On October 3, 1864, Archibald Gilchriste presented a paper to the Scottish Shipbuilders' Association in Glasgow titled, "An Early Example of Iron Shipbuilding."

The paper describes the iron barge *Vulcan,* launched on May 14, 1819, entered service on September 15, 1819, for the Forth and Clyde Canal Company, and served for several years as a passenger boat on the Glasgow to Edinburgh run, carrying 200 passengers and cargo. The ship had a BP length of forty-five meters, and a displacement of about 900 tons. This was considered a large ship at that time, and the first real iron ship.

Steel making in Britain was of vital importance, because it established iron shipbuilding in the country during a time when natural resources of timber in the British Isles had become seriously depleted, and when the need for a merchant navy was extremely important to the country. It was also of great importance because the size of wooden ships, from the technical point of view, had reached a limit of around eighty meters long. This limited the cargo carrying capacity of the merchant fleet.

The pioneering efforts to build small ships of iron led to the formation, first in the U.K. and later in Europe and the United States, of a massive iron shipbuilding industry. The true age of iron shipbuilding took place in Britain from 1830 to 1880, and in the United States form 1830 to 1898.

Steel in shipbuilding in Britain was introduced in 1858, and shipbuilding quality mild steel was introduced in the late 1870s. This type of mild steel was produced by the Siemens or Bessemer process. It was during this time that steel's superior strength, versatility, and ease of fabrication was fully realized.

The first proposals received at Lloyd's Register for building steel merchant ships was in March 1877. The scantlings were approved at a twenty percent reduction from those adopted for similar iron vessels. Apparently, these ships performed well, and the verdict was, "experience had shown the great superiority of mild steel as compared with iron."

By the end of the nineteenth century, mild steel had become established as a far more economical material for ship construction than iron. Weight and economical advantages, however, were not gained without some cost. Compared to iron, mild steel was found to be more susceptible to corrosion and consequently needed more careful protection against the harsh marine environment in which it is used.

The Higher Strength Steels

Between 1907 and 1937, Cunard Liners *Mauretania* and *Lusitania* were built in part of higher strength steels, mainly in the superstructure, with a view to reduce topside weight.

In 1928, the German ocean liners *Bremen* and *Europa* utilized higher tensile steel in the bottom, tank top, upper strength decks, and upper side shell. In the 1930s, shipyards in Italy, France, and the U.K. used this type of composite structure, that is mild steel and higher tensile steels, for the ocean liners constructed at the time, including the *Queen Mary* and *Empress of Britain*. In the United States, a limited amount of higher tensile steel was used in 1936 in the construction of the tankers *R.P. Resor* and *T.C. McCobb*.

By the mid-1930s, welding mild steel was an established practice in the U.S. shipbuilding industry. Higher strength steels, however, became available for commercial ships when the World War II emergency ended. Prior to this period, most of the available higher tensile steel was reserved for naval construction. The few commercial ships built of higher tensile steel during this period had been ordered before the United States' entry into World War II.

The growing use of higher strength steels for hull construction during the 1970s is considered to be no less significant than the move from iron to mild steel. The American Bureau of Shipping states in a recent publication:

> Metallurgically, the high strength is generally achieved by means of microalloying with elements such as Aluminum, Columbium, Vanadium and Titanium. These elements tend to form finely dispersed carbide, nitride and carbonitride particles, which strengthen the steel by several mechanisms, including refining the ferritic grain size. Solid Solution alloying is also used to achieve the desired properties such as manganese, is added to increase the strength and toughness, and nickel to increase toughness. Concurrently with the above strengthening mechanism is the reduction in carbon that adversely affects the weldability of the steel.

Early in 1986, ABS completed a study for the U.S. Maritime Administration on high-strength, low alloy steels produced by advanced metallurgical processing methods. The processing is designed to achieve high strength and excellent low-temperature toughness with the use of smaller amounts of such elements as carbon, nickel, chromium, vanadium, and titanium than would normally be present in conventional high strength steels. The low alloy content provides for an increased ability to weld without cracking under restrained conditions.

The U.K., with over 150 years of steel making experience, steel development, and innovation, led the way to the development of direct air-cooled steels, which, with microalloying additions, are capable of achieving suitable mechanical properties without subsequent heat treatment. British Steel Engineering, in collaboration with Lloyd's Register, ensured that the shipbuilding steel produced would meet the industry's requirements. Because of its higher strength, this type of steel influences the structural configuration of the hull in such parameters as frame spacing, girder proportions, bulkhead spacing, double bottom depths, and deck heights compared to a hull constructed entirely with mild steel.

Advances in metallurgical processing methods such as thermomechanical controlled processing (TMCP), especially the nonaccelerated cooling method, has produced a low alloy high tensile steel of 50 kg/mm^2 and is well suited for use in ship construction because of its superior weldability and notch toughness. This type of higher tensile steel has advantages over the conventional higher tensile steels such as HT-32 and HT-36, because a lower carbon equivalent reduces the hardness of the heat-affected zone in the weldments, and this increases its ability to weld without cracking under restrained conditions. In addition, because of its superior notch toughness, the steel produced by the TMC-Process is more applicable to high-heat input welding than the conventional higher tensile Strength Steels.

The most significant feature of TMCP steel is that its weldability is greatly improved due to lower carbon content, or lower carbon equivalent (Ceq) in its chemical composition. Also, TMCP enables the steel makers to obtain high toughness in a stable manner. This eliminates the normalizing process required in the manufacture of grade E steel in the conventional process. The TMCP process achieves satisfactory levels of toughness at heat affected zones against large heat input welding.

In the early 1990s, a new type of steel plate was developed by the Japanese steel producers. They claimed it had an ultra-high crack arrestability, and that it would be effective in preventing catastrophic extension of steel fractures in the event of a collision or grounding accident, with attention being focused on the effectiveness of shear lip formation in the brittle crack arrest mechanism. The new type of plate has surface layers with an ultrafine grain ferrite microstructure, which provides excellent fracture toughness even at cryogenic temperatures. They also claim it is superior to the conventional higher strength steels.

Today, unfortunately, the percentage use of higher tensile steels on VLCC hull structure has increased to more than seventy-five percent in a mix of HT-32, HT-36 steels, along with the addition of mild steel. The extent by which scantlings of tankers have been reduced is best illustrated by the reductions in steel weight. A VLCC built in the mid-1970s with similar dimensions to a VLCC built today would have a light weight some 6,000 tons heavier. While much of this difference is due to the increased depth of the hull, the use of higher tensile steels and structural optimization also has a significant effect.

From the shipbuilder's point of view, there are advantages to use higher tensile steels. For the tanker owner, the possible consequences may be summarized as follows:

- Lower corrosion margin

- Increased corrosion rates

- Higher magnitudes of stress in ship structure

- Deflection of primary structure is significantly increased, leading to increased stress in secondary structure

- Probability of higher magnitudes of as-built panel deformations

- Increased probability of buckling being the limiting design criteria

Neither the International Association of Classification Societies (IACS), who in 1980 agreed as a unified requirement to use a reduction factor in the calculation of longitudinal bending for the substitution of higher tensile steels for mild steel, nor the shipyards themselves have the experience or the resources to accurately determine the effects of such substitution. An example of this are the problems encountered by some VLCCs built by a reputable shipyard in the Far East recently, where the hull structure had to be reinforced with a great deal more steel after being in service for a short period only.

What is also of concern is the fact that the major classification societies can, in most parts of the hull structure, allow the same percentage thickness loss due to wastage for higher tensile steel as they can for mild steel. But being higher tensile steel, it is thinner than mild steel would have been, so each millimeter of loss is a greater diminution in percentage terms.

In addition, because of the greater flexure of higher tensile steel structures in service, they will generally corrode quicker than their mild steel counter parts. This in effect means that in the case of higher tensile steel structure, the allowable percentage waste margin will now be used faster than before. It is therefore extremely important for the hull designer to be careful on the extent and location higher tensile steel is used in a design, first because of the effect that the lighter scantlings will have on corrosion margins and therefore on the ship's life.

Secondly, the fact that because higher tensile steels do not show a significant gain in fatigue performance, particular care must be exercised in area of detail design, bearing in mind that the lighter scantlings used in primary and secondary hull structural elements, will include increased levels of stress magnitudes in structural components.

It is also important to keep in mind that a tanker structure, particularly that of a large tanker, is subject to complex motions and external as well as internal forces. The potential of resonant sloshing of the cargo in a tank that may be partially full or completely empty, is now becoming more evident. The cyclic, wave-induced loads, created by the passage of waves along the ship's sides when under way at sea, have also become more apparent.

When mild steel was the dominant mode of construction material, yielding was the dominant mode of failure for a ship structure. Design was directed towards preventing yield, while buckling and fatigue could, for the most part be ignored. The heavy construction required of a mild steel ship structure effectively prevented failure from buckling or fatigue.

Another important factor that affects a hull structure is the fact that, whereas the hull structures designed in the 1970s were not highly optimized due to relative slowness of the computer analysis of the time, today because of advances in computer technology, the peak stresses in the various parts of a modern highly optimized hull structure will all be close to maximum allowable stress. Although such structure may be absolutely safe, it is lighter and thereby not so generally robust. Consequently the life span of this modern structure will not be quite as long as that of the unoptimized earlier designs.

What must be recognized by the tanker industry is that the shipbuilder will opt for maximum utilization of higher tensile steels in the hull structure and maximum optimization of a design allowable by IACS. In that way, the finished product is built to the minimum standards of strength required by the classification society.

From the above, it is clear that because of the universal adoption of higher tensile steels in shipbuilding and the highly advanced computer technology enabling the shipyard to optimize a tanker design, there are profound commercial implications. One such implication is the close scrutiny required during construction by the classification surveyor, because highly optimized higher tensile steel designs require finer construction tolerances than are appreciated for unoptimized mild steel designs.

The view amongst the leading classification societies today is, "We have established standards for the construction of ships which have evolved/developed over the years to the best of our ability. The standards are being continuously updated to keep pace with technological developments, and better understanding of the ship structures as they evolve. These are minimum standards available to the shipbuilder to be used for the design and construction of ships offered to a shipowner. It is up to the shipowner to decide whether he wants his new ship to embody implicit and explicit margins appropriate to a safe but short life for his ship. That ship should be built to the minimum standards, but of adequate strength, acceptable to the classification society; or invest more money to increase the corrosion margin, and apply extra coating protection to the ship's structure."

It was this philosophy that guided my request of Mr. Onassis for extra investment when discussing technical specifications with shipyards for new VLCCs even with mild steel hull structure.

Computers of course do assist in the design of a tanker hull structure, but they do not result in a major change in steel weight. They do, however, redistribute the steel more appropriately throughout the structure, away from the least stressed and into the most critically stressed locations in the structure.

At the Tanker Structure Cooperative Forum (TSCF), in October 1991 in London, the Japanese classification society, Class NK, presented their findings on higher tensile steel tanker structures. Their field surveys on tanker side longitudinals of second generation VLCCs (built during 1980s) found cracks at the face plates at the end connections of the side longitudinals, where the cracks extended from that point toward the web plate. The cracks were found at the intersection of side longitudinals with the transverse bulkheads. The majority of cracks were found in the cargo oil tanks amidships, with fewer such cracks in the ballast tanks. The cracks found were more numerous on the starboard side. The age of the tankers surveyed was around three years, and the side longitudinals were constructed of HT-36 and HT-32 higher tensile steels. Class NK stated that no such damage was ever recorded on first generation VLCCs where mild steel was used. The damage observed was attributed to the long term distribution of wave pressure on the side shell where the transverse deflection of the side structure is larger.

A recent study by the U.S. Ship Structure Committee, prompted by reports of extensive fatigue fractures found in tanker hull structures of recent construction where higher tensile steels were used. The investigation called attention to the problem areas of higher tensile steels details in tanker hull structures. Results of the investigation were published in a document titled, "Effect of High Strength Steels on Strength Considerations of Design and Construction Details of Ships" (SSC-374-March 1994).

The major component in the cost of building a tanker is the cost of steel. The basic purpose of using higher tensile steels in commercial shipbuilding today is the steel's higher strength that allows scantlings reduction. This in turn results in a lighter hull and therefore greater cargo carrying capacity, in addition to reduction in the power required for a given speed. The primary arguments for advocating the use of higher tensile steels for tankers are those of weight and cost reduction in a design, and to some extent fuel economy. For example, the difference in net steel weight of VLCCs of similar dimensions built in the 1970s and a VCLL built today is 6,000 tons. Practically all hull structure higher tensile steel applications are selective, with the higher tensile steel being distributed in areas where the direct stresses are the highest such as the strength deck and bottom structure around the cargo tanks.

Weldable shipbuilding steels are designated by two key parameters: the yield strength and the steel's toughness. Toughness is measured by the Charpy impact energy test, and is the most commonly used measure of steel toughness. It is simple and inexpensive to perform and is widely used for quality control purposes in fabrication. It is a measure of the resistance of the steel to both crack initiation and propagation. It is a measure of energy absorption in manufacturing a notched steel specimen of defined dimensions at a specified temperature. The higher the energy absorption rate, the tougher the steel is. Similar considerations apply to the weld metal to be used, especially toughness which should not undermatch that of the parent metal.

In recent years, designers have used the fracture mechanics approach, which is considered more realistic. It gives more consistent results than the Charpy test, whose limitation is that it does not assess the ability of a steel to resist or arrest cracks under high rates of loading. The fracture mechanics approach, also known as the crack-tip-opening displacement test, requires fatigue cracks to be initiated in a shaped specimen and is a costly test because it requires the application of three dimensional elasto-plastic finite element analysis to the structural specimens. Fracture is a failure mechanism that involves rapid unstable situation and propagation of a crack. The underlying premise of fracture mechanics is that the behavior of a crack is governed by local conditions at the tip of a crack.

Today's quality of shipbuilding steels supplied by a modern reputable steel manufacturer is of better quality than steels that were available in the past. Weldable steels are manufactured to conform to the standard range required by the leading classification societies, both for material properties and the manufacturing process employed by steel manufacturers.

Steel Fatigue Analysis and Hull Design

SNAME's Technical and Research Committee sponsored a project titled "Definition and Validation of a Practical Rationally Based Method for the Fatigue Analysis and Design of Ship Hull." (T&R Report No. R-41, February 1993). The objective of this project was to develop, "an efficient rationally-based design method which includes wave and ship motion induced fatigue cracking."

The need to develop such a method was necessary because traditional classification-rule-based structural design used specified loads for various ship types and load parameters that each ship type must be capable of withstanding. Such loads reflect the experiences of many ships over long periods of time and it is for this reason that rule-based criteria may not be available when considering new ship types or may not be appropriate when operating conditions cannot be considered typical. A rationally based design method, in which actual, anticipated loads is developed by this project to analyze a specific structural design.

Further justification for the rationally based design arises, when cyclic loading and the resulting fatigue failures are considered. In practice today, the occurrence of fatigue cracking is minimized or avoided through quality control of welds and careful design of connection details.

Another difficulty that arises when applying Rule-based criteria is when extensive use is made of steels with higher yield stress. When such steels are used, classification societies allow higher levels of total stress because of the higher static strength of such steels, which means larger values of cyclic as well as static stress.

Combining ordinary shipbuilding steel (mild steel) with higher yield steel in a ship hull structure must be carefully and properly evaluated, because engineers have established that fatigue strength can actually decrease with an increase of yield stress. This in effect means that fatigue stress, which may have been acceptable for ordinary shipbuilding steel, is not necessarily acceptable for other steels and may result in fatigue problems in the hull structure. On the other hand, structural analysis by way of finite element methods is better developed, and its results can be viewed with greater confidence. FEM, however, should not be extended to buckling and fatigue, which is less predictable with regard to the structural behavior, and it must be closely scrutinized.

In November 1992, ABS published a guidance document for the "Design and Evaluation of Double-Hull Structures" applicable to double-hull tankers in the range of 190 to 500 meters in length with a length-breadth ratio not less than 5.0 and breadth-depth ratio equal to or less than 2.5, intended for unre-stricted service. The equations and formulas for determining design loads and strength requirements as specified in Section 3 and 4 in the document, may also be applied to single-hull and mid-deck tankers, provided the parameters defined there are properly adjusted to the structural configuration and loading patterns of such tankers. In general, the strength assessment and failure criteria as specified in section 5 of the document are applicable to all types of tankers.

As the majority of new designs of tankers produced by shipyards in Europe and the Far East, incorporate a mix of Mild Steel and higher tensile steels in the hull structure, the material conversion factor when calculating the hull-girder Section Modulus is for:

Ordinary Mild steel	1.00
Grade H 32 steel	0.78
Grade H 36 steel	0.72
Grade H 40 steel	0.68

In general, the above mentioned guide provides a standard for the design and assessment of the hull structure that can be used as an alternative to the ABS "Rules for Building and Classing Steel Vessels." The classification require-ments for materials, fabrication, survey, and hull structure not covered by the guidance document are to be in accordance with the ABS rules.

Fatigue and Brittle Fracture

Fatigue is a process by which cracks grow through a structure when it is subjected to fluctuating stresses. Wave action is the most significant stress factor that contributes to structural fatigue on a tanker's hull structure. It is for this reason that analysis of wave data likely to be encountered is essential in order to predict the fatigue life of the structure. Especially for tankers where extensive use of higher tensile steels has been made in a design, fatigue has become a key failure mode. During the 1960s and 1970s, when tankers were built using exclusively mild steel, fatigue failure was not much of an issue.

Brittle fracture is a failure mechanism in which a crack suddenly becomes unstable and may result in the structure breaking in two. All welded steel structures contain crack-like defects, although significant improvements in the production of fracture-resistant steels have been made since the early 1940s. Modern steels are still prone to brittle fracture if critical combinations of crack size and stresses are exceeded. The material property that provides a measure of the resistance to brittle-fracture is toughness. Toughness and the critical defect sizes increase significantly between A to E grades of steel. The hull structure designer must therefore be careful when selecting grades of steel for the design.

Particularly during the building period of the second generation VLCCs and ULCCs, no rational design procedure for the use of either mild or higher strength steels existed for the hull structure. It is for this reason that the most important factor in maintenance and repair work on such structures is to know precisely which steel grades have been used and where each grade is fitted in the structure. Also the original welding procedure must be known, understood, and duplicated in order to accomplish successfully repair work. Such information should be carefully compiled during construction to be used for repairs in the future.

The problem of cracks in the structure of VLCCs and ULCCs first appeared in the late 1980s. Crack problems in structural members were most common in the first tankers delivered after 1985. The findings alerted one of the leading classification societies, who conducted detailed examinations of wide spread cracking in the longitudinal sections of more than sixty-five second generation crude oil carriers. The study concluded that the causes ware defective design, defective workmanship, or rough sea conditions.

It is important to bear in mind that structural inspections of large tankers are difficult and costly because of the sheer size of the task in terms of the area of the structure to be inspected.

The importance of ensuring adequate and safe access for the inspection of the structure at the design stage cannot be overemphasized. In a VLCC or ULCC structure, the physical obstacles to ascertaining internal steel work condition are enormous. Careful thought must be given to making this operation less dangerous and time consuming.

The current practice of carrying out tanker hull structure surveys is based on experience from the past. In view of recent experiences, where degradation of the steel due to corrosion and fatigue cracking has created concerns, survey practices warrant revision. The frequency of surveying tanker hull structures has been established through the years, based on in-service experience of various types of ships by the class societies. Different analytical procedures have been developed for the offshore structures and aircraft industries to determine inspection intervals for components that are subject to time dependent failure modes, such as corrosion and fatigue. Engineers are interested now in applying the same techniques to ship structures, where fracture mechanics methodology may be used to determine an optimal survey interval for fatigue cracks as a rational method for tankers. There are some constrains however in the use of fracture mechanics methodology, one of which arises from the special characteristics of crack growth in structures with large redundancy.

During the periodical hull structure inspections, the areas where higher strength steels is used should be given special attention, because there is no empirical data on the long-term impact of the extensive application of such steels, especially in the large structure of VLCCs or ULCCs. The more critical areas of the higher tensile steel structure are the welds, particularly in the multiaxially loaded welds. As regards pitting corrosion, this should be treated differently than general corrosion in regard to determining survey intervals, because localized pitting is not considered a threat to structural strength.

The single most important factor in the maintenance and repair of higher tensile steel hulls is that of knowing precisely which steel grades have been used, and where each grade of steel is fitted. Also the original welding procedure must be known, understood, duplicated, and compiled during construction of the vessel, and this log should be maintained on board throughout the tanker's life.

Steel Corrosion, Prevention, and the Corrosion Margin

The disadvantage in using steel for a tanker is that it corrodes. Corrosion protection of a tanker's hull structure, therefore, is vital to preserving the basic functional integrity and operating status of a crude oil carrier. Anticorrosive paint coatings are a vital part of an effective maintenance culture, because protecting the tanker hull structure is one of the determining factors of the tanker's service life. This is particularly true for double-hull crude oil carriers, where the integrity of the ballast tank structure is of paramount importance to their safety, because ballast tanks completely surround the cargo tanks, presenting an enormous critical area that must be protected.

Ballast tank integrity is equally important in the single-hull crude oil carrier structure. The distinction, however, is that single-hull tankers with segregated ballast tanks present less bulkhead area in contact with cargo spaces. Crude oil cargo tanks are seldom coated. Some owners, however, do coat horizontal surfaces as preventive maintenance to reduce the effects of acidic content of the cargo carried.

Coating the structure of a crude oil carrier is primarily applied to prevent corrosion, and to maintain the hull strength. Coating also serves a cosmetic function, covering decks and the exterior and interior of other parts of the tanker structure. It is advisable during ballast voyages to keep the ballast tanks completely full or completely empty, because, apart from the dangers of sloshing action, the tanker's motions can eventually wear the protective coating of the steel surface in the ballast tank.

The International Maritime Organization (IMO) has mandated ballast tank coating with special recommendation that for crude oil carriers, light colored coatings be used to ease inspection and to detect coating break down as it occurs. Especially in double-hull crude oil carriers, a crack in a bulkhead could, over time, allow ingress of hydrocarbons, creating an explosion risk.

Early in 1994, the IMO drew up guidelines for the selection, application, and maintenance of corrosion prevention of dedicated seawater ballast tanks (DSBT). The draft, developed by the Subcommittee on Ship Design and Equipment, was submitted to the Maritime Safety Committee, who sent it to the IMO Assembly for formal adoption. Debating the issue of coating application to prevent corrosion, the argument revolved around, "who is ultimately accountable for corrosion prevention in a ship's structure." A coatings working group, under the aegis of the Hong Kong Shipowners Association, first convened in early 1994 and devised minimum standards pertaining to the extent of examination, thickness measurements, and tank testing, especially for ballast tanks and other vulnerable areas.

Blaming the paint supplier, shipbuilder, or ship repairer after the event, does not help the shipowner. These people can only give the owner a limited guarantee period for a paint job. It is the shipowner's responsibility to ensure from the outset, that he has a good paint specification and that the anticorrosive coating system is correctly applied, under the supervision of a trained paint inspector. Painting the hull structure of a crude oil carrier is a costly affair, and some owners find this out all too late.

There are a number of factors to be considered in the coating selection process that define a coatings' value. A major factor in determining such value is the ability of a coating or coating system to meet the requisite performance as defined by the owner. One method is to match the coating system's performance attributes and limitations with the anticipated exposure conditions. For this, it is most important to discuss carefully the paint specification with the paint supplier and with the shipyard before deciding on the coating system to be adopted, especially today, with the change in coatings' application form multicoated thin-film technology to single or dual thick film technology. It is also important to ensure inspection of the paint work is carried out by a properly trained paint inspector.

Steel Surface Preparation

Proper steel surface preparation is essential because even the best protective anticorrosive coatings are never better than the quality of the preceding surface preparation. In most cases premature failure of a protective coating system is caused by substandard steel surface preparation. Factors that are known to affect the performance of coating systems are:

- thorough cleaning of the steel surface, which means removal of mill-scale, rust, old layers of paint, as well as contaminants such as salts and chlorides, dust, oils, and greases.

- creating a profile on the steel surface known as "anchor pattern."

In the past, sand was used as abrasive media, and even today, the word "sandblasting" is used to describe the method for steel surface preparation. The description is no longer correct. The Silicosis Law was enacted in Holland in 1957, forbidding the use of material containing more than one percent free crystalline silica for blastcleaning. Aluminum silicate grit, produced in Holland by Eurogrit B.V. is now used and is considered a safe blasting medium.

Steel will not start to oxidize without a catalyst, and a polluted environment contains many airborne catalysts that promote reaction of the cleaned steel surface forming an oxide layer and starting corrosion. It is important therefore that blastcleaning is done in as pure an atmosphere as possible, because this will prevent the steel surface from oxidizing before it is coated. The normal procedure before commencing steel surface blasting is to hose down the substrate with fresh water in an attempt to rinse off as many of the chlorides as possible.

In a new building, blastcleaning of the steel surface is of great importance, because all marine coatings adhere to the substrate through mechanical adhesion. A well organized shipyard will go to great lengths to ensure their paint shop is properly equipped for steel surface preparation and for the painting of a steel assembly before it is moved to the building site. Painters recognize that steel blasted in a pure atmosphere will resist oxidation for a long time.

Preventing Corrosion

Steel corrosion is a natural and unavoidable occurrence in steel structures once they enter service. It is the natural predator of all steel structures operating in a marine environment, and it is the most dominant factor affecting the physical life of a ship's steel hull. In the case of marine structures, oil tankers and bulk carriers are the two types most affected by corrosion, while in container ships and gas carriers, the effects of corrosion are less severe.

Scantlings corrosion is the result of tanker operation and varies between horizontal and vertical surfaces, and between locations of similar surfaces in the same tank. Assessing corrosion, therefore, is a complicated process because of its lack of uniformity. Other factors involved cause corrosion rates to differ from tanker to tanker. Corrosion pitting, which is caused by water and sulfur from the cargo and the inert gas systems, generally occurs on the bottom structure of the tank, such as the inner side of the bottom shell and face plates of the bottom longitudinals.

The established methods to prevent steel corrosion are paint coatings or coatings in combination with cathodic protection. Both methods are expensive but a necessary investment to ensure the steel structure is maintained in good condition throughout the tanker's operational life. Paint coatings are intended to form a barrier between the steel surface and the sea water. It is the degree of permeability of the particular coating that determines its effectiveness. The coating permeability is reflected in the type of material used and the thickness at which it is applied. Successful adhesion to the steel structure is of vital importance. It is equally important to ensure a high standard of steel surface preparation and the conditions of coating application. Today's paint coatings, when applied correctly, do control steel corrosion. However, corrosive cargoes and mechanical damage can cause the degradation of a protective coating and contribute to the onset of the steel structure corrosion.

Ballast tank corrosion is an obvious danger on a double-hull where the space exposed, is more than twice that of a single-hull VLCC. Even with a coated steel surface, the chances of severe corrosion can cause serious wastage of steel.

There are a number of factors that have been giving cause for concern. These fall under five main headings.

- Decreasing maintenance on older tankers as they approach phase out
- The need for higher maintenance of the increased ballast spaces on segregated ballast tankers and double-hull tankers

- Lower corrosion margins due to optimization of scantlings
- The interactions between the outer skin and the inner skin of double-hull tankers
- Fatigue performance of structural details in hulls where a large percentage of higher tensile steels has been used in the hull structure

Structural deterioration also depends on the rigors of service. This is particularly important in double-hull tankers where a large percentage of the steel surface requires protective coatings. Such tankers require a higher commitment from the owner/operator than the pre-MARPOL tankers. To ensure good structural performance, planned inspections and planned maintenance are the most economical route. The idea of extending the tanker's inert gas system into the ballast tanks has drawbacks. Any sulfur in the inert gas could mix with the water remaining in the ballast tank producing a corrosive liquid, and this may outweigh the use of inert gas.

When the time comes to seriously consider steel renewals because the structure has reached a certain level of deterioration, it is critical to consider carefully the changes to the network of stresses in the structure. Large areas of steel that need to be replaced could aggravate a situation already made delicate by large areas of corroded structure. In such situations, it is wise not to spare the pennies. Every effort must be made to ensure structural continuity between materials that may have different properties and may be of different thickness.

There are two types of corrosion, general and localized or pitting. Generally, pitting is not considered a threat to structural strength. It is more of a pollution risk that has the potential to cause cargo leakage when the steel plate is pierced. It is the general corrosion that is the most pervasive type of tanker structure problem, and there is no easy solution to corrosion prevention in a tanker steel structure. In recent years, the tanker industry has been paying more attention to a third and less well-known phenomenon, the microbiologically influenced corrosion (MIC). Corrosive bacteria thrive in low oxygen and oxygen-free environments, in the water layer at the bottom of oil tanks, and in the sediment in ballast tanks. The bacteria produce acids, destroy paint coatings, create corrosion cells, and produce hydrogen sulfide. They can double their mass every twenty minutes and can corrode steel by four mm in one year.

Acid producing bacteria (APB) and sulfate-reducing bacteria (SRB) are the main culprits. The former colonize on the steel's surface inside ballast and cargo tanks and feed on organic compounds, including oil and oil products, to form organic acids. If there is little oxygen in the atmosphere, they grow faster. The sulfate-reducing bacteria thrive in an oxygen free environment. They also use hydrocarbons as a food source, but prefer the organic acids given off by the acid producing bacteria.

Recent strong evidence suggests that cargo tank areas of fairly new tankers have experienced high rates of (MIC) corrosion that resulted in deep pitting on uncoated horizontal surfaces, such as tank bottom plating and bulkhead stringers. The American Bureau of Shipping issued an advisory warning sometime ago that unusual corrosion rates and patterns were occurring in some quite new tankers, both of single and double-hull construction.

Corrosion Margin (Corrosion Allowance)

Corrosion reduces steel thickness, and this affects the strength performance of the hull structure of a ship and results in other forms of failure. To ensure a ship's structural reliability after commissioning, with respect to steel thickness reduction due to corrosion, efforts are being made to establish criteria for permissible corrosion levels. Shipbuilders are also setting standards to be used for maintenance work, especially when decisions have to be made on the extent of work that has to be carried out to renew steel parts.

In order to maintain the strength of the designed hull structure throughout the structure's operational life span, a corrosion margin is introduced to the designed scantlings in the form of added thickness to the net material or net scantlings designed for a particular structure. The added material is used to compensate for the predicted thickness diminution during the ship's life span as one measure to address the problem of corrosion. The criteria generally used to determine rational corrosion margins are based upon probabilistic corrosion models for corrosion levels. Such models have been developed in order to evaluate the extent of scantling thickness reduction in a structural member due to corrosion during the first, second, third, and fourth special survey of the ship's twenty-year lifespan.

It is to be noted that significant difference in corrosion rates can be observed between mild steels and higher strength steels. To ensure good structural performance, a rational corrosion protection system for water ballast tanks and other spaces such as holds, machinery spaces, pump rooms, and cofferdams is essential and should be designed into the building specification. A tanker hull structure effectively protected against corrosion minimizes the risk of failure or major renewals during the tanker's expected operational life.

Oil tankers are normally designed for an operational life of twenty years plus, and this can be achieved by applying a complex set of measures that are based on the material properties, careful engineering, and fabrication technology. Additionally, such measures must be combined with periodic surveys that take into consideration age and structural condition. In this context, the corrosion allowance presents a significant gain in the safety margin of the structural design.

Is there a corrosion-proof steel structure? The answer is yes. If an owner can afford it, the problem of corrosion in a tanker structure may be solved by using titanium alloyed steels, which are well known for their outstanding resistance to corrosion in a marine environment as well as being light, yet strong, tough, and fatigue resistant. As a result, titanium needs no corrosion allowance (corrosion margin) and a structure built with titanium alloy should be designed to minimize thickness of material to satisfy strength requirements.

Cathodic Protection of Tanker Hull Structure

When two metals are electrically connected in an electrolyte such as sea water, electrons will flow from the most active metal—the anode—to the less active metal—the cathode. The flow is due to the difference in the electrical potential.

When an anode supplies current, it will gradually dissolve into ions in the electrolyte, and at the same time produce electrons which the cathode will receive through the metallic connection with the anode. The result is that, the cathode will be negatively polarized and hence will be protected against corrosion. Such protection can be achieved either by "sacrificial anodes" or "impressed current." In practice, steel is protected by the supply of electrons from metals such as zinc, aluminum, and magnesium, which are sacrificial anode materials.

In steel protection using the impressed current system, the steel is coupled to the negative pole of a direct current source, while the positive pole on the direct current source is coupled to an auxiliary anode. This anode will dissolve at different rates in the electrolyte, depending on the type of auxiliary anode material.

Sacrificial anodes are the accepted practice for the internal protection of all types of ballast tanks. In the case of unpainted ballast tanks, cathodic protection will require a large amount of anodes well distributed throughout the tank structure. If cathodic protection is to be combined with paint coating, the amount of anodes will be reduced in line with increased thickness and quality of the paint system used. In such cases, it is vitally important for the designer of the cathodic protection system to have a very good knowledge of paint coatings in order to achieve a good balance of both systems of protection and optimize installation costs.

Zinc or aluminum anode performance is practically the same. Aluminum however, has the advantage of being one-third lighter than a comparable zinc installation. The disadvantage of the aluminum alloy anode, however, is that of a spark hazard, which a falling aluminum anode can create. For this reason, classification societies impose certain restrictions in the use of aluminum anodes. One such restriction is that, an aluminum anode having a weight of 28 kg or more, cannot be installed higher than 1.40 meters above the bottom of the tank. Securing the anodes in place can be arranged either by clamping or welding to the structure.

One advantage using a well designed impressed current system instead sacrificial anodes to protect the steel structure is that, once the anodes are in place, they may be forgotten until the next dry-docking. For best results, the owner should consult a reputable cathodic protection system supplier. The supplier can offer optimum combined solutions and guarantee results of the recommended protection system.

Electrolytic Descaling of Steel Structure

Descaling of uncoated tanks can be accomplished using magnesium strips. This can be done during a ballast voyage prior to dry-docking. Such a method has been found to be successful where the steel structure has extensive formation of rust or in coated tanks where corrosion has caused paint breakdown representing seventy percent or more of the area. Electrolytic descaling can be achieved in about fourteen days.

The procedure is rather simple. The magnesium strips are welded or clamped to the steel structure and produce a strong electrical current in the tank. Hydrogen gas is evolved at the steel surface and causes breakdown of the scale and rust, and a soft calcareous layer forms on the steel surface. This forces the rust scale loose from the steel surface and it then drops to the bottom of the tank. The tank is emptied and washed down with fresh water as soon as possible. This will remove rust scale, salt, and the calcareous layers that form under the rust scale during the descaling process. Descaling of the rust takes place while the magnesium strips are being sacrificed. Here again a reputable supplier should be consulted.

Electric Arc Welding in Shipbuilding

The advent of electric arc welding and its application in ship construction must rank as perhaps the greatest major advancement in steel hull construction. It stemmed largely from the outstanding success of the *Liberty* ship and T-2 tanker construction program initiated in the United States during the Second World War. It was during the early years of World War II that electric arc welding for ship construction came into its own. The procedure was adopted and refined in the United States by the Maritime Commission to meet the needs of the time for the construction of cargo ships and oil tankers.

Electric welding for hull construction at a time of growth in ship size was not without its problems. Tankers built during and immediately after World War II, became prone to major hull cracks, such as that of the T-2 tanker *Schenectady* and the tanker *World Concord* and broke in two. The phenomenon, which can be traced to the classification societies extrapolating old rules designed for smaller vessels, was one of the catalysts for the leading classification societies to review their rules and develop new ones early in 1950, on a more "Scientific Basis."

Electric arc welding soon became the standard shipbuilding technique. With the assistance of automatic welding, large subassemblies were fabricated away from shipbuilding berths or docks, limited in size only by crane or transporter capacity. Some shipyards that were physically constrained by short building berths—in Yugoslavia and in Scotland, for example—developed systems of building large hulls of more than 200,000 dwt in two halves and welding them afloat.

One of the ship classes that played a key role in post-war years in maritime technology was the large crude oil carrier. In Europe, early in the 1960s, the Gotaverken Arendal yard in Sweden, pioneered a new trend by joining together subassemblies under cover and jacking them out horizontally into a dock until a complete tanker was assembled. During the same period, the Japanese yards preferred to transfer their subassemblies by crane into building docks. This method, enabled the yards in Japan to press the tanker size relentlessly up where, by the 1970s, the half million dwt tanker was a reality. In fact, in shipyards in Japan, South Korea, and Europe, building docks were being readied to accommodate tankers of one million dwt. (See Chapter on the million ton tankers.)

Precision cutting of plates and sections is very important because it improves fit-up, reduces the possibility of misalignment, and minimizes fatigue cracks in the hull structure. Such precision engineering enables the shipyard to robotize their operation for automatic critical welding of the hull parts, and can be controlled and monitored in the yard's computer integrated manufacturing system (CIMS).

Automatic welding is superior to the traditional manual welding because it obtains consistently deeper penetration and leaves a much smoother weld surface than manual welding. This in turn minimizes the possibility of surface mini-cracks that can initiate failure. In addition, a smooth surface is necessary to ensure protective coating durability.

A prerequisite to fabricating welded structures is the evaluation of the toughness of the steel to be used and their welded joints for the selection of suitable welding techniques. Today, all such work is done easily and rapidly using computer aided material fracture toughness evaluation system, which stores the strength and toughness of the steel used in the past, together with the specific type, style, and locations of welded joints.

Leading shipyards in Japan today have developed structural systems substantially enhancing hull structure design efficiency by integrating accumulated design know-how into a database, and incorporating it into the computer-aided design system of the yard for future use. Efforts are also being made to eliminate faults that have been identified at the design stage and during the production process under unified management on an in-house network, and to visualize how these faults are addressed.

In today's highly competitive shipbuilding market, cost saving is one of the major requirements in the industry, and a great deal of attention is focused on production techniques. Electric arc welding is one of the most significant and important aspects of ship construction. As a consequence, changes in the process of welding have been driven by the need to improve quality and productivity. Success of this mature and important sector of ship construction is due to increased understanding of the physics of electric arc welding, which has allowed the welding technology to be translated into improvement in welding techniques. Because of the advances made in the application of the process, which is focused on panel assembly/production, the panel-line concept has been used as a basic production format, and has been highly successful.

Using process-control form cutting through the several stages of assembly, it is possible to minimize or eliminate changes in welding parameters due to deviations in accuracy, and use these changes for correction, using sensors that maintain geometry and penetration of the weld metal. Improvements in such electric welding practices have resulted in reliable welded joints in the ship's structure, with a minimum of deformation and distortion caused by residual and thermal stresses. The end result is an accurately finished assembly.

Recently, a state-of-the-art robot welding system controlled by an advanced visual sensing and guidance programming system has been developed. It is a part of the automatic vision-guided robot welding system developed in Finland. Developers claim the system will open up a new era in shipyard production for the fabrication and welding of hull parts and subassemblies.

A Tanker's Operational Life

What is the expected operational life of a crude oil carrier? How long is a string?

Depending upon the circumstances, crude oil carriers have been known to have lifetimes varying from ten to thirty years. The three criteria that determine a tanker's operational life are economic, physical, and regulatory obsolescence.

In theory, there is no limit to the durability of a tanker, because everything is replaceable. In practice, economics and regulation will determine life span. Statistically, the critical fifteen to twenty-five year age bracket has proved the most susceptible to damage or casualty.

As far as physical obsolescence is concerned, the operational life of a crude oil carrier is a function of how well the hull structure has been designed, built, and maintained. Some independent tanker owners are entrepreneurs by nature who, in a high risk business, have only one objective—to make a profit on their investment in the shortest possible time. The prudent and serious tanker owner, however, puts considerable effort into meeting a planned economic objective.

In the case of a tanker, more than any other field, structural condition determines the remaining operational life of a tanker. Efforts to monitor the condition of the structure will enable the owner to have a clear understanding of the state of the internal structure in the tanks at all times. For this, the owner must have a ready means of updating information to assess the economic life of the tanker, and consequently the return on investment must be carefully and constantly evaluated.

In the 1960s and 1970s, when large tankers were built, they were assumed to have a lifespan of between twenty to twenty-five years. Such predictions have had more to do with performing investment calculations than a detailed technical prediction. In our company, we considered that with a good specification and good maintenance, the nominal life of a crude oil carrier would be at least twenty years. In the 1980s the trend was toward short life, lighter scantlings tankers, with a significant proportion of higher tensile strength steels incorporated in the hull structure. In such hull designs where scantlings are optimized, resulting in smaller corrosion margin in absolute terms, the life of hull structure will be shorter if the steel is not protected carefully.

Life Extension

In the early 1990s, with new building prices too high, owners with tankers approaching their fourth hull special survey were faced with the dilemma whether to extend the life of their tankers or recycle them (scrap them). During this period, it was estimated the average repair bill to complete the fourth hull special survey for a VLCC was around US$8.0 million. At that time the view was supported that a well built and properly maintained VLCC of the mid-1970s vintage represented a sound investment in the medium term, because possible life expectancy of the hull structure was in excess of thirty years. Only regulatory requirements would have curtailed the VLCC's life by the need to satisfy protective location requirements when they were twenty-five years old, and double-hull equivalence when they were thirty years old. This was also the period when the importance of building a tanker to a good specification and proper maintenance was appreciated. A well built and maintained tanker of the same age was able to trade up to and beyond the fifth special survey.

Leading classification societies were offering schemes for hull renovation and life extension, which was viewed as basically a longer term maintenance approach. In general, life extension programs started with a thorough initial survey assessment of the tanker, which enabled the class society to designate the actual renovation and renewal work to be carried out. The emphasis was on the hull structure. Propulsion and other equipment were also covered.

The class societies were more than willing to establish condition assessment and hull renovation schemes with complete disregard as to whether this was a justified expenditure by the shipowner in terms of results. The class societies were either ignorant or were not in a position to assess the changes to the network of stresses in the hull structure brought about by the renewal of large areas of steel to a variety of hull designs.

Failure of these programs became apparent later on, and the class societies were pointing the finger at the repair yards, blaming them for poor workmanship. They ignored the fact that work of such importance was carried out under class society's approval and supervision. What also was overlooked was the fact that there was an inability to correctly establish critical stress areas in the many hull designs constructed during the rush period of the early 1970s to build tankers. Also, no consideration was given to the interaction between sections of new replacement material and the adjoining existing material of reduced scantlings, which in some cases was either pitted or notched to some degree. The disappointment of the owner for failure in the system of hull renovation became apparent later when he was confronted with the specter of hull repairs that should never have been encouraged in the first place.

Tanker Hull Structural Failures

The three classes of structural failures as defined by the U.S. Coast Guard are:

1. Class 1

    Any fracture or buckle in the main hull of the vessel. For this standard, a fracture is one that is visible and of any length which either indicates in or has propagated into the main hull of a vessel. The main hull of a vessel consists of the strength deck, side shell, and bottom plating.

2. Class 2

    A buckle or fracture of any length that either indicates in or has propagated into a strength member of a vessel's support structure. For this standard, strength members are the center vertical keel, deep web frames, transverse bulkheads, side longitudinals, underdeck longitudinals on the strength deck, longitudinal bulkheads, and bilge keels.

3. Class 3

    Any buckle or fracture not meeting the definition of a Class 1 or Class 2 structural failure.

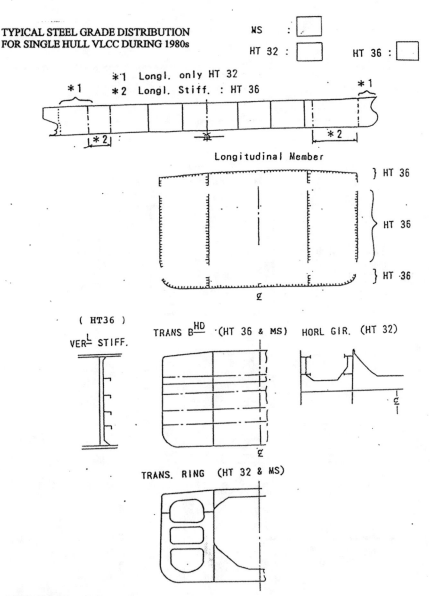

TYPICAL STEEL GRADE DISTRIBUTION
FOR SINGLE HULL VLCC DURING 1980s

MS :
HT 32 :
HT 36 :

*1 Longl. only HT 32
*2 Longl. Stiff. : HT 36

Longitudinal Member

} HT 36
} HT 36
} HT 36

(HT36)
VER⊥ STIFF.

TRANS B^HD (HT 36 & MS)

HORL GIR. (HT 32)

TRANS. RING (HT 32 & MS)

MILD STEEL – 27%
H.T. STEEL 32 – 26%
H.T. STEEL 36 – 47%

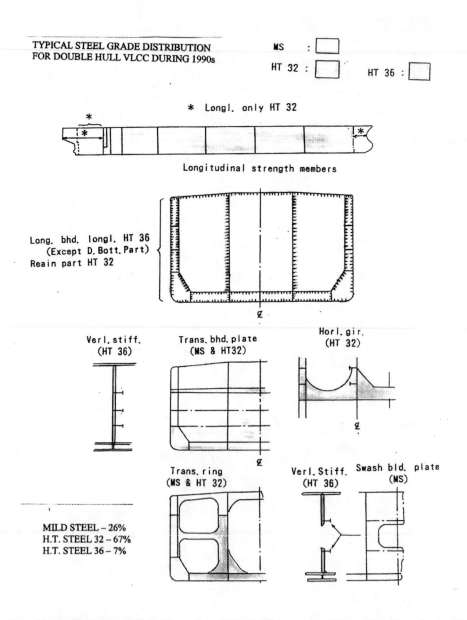

TYPICAL STEEL GRADE DISTRIBUTION
FOR DOUBLE HULL VLCC DURING 1990s

MS :

HT 32 :

HT 36 :

* Longl. only HT 32

Longitudinal strength members

Long. bhd. longl. HT 36
  (Except D. Bott. Part)
Reain part HT 32

Verl. stiff.
(HT 36)

Trans. bhd. plate
(MS & HT32)

Horl. gir.
(HT 32)

Trans. ring
(MS & HT 32)

Verl. Stiff.
(HT 36)

Swash bld. plate
(MS)

MILD STEEL – 26%
H.T. STEEL 32 – 67%
H.T. STEEL 36 – 7%

TWELVE

Ship Classification and the Classification Societies

It all began in 1760 at Eduard Lloyd's coffee house in London, U.K., when the Register Society was formed by the customers of the coffee house. The Society printed the first Register of Ships in 1764 in order to give both underwriters and merchants an idea of the condition of the vessels they insured and chartered.

In 1834, the organization was restructured as Lloyd's Register of British and Foreign Shipping and the first "rules" for the survey and classification of ships were published. During the first year of its operation, the Society employed sixty-three surveyors, and by 1840, 15,000 vessels had been surveyed in accordance with the Society's Rules. In 1828, the French classification society, Bureau Veritas, was formed at the initiative of two Antwerp underwriters, but in 1831, the Society's head office was transferred from Belgium to Paris in France. Until around 1870, it introduced itself to the English-speaking community as "French Lloyd's Register of Continental and American vessels."

In the 1860s, four more classification societies were formed:

- Registro Italiano Navale (RINA) in Italy
- American Bureau of Shipping (ABS) in United States
- Det Norske Veritas (DNV) in Norway
- Germanischer Lloyd (GL) in Germany

In 1899, the Japanese classification society, Nippon Kaiji Kyokai (class NK), was formed in Japan, although this society did not start ship classification until 1915.

Today, there are fifty-five classification societies worldwide, including the Polish Register, Russian Register, Hellenic Register, Korean Register, Indian

Register, and others. Each of these societies class a substantial amount of tonnage in their national fleets, although they do not have the worldwide coverage of surveyors provided by the long-established classification societies.

Classification societies are considered to be independent, risk management organizations providing risk-assessment systems certification around the world. They are considered to operate independently of any government or other body and are able to assure absolute commercial impartiality. They are nonprofit distributing organizations, and in their contractual relationship with the shipowners, it is generally understood that their job is satisfying underwriters that their ships are acceptable risks. They give the responsible owner the assurance that his ship is sound.

The class societies also provide a great deal of technical support and advice in the process of classification. Their knowledge and experience enables them through IACS to assist the IMO with draft safety regulations that provide the basis of flag state regulations for safety at sea, and to conduct statutory survey work for a flag state.

Catastrophic disasters at sea in recent years have raised serious questions on the ability of the classification societies to ensure the safety of ships they class. The proliferation of roles for classification societies has increased the arenas for competition with all its potential down sides. Such expansion of functions and the influence of the class societies raises two questions: "Whom do the societies serve?" and more importantly, "Whom should they serve?" The dilemma confronting the shipping industry for some years now has been the quality of service class societies provide to the shipping industry and performance of the societies generally. The reaction to the criticism by the classification societies has been, "classification societies are accustomed to being disparaged for having commercial motives. It has been implied that responsibility for safety can only be exercised in an environment from which all commercial considerations are excluded. What has been overlooked is that the safety business is a real business and that, even those with the most direct responsibilities for safety must be aware of commercial considerations and respond to them. It is also recognized that any one who carries obligations for safety of human life, of property and of the environment, must never allow financial considerations to distract them from setting and applying acceptable standards."

These are fine words. The shipping industry however has been very disappointed with the classification societies' performance of the ethical and social responsibilities that the class societies carry. One has to view documentary films such as that produced by BBC in the U.K., titled *Scandal of the Seas,* to realize that the credibility of the classification societies has suffered serious setbacks. The class societies response to such evidence has been, "the balance between technical and commercial factors is a difficult one to maintain on a consistent basis, especially when it is certain to be disputed by people who have a legitimate interest in the safety judgment, but can see things solely in technical or commercial terms." Such statements did not help the shipping industry's feelings that "ship inspection and surveys are dead," and that classification societies cannot be relied upon to carry out flag state inspections.

In response to justified concern by the London Hull Underwriters at the condition of some of the ships, the Committee of Hull Underwriters considered various technical solutions, such as stress monitoring. From the committee's findings it seemed that, in this case, such solutions were not available and the one unassailable fact that emerged was that independent surveys of suspect vessels were the only practical answer. To this end, the underwriters consulted with the London Salvage Association for advice and guidance on the various aspects of the proposed surveys. This resulted in the emergence of the Structural Condition Warranty which reads:

> Warranted the Salvage Association's Structure Condition survey to be carried out within 30 days from......(as required by the Underwriters), or at the next port or place, etc. etc. The survey to be on the Assured's instructions and on their behalf, but Underwriters should be entitled to receive a copy of any recommendations and/or reports direct from the Salvage Association.

A presentation at a Plenary Session of the Society of Naval Architects and Marine Engineers (SNAME) in the United States in 1997 titled "The Changing Role of Classification Societies," prepared by the Advisory Public Service Committee, began with this quotation from Thomas Babington MacAuly: "Men are never so likely to settle a question as when they discuss it freely."

Those involved in the debate failed to appreciate the fact that there is nothing wrong with constructive dissent. Because of intimidation, the debate simply fizzled out.

Classification societies are unique organizations that provide professional services in the field of ship safety. As third parties in a complex business such as shipping, they have the difficult task of balancing various interests, and at the same time maintaining quality in all surveys, using the most appropriate technology to determine marine safety standards. Historically, class societies' are deemed to represent and administer the high standards of safety-at-sea and protection of the marine environment, required by governments and underwriters, and expected by responsible shipowners and the general public. Over the years, the class societies have become the principal repository of technical information for the shipping industry, and because of their worldwide network of classification surveyors, they are able to carry out classification as well as statutory surveys. The class societies have been criticized strongly in the European maritime press for disasters at sea resulting in loss of life and extensive marine pollution.

Enter "IACS"—International Association of Classification Societies

There are fifty-five ship classification societies worldwide; eleven are members of IACS, an exclusive organization whose members are considered to have higher technical capabilities and professionalism. In April 1993, there was a threatened schism in IACS by three of its members—Germanischer Lloyd, Bureau Veritas, and Registro Italiano—followed by a second threat to split the Association in March 1995, by three other members of the Association—Lloyd's Register, American Bureau of Shipping, and Det Norske Veritas. The reason given for this threatened split was, "Instead of working through IACS, to formulate and implement the various initiatives within the normal IACS forum, a smaller group of societies would expedite progress to achieve improved levels of maritime safety and restore class society credibility." The other IACS' members strongly criticized the action calling it a "clever marketing move." Reconciliation took place at IACS' Paris meeting in June 1995. In March 1997, the international shipping community faced another classification society war. Competition amongst class societies became increasingly fierce and the battle for market share and profits intensified.

In May 2000, the IACS Council met in London with leaders of key shipping industry organizations to discuss one of the key issues confronting the Association, namely, "the loss of trust in the system of ship classification, and the growing realization that the whole shipping industry is right up against the wall, pinned there by the regulators and the public at large." The assembled executives stressed the need for fundamental change in thinking. Attendees pointed out that the criticism was not simply a class-bashing exercise. Shipping industry's organizations at this crucial round-table meeting mentioned that the Oil Companies International Forum (OCIMF) no longer recognized IACS. Others mentioned that the regulators, the public, and even the shipowners were losing confidence in the classification system.

What did shake the classification societies, however, was the progression of a wide range of maritime safety measures by the Parliament and Council of the European Union in Brussels, as part of its response to the marine pollution caused by the tankers *Erika* in December 1999 and *Prestige* in November 2002. This was a signal to the class societies that the legislators had lost faith in the performance of the class societies. The classification societies' view is that a class society benefits the owner with the means of satisfying underwriters that the ships they insure are acceptable risks. They also provide technical support and advice in the process of classification from the time a ship is planned to the end of its life. This is a fair response and there is merit in such view.

Despite efforts by IACS to portray itself as a strong, dynamic, united organization, the IACS Council meeting in May 2000 in London scrapped its agenda on the spot to focus on one key issue, the loss of trust in the shipping classification system. Leaders of key shipping industry organizations emphasized ; the growing realization that the oil companies, the regulators and the public no longer had faith in the classification societies. A review released by the International Chamber of Shipping in London, (ICS Review of 2001-02), states that the mistrust that is evident in the relationships between class societies, flag states, and the maritime industry is having an adverse effect on efforts to improve working practices. The review mentioned that class societies are vital to the maritime industry, but efforts were needed to improve their image and help them to regain respectability. Industry organizations are too often finding that class society politics take precedence over commitments to cooperative working practices. The ICS more or less told class societies to stop their internal squabbling, because nobody benefits from this lack of mutual confidence. "If the shipping sector is to have any prospect of returning to the days when professional integrity of class was accepted without question, all parties will have to pull together more effectively than at present."

An official of a leading classification society attending the World Maritime Forum in St. Petersburg, Russia, in the spring of 2003 stated, "If class is to remain relevant, it must remake itself for the modern world. Self regulation will continue to provide an effective method for establishing and enforcing standards only, if all elements of the industry recognize that substantive overhaul is needed." On another occasion in 2003, another official of a leading class society responded to the question, "What are the strengths and weaknesses of the existing system of ship classification?" The official responded, "In due time, there will be changes in the manner in which class establishes and maintains standards in the future."

Many hope that these changes will take place soon, because failure in safety at sea and protection of the marine environment are an urgent summons to action. The constant squabbling and struggle for supremacy, amongst the leading classification societies has raised serious questions in the shipping industry as to whether the class societies will ever be able to achieve the badly needed, universally acceptable, structural safety standards, particularly for bulk carriers and tankers. An important consideration facing the shipping industry is the difficult task of decision making concerning safety standards for ships, because the gap between research and application of an innovation or change has now narrowed. The industry is at the point where there is little time left to evaluate the level of safety afforded, and to demonstrate the application of such innovation or change in a design. An example is the OPA '90 legislation which was adopted with insufficient knowledge and experience with the double-hull design.

While it is generally accepted that eighty percent of accidents at sea that result in loss of life and oil pollution are caused by human error, and approximately twenty percent by mechanical or structural failure, changes are necessary to deal with the issue of tanker and bulk carrier disasters. In November 1993, I made a presentation at a joint session of the Royal Institution of Naval Architects and the Institution of Engineers and Shipbuilders in Scotland titled "Oil Tankers and the Environment," in which I proposed, an International Tanker Evaluation Council (ITEC) be established to coordinate efforts and to harmonize work for the design of tanker hull structures. A broadened form of ITEC to take care of the bulk and combination carriers would include a panel working closely with, and be part of the ITEC team.

ITEC would not seek to supplant the role of the class societies or of IMO, or pose a threat to their roles. On the contrary, ITEC should be viewed as a valuable source available to them. It would be a fully operational nonprofit entity and must operate and report without fear or favor the results of its findings on the subject of producing safer tankers and bulk carriers. The ITEC's commitment will be to improve oil tanker and bulk carrier design and enhance safety at sea through serious and sustained research and development. It should also be able to create a strong consensus in the international maritime community, making it easier to enforce international standards.

Such an undertaking requires financial resources as well as highly trained and motivated personnel. The European Commission spends large amounts of money every year on shipping related safety and environmental research, with growing emphasis on a risk based approach. Helping to finance the ITEC would be a worthwhile expenditure. It is the responsibility of flag states, by virtue of the International Law of the Sea Convention (Article 94), to ensure safety at sea with regard to the construction, equipment, and seaworthiness of ships. Other entities such as the major oil companies, and tanker and bulk carrier owners should assist in the financing of ITEC, bearing in mind that shipping is the delivery mechanism of international trade which is vital to the global economy.

The ITEC's objectives would be to create a framework within which ship construction and maintenance standards are established, so that commercial ships can operate safely with minimum negative impact on the marine environment. In order to further enhance its independent nature, ITEC could be based in an area with facilities such as those found in London, U.K., which is home to the world's leading maritime organizations adept at working together. London also offers a large and diverse maritime community that can offer expertise and experience across the entire range of international shipping services, including the advantage of an English legal system that enjoys a widespread confidence in the international maritime community.

Unified Rules by IACS and Goal-Based Ship Construction Standards by IMO

Recent reports in the world's maritime press indicated IACS is committed to the introduction of unified or common structural rules for tankers and bulk carriers. The new rules for tankers and bulk carriers would enter into force around January 2006.

The move towards the new rules is of great significance and one of the most fundamental changes in the system of ship classification since the inception of self-regulation. It is a move away from the traditional prescriptive rules that are based on experience. With today's powerful computers, any loop holes in the prescriptive rules grew steadily wider, giving the hull structure designer the ability to optimize a design. Such optimization was exploited by most shipyard hull structure designers who chose to interpret "optimization" as meaning minimum possible scantlings instead of redistribution of the steel in a design to areas in the structure subject to the greatest stresses. The unfortunate part of this rather sad story is that the class societies gave their blessing to such designs.

It is encouraging to note the changes in class societies thinking and hopefully will lead to other improvements in ship classification, particularly in the professionalism of survey work. The change will also remove the "shadow" of the International Tanker Evaluation Council's involvement mentioned earlier in this Chapter.

Another recent and equally important development has been the IMO's Maritime Safety Committee (MSC). At the 79th Session in December 2004, the Committee Working Group developed goal-based standards for building and equipping new ships. The group's objective is to develop standards, bearing in mind human and environmental issues. This will enable the IMO to play a larger role in determining the fundamental standards to which ships are constructed and equipped.

It has been made clear, however, that IMO has no intention of interfering with the work of the classification societies, but rather state what has to be achieved, leaving the shipping industry to decide on how to meet the required standards. The aim of the MSC's group is to introduce a mechanism so that, internationally agreed upon ship construction standards are uniformly and harmoniously applied by the shipbuilding industry.

Recently, there has been criticism by some independent shipowners who have been around a long time, of the way ships are designed, built, and blessed by the classification societies. Such criticism is, in my view, unfair, for the simple reason that "you get what you pay for." More importantly, it is up to the shipowner to ensure his ships are properly designed, built, and maintained. For the prudent and serious owners, organizations involved in rule making in the maritime industry should not be held accountable. It must be kept in mind that all such organizations are made up of personnel who represent the shipowners, and their rules are intended to help and guide the owners. It is up to the owner how he interprets and uses these rules which require or allow for a minimum standard. Some owners however, flaunt even these standards. What is also important is the fact that *all* rule making organizations have big owner representation in their committees, and support the organizations with executive time.

IMO's Goal-Based Standards

The idea to develop goal-based standards was presented to IMO by members of that organization with a view for the IMO to assume responsibility of setting standards for future new buildings. The standards are to include safety and environmental performance objectives for new ships, which, until now, have been determined largely by the classification societies.

There were concerns on the part of class societies that governments might take over functions that are currently the preserve of these societies. During IMO's December 2004 debate, in which the International Chamber of Shipping, Intertanco, BIMCO, and Intercargo participated, efforts were made to define clearly the standards, which will include, but not limited to the following:

- Design life
- Quality of construction
- Structural safety and access
- Environmental conditions

IMO's Maritime Safety Committee, in introducing the above list emphasized it was a first attempt to identify the major elements of the work to be accomplished during the next six year period—2004 to 2010. It was pointed out that a full discussion of all the elements, including the pros and cons, is essential to gain widespread support to carry forward this fundamental methodology on the use of goal-based standards. This will be a radically new approach to IMO's regulatory role prompted by the dissatisfaction in the international maritime industry because of the recurring ship casualties that resulted in loss of life at sea and major pollution of the marine environment.

Verification of compliance with the identified goal-based standards is another key issue that impacts directly on the essential relationship between IMO and the leading classification societies. The other important question to be decided is whether comprehensive goal-based standards encompassing the entire ship should be developed. This would mean extending the standards beyond ship design and construction, to include ship's machinery and electrical installations, fire protection, and life saving appliances.

A related issue concerns the future relationship for survey work for new buildings as well as existing ships and the goal-based standards. One of the IMO's aims would be to develop a Ship Construction File and a Ship Inspection and Maintenance File that would stay with the ship throughout its lifetime.

Enter the International Standards Organization (ISO)

Another recent, interesting development has been the proposal ISO-18072: Limit-State Assessment of Ship Structures. This is a new approach to ship's structure design, developed by the Geneva-based, International Standards Organization, which is a network of the national standards institutes of 146 countries, with a central secretariat in Geneva coordinating the ISO activities.

The ISO-18072 proposal is based on the allowable working stress design (WSD or ASD) and is intended to serve as a basis for defining a consistent and realistic level of safety margin for ship structures. It would work as a complementary tool to ship classification societies' unified design rules. The proposal would provide guidelines for limit-state assessment of ship structures in terms of strength modeling techniques related to, geometric and material properties, boundary conditions, loading conditions, finite element mesh size, fabrication-induced initial imperfections, and structural degradation due to age. The above proposal implies inadequacy in scantlings determination resulting from the present methodology, and will change the manner by which classification societies establish and maintain universally accepted structural standards.

The ISO-18072 idea constitutes a common basis covering aspects that address the limit-state assessments of ship structures, because it uses the limit-state approach rather than the allowable working stress (AWS) approach, where the shipping industry has experienced problems due to inconsistency of safety measures based on the working stress concepts. It supports the idea that the load and resistance factor design—LSD, also called LRFD—approach, is much better than an allowable working stress design approach. The latter relies on restricting stress levels to a portion of the material yield strength through the use of a simple safety factor. This provides a convenient tool by which to determine ship's scantlings but does not provide a means by which the true capacity of a structural component can be quantified. As a consequence, the structural reliability of a ship cannot be ascertained without recourse to limit-state principles.

Apparently the LSD approach has been adapted for the design of land-based steel structures for the past twenty years and more recently for fixed offshore steel as well as concrete structures. The ISO-18072 proposal makes it clear that the initial determination of structural dimensions and scantlings for a design are not included in this international standard. It assumes that procedures and guidelines that determine a ship's dimensions and scantlings are provided in detail in the relevant classification society's rules. The ISO-18072 proposal has been put forward for consideration by the shipping industry and has been termed a new tool to complement classification societies' rules, aiming to further reduce casualties and loss of life at sea.

The International Maritime Organization (IMO)

Background Development of the IMO

The purpose of establishing the IMO was to develop sensible and practical international standards in efforts to improve safety at sea and to replace the multiplicity of national legislation that existed previously. The primary role of the IMO is to act as a forum for the member states to meet and decide on collective action in establishing minimum criteria for safety at sea and to protect the marine environment.

The first International Conference on the Safety of Life at Sea (SOLAS) was held in London in 1914, followed by a second such conference in London in 1929. In 1948, a third (SOLAS) conference was held in London, where eighteen maritime nations participated. (I attended this conference as a member of the Greek delegation.) Following a United Nations Conference in Geneva in 1959, the Convention established the Intergovernmental Maritime Consultative Organization (IMCO) now (IMO). Today's IMO actually started to operate in 1959.

The IMO is a United Nations Agency whose objective is to provide the mechanism whereby the governments of countries with an interest in shipping can come together to decide on standards to be applied on ships engaged in international voyages. Although the governing of the organization is provided by the assembly and the council, the core of IMO's work is carried out in a chain of committees, subcommittees and working groups, to which the member governments send their experts. As well as the government representatives, nongovernmental organizations representing a wide diversity of interests from within and outside the shipping industry itself and intergovernmental groups that represent special interests also participate in IMO meetings. For a world merchant fleet consisting of around 46,000 ships, the vast majority operate safely within the regulatory framework that has been developed over the years by IMO.

When a new measure is considered to improve maritime safety or prevent pollution of the seas, the measure may begin as detailed discussion among experts in an IMO committee room, but the measure's eventual success will depend on the commitment, dedication, and skill of a whole range of people who make a contribution to the implementation of the standards that are agreed to at IMO. Maritime lawyers and administrators in the member states have the task of ensuring that new measures are properly incorporated into their national legal frame works, and that the appropriate infrastructure and expertise for whatever inspection, testing, verification and certification may be required, is in place. And then the responsibility for successful implementation spreads wider still, to a whole network of people embracing classification societies, port state control, harbor authorities and so forth. But, the final responsibility must eventually lie with the ship operators.

Today, IMO's highest governing body is the *Assembly*, which consists of all member states and meets once every two years in regular sessions. They may also meet in an extraordinary session if necessary. The Assembly is responsible for approving the work program, voting the budget, and determines the financial arrangements of IMO. Next in order of seniority is the IMO *Council*, which is the executive branch of IMO and is responsible, under the Assembly, for supervising the work of the IMO. Between sessions of the Assembly, the Council performs most of the functions of the Assembly. It also appoints the Secretary General, subject to the approval of the Assembly. Today (year 2003), membership of the Council has increased to 40 member states, from 32 in the year 2002. The enlargement was designed to ensure the Council better represents the interest of all 162 IMO Member States.

Council members are elected by the Assembly for two year terms. Reporting to the Council are the three main Committees:

- Maritime Safety Committee (MSC);
- Environment Protection Committee (MEPC); and
- Technical Cooperation Committee (TCC).

The MSC is the highest technical body of the IMO, and it consists of all member states. Its purpose is to consider any matters directly affecting maritime safety. There is also a Facilitation Committee (FAL) and a number of subcommittees are in place to support the work of the main Technical Committee.

The MEPC, which also consists of all member states, is empowered to consider any matter within the scope of the organization concerned with prevention and control of pollution from ships. In particular, it is concerned with the adoption and amendment of conventions and other regulations and measures to ensure their enforcement. The MEPC was first established as a subsidiary body of the Assembly, and raised to full constitutional status in 1985. The MSC and MEPC are assisted in their work by nine subcommittees, which are also open to all member states.

The Technical Cooperation Committee (TCC) is required to consider any matter within the scope of the organization concerned with the implementation of technical cooperation projects for which the Organization acts as the cooperating agency. It was established in 1969 as a subsidiary body of the Council.

The Facilitation Committee was established in 1972 and deals with IMO's work in eliminating unnecessary formalities and "red tape" in international shipping.

Within the basic overall structure, there are numerous working groups, correspondence groups, and informal meetings. All of this work is supported by the IMO Secretariat, a staff of about 300 people, who provide the member states with a host of services including interpretation, translation, and the production of documents.

Some 120 nationalities are represented on the Secretariat staff, which is structured in six divisions.

- Maritime Safety
- Marine Environment
- Technical Cooperation
- Legal and External Relations
- Administrative
- Conference

Effective Dates

SOLAS 1948	November 19, 1952
SOLAS 1960	May 26, 1965
SOLAS 1974	May 25, 1980
SOLAS Protocol 1978	May 1, 1981
MARPOL 73/Protocol 78 Annex I	October 2, 1983
1st Set of Amendments SOLAS 74	September 1, 1984
2nd Set of Amendments SOLAS 74	July 1, 1986

The work of IMO represents the collective efforts of several hundred people to ensure there is a comprehensive and effective frame-work of international standards for ships that are fair, effective, and which can be applied uniformly throughout the world. One of the unfortunate things from IMO's point of view is that the delay in the promulgation of marine accident findings and recommendations makes it virtually impossible for IMO to exercise its global standard-setting on the basis of risk-based, cost-benefit analysis. The proper way to rule-making should follow, not precede, proper casualty investigation. In the maritime industry, unfortunately, almost always, no firm conclusions about what has caused an accident become available, because there are many and complex reasons not to make such information available.

At the end of the year 2003, articles published in the U.K. maritime press were hinting that the IMO should be involved in producing technical standards for tanker construction, and for that matter, ship construction in general. Some years ago, IMO's Secretary General Mr. William O'Neil made it clear that, "the IMO wishes to concentrate on the human and operational considerations which contribute to tanker accidents rather than technical." Mr. O'Neil correctly sensed that the perfect ship in the care of incompetent crew will not survive the hazards of the untamed seas.

The Flag State or State of Registry

The primary statutory responsibility of the flag state is to ensure the safety of a vessel. The responsibilities, duties, and role of the flag state have been defined through the various international conventions that have set parameters for the role of the flag state as described in the following conventions:

- Prevention of Pollution from Ships (MARPOL 73/78)
- Safety of Life at Sea (SOLAS)
- Standards of Training, Certification and Watch Keeping for Seafarers (STCW-1978)
- Regulations for Preventing Collisions at Sea (COLREG-1972)
- Load Lines (LL-1966)
- United Nations Convention and the Law of the Sea (UNCLOS-1982)

These six instruments have become the Charter of Flag and Port State for safety at sea and protection of the marine environment. The Law of the Convention, clearly defines how a Flag State should operate within the system to prevent Port State interventions, and if an intervention does take place, how the flag state should react. (Articles 94 and 217 in the UNCLOS Convention). Article 94 outlines the jurisdiction and control the flag state may assert over the administrative, technical, and social matters of a ship flying its flag. It also establishes steps that may be taken by the flag state to ensure safety at sea; employ qualified surveyors and proper navigational equipment, maintain appropriate manning and crew qualifications, and cooperate in marine casualty and incidents of navigation.

Article 217 of UNCLOS describes the measures that may be taken by the flag state to enforce these standards, and specifies that a procedure must be established to ensure that ships failing to comply with the applicable international rules and regulations are prohibited from sailing. It also provides for immediate investigations and proceedings, in the event that a ship is found to be in violation of these standards. In March 1995, the UNCLOS Convention was sent to the U.S. Senate for ratification but has not as yet been ratified by the Senate. The United States however, does recognize its contents as applicable law.

In short, Articles 94 and 217, greatly contribute to a comprehensive understanding of how a flag state can work within the system to prevent port state intervention, and if an intervention does take place, how the flag state should react.

The Port State

The port state's duties and responsibilities are outlined in Regulation 19 of the SOLAS Convention where procedures that should be followed are set forth in cases of intervention. The regulation focuses in the port state's power to intervene and also provides the "caution" that, "when exercising control under this regulation, all possible efforts should be made to avoid a ship being unduly detained or delayed. If a ship is thereby unduly detained or delayed, it shall be entitled to compensation for any loss or damage suffered." The MARPOL 73/78 Convention, Article 6, however, contains a balanced description of how the systems of flag and port state should work together.

The prudent owner/operator should be in a position to contact, as soon as possible, the flag state's key marine safety personnel in the event of an intervention. The flag state administration should also provide Port State Authorities with the necessary information to ensure cooperation with the appropriate representatives of the Flag State administration. In cases where interpretation varies, port state personnel frequently find the opinions of the flag state and classification societies to be helpful. Some people feel the system may be flawed overall; however, flag and port states do work together effectively.

Environmental and safety-at-sea concerns have recently become major issues for many flag states and this resulted in many port states and coastal states adopting additional requirements above and beyond those imposed by international agreement. Despite the fact that there really is only one set of internationally accepted standards, and one system of enforcement, it would appear that many conflicting interpretations of these standards by both flag state and port state have developed.

In cases where interpretation varies, it is advisable to seek the opinions of the flag state and classification society, because they can be helpful especially where port authorities are about to detain a vessel or have already done so. In such a situation, the participation of the classification society is essential because the documents issued by the classification society either certify compliance with, or note departure from applicable regulations. It is important therefore for the system to work well, flag state, port state and the classification society working together to effectively resolve a problem when it does arise.

The International Safety Management Code (ISM Code)

Another important piece of legislation developed by IMO was the International Safety Management Code (ISM) for the safe operation of ships and for pollution prevention. The ISM Code was adopted by the Assembly during its 18th session on November 5, 1993. While not mandatory, the IMO resolution strongly urged governments to implement the ISM Code on a national basis as soon as possible, but not later than June 1, 1998.

This resolution revoked existing IMO Resolution A.680 (17) and the associated Guidelines for the safe operation of ships and for Pollution Prevention. The ISM Code contains thirteen sections covering marine management systems with regard to safety and pollution prevention. The objectives include the following:

- Providing for safe practices in ship operation and safe working environment

- Establishing safeguards against identified risks

- Continuously improving safety management skills and emergency preparedness both ashore and aboard

- Ensuring compliance with mandatory rules and regulations with applicable codes, standards, and guidelines taken into account

The code is intended to improve safety at sea and reduce pollution of the marine environment by influencing the way shipping companies are managed and operated. It establishes an international standard for the proper and safe management and operation of ships, and the implementation of a safety management system. As vessel size increased, virtually everything about a ship's operation was growing more complex and more challenging. The question was can the existing management arrangements be focused on how safety should be determined effectively and be relayed to those on board a ship so that operational hazards are avoided?

It was for such reasons that the 1978 International Convention on Standards of Training Certification and Watchkeeping (STCW) for seafarers was completely revised and updated in 1995. The objective was to significantly enhance maritime safety and the quality of the marine environment by addressing human element issues to improve performance.

It should be noted that when comparing the ISM Code with the ISO 9000 Code, which is an internationally recognized series of standards covering management and assurance, both codes address specific aspects of a company's management system for different purposes. As there is an overlapping of the two standards; compliance with both standards does not require two separate management systems. One system may be designed to meet both standards.

It should also be noted that despite the fact that the ISM Code has been in force for some years now, confidence in the beneficial impact of the code on standards has been subdued.

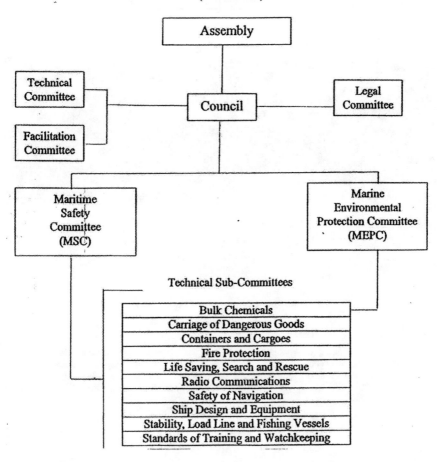

International Maritime Organization (IMO)
(Year 2003)

Assembly

Technical Committee

Facilitation Committee

Council

Legal Committee

Maritime Safety Committee (MSC)

Marine Environmental Protection Committee (MEPC)

Technical Sub-Committees

| Bulk Chemicals |
| Carriage of Dangerous Goods |
| Containers and Cargoes |
| Fire Protection |
| Life Saving, Search and Rescue |
| Radio Communications |
| Safety of Navigation |
| Ship Design and Equipment |
| Stability, Load Line and Fishing Vessels |
| Standards of Training and Watchkeeping |

In Session

*The International Maritime Organization's
highest governing body, the Assembly.*

Especially during the past decade, the IMO has succeeded in improving Maritime
Standards, and continues to provide a sound and well considered regulatory mechanism
which balances the demands of member states and the needs of the International Shipping
Industry, including the issue of Ballast Water Exchange, which was first introduced at
IMO in 1988.

THIRTEEN

Redundancy of Propulsion and Steering Equipment

Historically, most changes in international regulations for ship design and operation have been introduced as a result of major disasters, specifically when the disaster results in loss of life. The oil tanker industry disasters such as that of the *Torrey Canyon, Amoco Cadiz, Exxon Valdez, Erika, Prestige,* and others in between have unleashed, in their wake, a whole generation of tanker technology to improve the general safety of the oil tanker.

In the forefront of any new-ship project today is the issue of redundancy, where duplication of equipment and split machinery systems improves safety by adopting innovative thinking to make transportation of oil by tankers safer. It was suggested recently that the next mandatory requirement to be imposed by the regulatory bodies could be system redundancy.

Early in the 1990s, a team of European shipping industry experts carried out a study of the technical solutions and economics of building a much higher degree of a tanker propulsion machinery redundancy, that is, a machinery arrangement with surplus to requirements. The experts endeavored to assess the feasibility of employing the redundancy concept in commercial ships and began by identifying a number of factors common to a range of maritime incidents from statistics obtained from Lloyd's Register Statistics Department. It was established that of all total losses to tankers during 1976 to 1994, thirty percent were attributed to machinery related incidents, of which the largest single category was engine room fire.

The team's guiding principle was that tankers and passenger ships should not be designed with a machinery arrangement in which a failure of any one component would lead to the loss of the ship. It was pointed out by one of the team members that while most single-screw arrangements are supported by

313

service systems that contain some degree of redundancy, such systems do suffer breakdowns of various kinds, which result in the vessel being left without propulsion power for some period. The team concluded that a fully redundant system based on a twin-screw, twin-rudder arrangements with two engines in separate watertight engine rooms, with the auxiliary machinery also divided and separated, would preserve fifty percent of the tanker's total power except for the most catastrophic cases.

A tanker with full propulsion machinery redundancy should beneficially affect the casualty statistics and by extension insurance costs. The overall safer navigation from the redundant concept has implications in several of a tanker's voyage costs, including harbor dues, pilot dues, and tug costs. The exact influence however, is difficult to quantify. The study concluded, the most successful arrangement was one with twin-screws, twin medium speed engines, controllable pitch propellers, and large power primary shaft generators.

For a tanker owner, what the economics of operating a fully redundant machinery arrangement would be in practice today is a matter of conjecture. Here is where the risk and the cost come into the financial equation of installing and operating the fully redundant machinery arrangement.

Tanker system redundancy is not a new concept. It was implemented in the United States in the late 1950s when my company committed to build the 100,000 ton crude oil carrier at the Bethlehem Steel Shipyard in Quincy, Massachusetts. This was the 106,800 dwt tanker Mr. Onassis contracted to build for operation under the U.S. flag.

A brief history of the project is worth mentioning because this tanker, which, for a brief period, was the largest crude oil carrier in the world, became known as the S/T Manhattan. The contract was negotiated with Bethlehem Steel in New York in the late 1950s and the technical specifications were discussed with Bethlehem Steel's Central Technical Department. Construction was to be accomplished under Mar Ad's Construction Differential Subsidy. The principal dimensions were determined, and model basin tests were carried out at the David Taylor Model Basin in January 1958.

The principal characteristics were:

LBP: ....895' -0"
Breadth: ....132' 0"
Depth:..67' 6"
Draft: ....49' 1"
Block Coefficient:..0.791
Displacement: ....137,200 tons (salt water)
Deadweight: ....106,800 tons

Total Horsepower:..43,000 hp
Maximum Speed:..19.00 knots
Twin-Screws, fixed pitch propellers.
Twin-Rudders, canted 4 degrees out board.
Adequate provision had been made in the arrangement of the auxiliary machinery to ensure survival in the event of equipment failure.

A most interesting presentation was made to SNAME members in New York in November 1960 titled "Some Aspects of Large Tanker Design" by Bethlehem Steel's Central Technical Department, where I contributed to the discussion that followed the presentation. Because of the deteriorating tanker market, Mr. Onassis decided to substitute the large tanker by two smaller tankers of 56,000 dwt, which we named, *S/T Mount Vernon Victory* and *S/T Mount Washington Victory*. The large tanker was taken over by Manhattan Tankers Co. of New York, hence the name *Manhattan*, and for a period the tanker was used to carry grain cargoes. It was later taken over by Humble Oil on a bareboat charter with an option to buy. It was later reconstructed and strengthened for ice navigation by Standard Oil of New Jersey, now ExxonMobil, and in the Summer of 1969, commenced trial runs, in ballast, in an effort to open the Northwest Passage into a year-round trade route.

FOURTEEN

Risk Assessment in Ship Design and Operation

Risk is defined as the chance that something will happen, and arises from events with the potential to cause harm. When harm does occur, this is known as a hazard. Risk is the product of the frequency of occurrence of the hazard and its consequences.

In ship design and operation, what is normally considered a common sense approach to hull structure design and ship operation, has now been made into a new discipline called risk-assessment and risk-based approach, supporting ship design and operation. The discipline is widely applied in safety and environmental assurance in other industries, and has found increasing acceptance in the marine industry. The discipline enables all those involved in the marine industry to share a common understanding of hazards and risks. It provides a means of ensuring that life, property, and the marine environment are respected and protected, and that adverse situations that may arise can be examined and their impact properly controlled.

In shipping, hazards can arise for all sorts of reasons, both from the operation itself and from external factors. To be in a position to manage the risks from these hazards, it is necessary first to recognize these hazards, and to be able to rank them in order of importance. This approach is known as risk assessment, and the most effective time to apply this process is during the design stage. This is when it is easiest to make changes and build into the design low-risk strategies.

Risk assessment and analysis provides the process of identifying hazards, that is, events with the potential to cause harm. The process answers three basic questions:

- What can go wrong?

316

- What is the likelihood that it will go wrong?
- What are the consequences if it does go wrong?

Varying consequence categories may be evaluated including the following:

- Loss of life
- Injury and illness
- Economic loss
- Performance failure
- Environment impact

In shipping, there are basically two types of risk: technical risk requires a ship design engineering and operations approach; business risk requires financial approach. In ship design engineering, the judgment of what is acceptable standard of safety must take commercial factors into account. The hull designer must seek the least expensive way of achieving an acceptable standard of performance and safety and to improve safety at affordable cost.

Leading classification societies provide the owner/operator with risk management services focusing on an analysis of the risk-contributing factors.

The International Maritime Organization (IMO) has recognized the process known as Formal Safety Assessment (FSA) and has issued guidelines for the application of FSA to the IMO rulemaking process (MSC circular 829 and MEPC circular 335).

The FSA defines five steps:

- Identification of hazards
- Risk assessment
- Risk-control options
- Cost-benefit analysis
- Recommendations for decision making

The IMO defines *formal safety assessment* as "a rational and systematic process for assessing the risks associated with shipping activity, and for evaluating the costs and benefits of IMO's options for reducing these risks." The process, which involves the politically sensitive topic of regulations and standards, was introduced at IMO to assess the risks of the shipping industry's various activities, and to evaluate the costs and benefits of the identified risk management options. One application of risk methods to regulations and standards involves the shift from prescriptive design standards to performance standards using a risk-based approach. It must be recognized that the major disasters at sea have focused attention on the formal safety assessment.

Application of FSA is particularly relevant to proposals for regulatory measures that have far reaching implications in terms of costs to the maritime industry, or the administrative and legislative burdens that may result. The basic philosophy is that risk assessment can be used as a tool to facilitate a transparent decision-making process. The process also provides a means of being proactive, enabling potential hazards to be considered before serious accidents occur. Whereas in the past, actions taken by IMO were due to public opinion and political considerations rather than technical, FSA is now being applied to the IMO rule making process. Corrective actions stemming from the FSA are based upon realistic considerations and give due regard to the market realities.

The reason for this evolutionary trend in the shipping industry is the fact that while design standards and technical solutions are improving, major accidents continue to occur, despite the introduction of the International Safety Management (ISM) Code. The (ISM) Code does not require specific safety studies such as hazard identification or risk assessment. It does however require "safeguards to be established against all identified risks." The requirements imply that these hazards and risks be identified.

Risk of failure in a tanker hull structure can be identified using past experience, stress monitoring, and analytical studies using theoretical techniques.

In an effort to identify the risk of hull structural failure, and to examine the structural aging of a tanker, the technical staff of a major oil company monitored and analyzed the hull behavior on one of their VLCCs under way at sea during 1990. The objective of the monitoring was to measure hull structural responses to the environment, for use in correlating the measurements with analytical predictions. The analysis also helped provide guidance to ship's personnel for tactical decisions to be made in severe weather and avoid reaching or exceeding preset stress thresholds. From this monitoring, the study also concluded that, for a VLCC, steel as little as 100 to 150 tons objectively replaced can offer better technical value than many times the amount of steel randomly renewed.

With today's knowledge of tanker hull behavior and hull response to loads, scantlings redistribution will be likely compared to the designs of hull structures of the 1970s. The changes represent a better understanding of the loads on, and strength of, the various structural members of a tanker hull.

Successful aging and durability of a tanker hull girder can be achieved by the following:

- Quality and prudent distribution of steel to be used for the structure

- Adequate stiffening to avoid buckling or permanent distortion during the tankers service life
- Good coating protection of steel against corrosion

Prudent tanker owners have accumulated a library of finite element models, mainly to improve their efforts to repair and eliminate fatigue cracks. With regard to fatigue, because of the many variables involved, it is not possible to evaluate exactly the fatigue life of a specific structural member.

The Management of Technical Risk

Risk management is the discipline which enables the naval architect or hull designer to understand hazards and risks. It provides a means of ensuring that safety and the marine environment are protected. When adverse situations arise, they can be examined and their impact properly controlled. It has at last, been realized by the shipping industry that learning from failure and disasters is a very costly way to make improvements. Management of risk enables the shipping industry to implement strategies necessary to achieve a risk-based, decision-making culture. Such culture will improve the industry's image, not because the improvements are forced on the industry by regulations, but because it makes good sense.

The concept of risk management is relatively new to the shipping industry. The question arises, why now? The answer is, because in the past there has been lack of understanding of risk management in the shipping industry. A good example is that of the liner *Titanic*, where the risk of the vessel sinking was considered to be so remote that when the ship entered service, there were only sufficient lifeboats for half the passengers and crew.

Risk assessment and management is a new way to evaluate and to control risks in the shipping industry. The naval architect and tanker hull designer is afforded greater flexibility in the preparation of a design, because he is able to consider alternative design approaches that provide a level of safety in the design equivalent to that called for in the classification rules. Leading classification societies have introduced risk evaluations and offer advice on defining the objectives, conducting a basic risk assessment, and if necessary, a more detailed risk assessment. The basic risk assessment can be done in the very early stages of the design and later, detailed evaluation may be carried for a limited scope of issues identified during the basic Risk Assessment.

Managing a technical risk is like picking over bones of past accidents or near misses and drawing lessons to ensure that those particular mistakes are not repeated. In ship design engineering and ship operation, risk exists on many levels and takes many forms. The way to minimize risk is through awareness and the ability to identify important hazards and their consequences, so the vulnerability can be reduced by design and operation. An example is the loss of the motor tanker *Braer*.

This tanker, loaded with 84,700 tons of light crude oil while on a voyage from Norway to Quebec, Canada, lost power on January 4, 1944, and went aground on the Shetland Islands in Scotland. The vessel was heavily damaged and sank, spilling the entire cargo of oil. The loss of power was due to contamination of the diesel fuel by sea-water that had entered the fuel tank through a broken air pipe on the upper deck. This air pipe that led to the diesel oil tank was broken by steel pipes that were left unsecured on deck. With the rolling of the ship, the loose pipes broke the air pipe. Contamination of the diesel fuel caused main engine failure, and a few hours later the diesel generators failed for the same reason, that is, contaminated fuel. It would appear that those on board the tanker failed to take action when it was known that the spare pipes stowed on the upper deck aft, had broken loose.

In recent years, some underwriters have taken a wider view of risk, examining the total risk present in the owner/operator applicant. To underwriters, risk may not always be risk to safety, but it is always risk to assets. For the owner/operator, safety is a form of asset protection and the safety benefits are worth the cost of improving a design.

As the marine industry is taking a more serious view of safety enhancement, the marine insurance industry examines how enterprise risk management (ERM) might be used to reduce claims. By developing a risk profile for an owner/operator, the underwriter is able to differentiate among manageable risks helping their clients to develop risk management systems.

The Management of Business Risk

What causes risk to exist in marine capital investment? The principal problem in carrying out a marine capital investment analysis is that of estimating the values for the key elements that determine the investment's outcome. These elements include the following:

- The initial investment
- Operating costs
- Capacity utilization
- Freight rates
- Economic life of the ship
- Residual value of the ship

It is the uncertainty that surrounds such values that cause risk in marine capital investment and that surrounds the future values that makes an investment's outcome questionable. Forecasting future costs and revenues is generally the most difficult and critical task in an investment analysis.

Judgment and intuition frequently play a large part in the estimation of many of a ship's significant variables such as:

- Time in service each year
- Dry-docking frequency and costs
- Amount and timing of major steel renewals
- Availability and relevance of historical data
- Personal experience of the estimator

The problem of decision-making in the face of uncertainty is heightened when the decision maker is not the person who estimates the most likely values upon which investment analysis has been based. In economic terms, risk can be viewed or defined as the possibility of not achieving the minimum acceptable rate of return on the investment. Uncertainty or doubt encompasses the key elements in an investment, such as costs, revenues, and project life, which in this case is the life of a ship.

Between the risk and uncertainty are other uncertainties; the most relevant to marine capital investment are attributable to the following:

- Technological developments
- Competition
- Economic environment

- Political developments

In marine capital investment analysis, because of the critical importance of dealing effectively with risk and uncertainty, any evaluation technique must be combined with sound managerial judgment if rational investment decisions are to be made. For example, in the early 1950s, Mr. Onassis, in addition to oil tankers and bulk carriers, owned and operated a whaling fleet that consisted of twelve whale catchers and one mother ship, the *Olympic Challenger*. This was a converted T-2 tanker and was used to process the whale parts into whale oil and store the oil on board.

During one of the expeditions in the Antarctic and just before the end of this expedition, the *Olympic Challenger* was arrested by the Peruvian Navy, because the Peruvian authorities claimed the Onassis whaling fleet were poaching in Peruvian waters, that is, the fleet was catching whales inside the 200 nautical miles that the Peruvians claimed as their territorial waters. Onassis claimed that the Peruvian action was illegal and brought the case before the International Court of Justice and won the case.

Onassis, prior to the start of the expedition, in addition to insuring the fleet for the usual marine hazards such as damages due to heavy weather, and so forth, had insured this operation with Lloyd's of London against such contingency, and the underwriters compensated Onassis accordingly.

Tolerability of Risk/Permissible Risk

The tolerability of permissible risk is as follows:

- The nuclear industry tolerates a chance of one death in a million per year.
- For death by road accidents is one death in ten thousand per annum.
- For lightning strike, it is one in ten million per annum.

Epilogue

In writing this book, my intention was to put on record the development of the crude oil carrier in the past 60 years. Researching ship design and construction, inevitably led me to the realization that our industry has been in a somewhat chaotic situation as a result of the tragedies at sea with heavy loss of life and disastrous pollution of the seas. The reason for the sad situation is the standards, and application of these standards has obviously been inadequate.

The shipping industry is an international self-regulated, self-sustaining industry inherited from the days when ships embarked on maritime ventures into the unknown, out of contact for weeks or months at a time. Today the industry has one important fundamental strength: it carries more than ninety percent of the world's trade. As long as there is world economic growth, trade will expand and develop. Shipping is both the least expensive and most popular form of transportation.

From the preceding chapters, the reader will see that ship design and construction is a constantly evolving science with few or no absolutes. It is a constant learning process. Learning from failure, however, is a very costly way to achieve progress, especially where public and seafarers' lives are involved.

The grounding of the tanker *Torrey Canyon* in England in 1967, due to faulty navigation, alerted the maritime world to the dangers posed to the marine environment by oil tankers. The disaster led to the adoption of the "load-on-top" system, which saved the oil companies some oil cargo that was otherwise dumped into the seas. It was also effective in reducing operational pollution, but the system could do nothing with oil pollution arising from grounding accidents.

The explosions on the Shell Oil's VLCCs *Marpesa* and *Mactra*, and the Norwegian VLCC *Kong Haakon VII* in 1969 while gas-freeing in the Atlantic, led to the introduction of the "inert gas system," while the grounding of the Exxon-Mobil VLCC *Exxon Valdez* in Alaska in 1989, as a result of faulty navigation, led to the U.S. OPA '90 legislation, which requires a double-hull for all tankers trading in U.S. waters, and which is now accepted as universal oil tanker design.

The sinking of the oil tankers *Erika* and *Prestige,* which caused massive oil pollution in France and Spain in 1999 and 2002 respectively, led to the accelerated phase out of the single-hull oil tankers. Regulations stemming from these disasters placed many of the existing oil tankers that are still structurally sound into the process of regulatory obsolescence.

Despite noticeable improvements in safety lately, the industry still faces important problems of safety, which may be defined as the quality that determines to what extent the design, construction, and operation of a ship is free of danger to life, property, and the marine environment. The shipowners and operators of quality tonnage have always had enviable safety and environmental records without being forced into it by national or international regulations. Such owners and operators consider reliability of their ships a form of asset protection.

One of the fundamental elements for a safe ship is adequate strength and buoyancy. With the development of new technologies, new designs, and the use of new materials, the problems encountered to ensure structural integrity require different approach to obtain robustness and reliability. The other fundamental element is the availability of data obtained from real service experience, such as hull-monitoring that is crucial to the quantification of risk. During a ship's operational life, the hull structure, as well as the equipment on board, is subject to a number of aging factors that must be regularly monitored to ensure continuity in safety.

The decision by IACS members to cooperate and use a proactive approach in the development of goal-based classification standards is encouraging, and this is of importance to the Maritime Safety Committee at the IMO. In a presentation in London, at the President's Invitation Lecture to the Royal Institution of Naval Architects in November 2004, the new chairman of ABS, Robert D. Somerville, stated, "the whole principle of modern ship classification is due for a thorough review." Another delegate stated, "a Round Table meeting of IACS' Council will take place in London in December 2004 in efforts to improve the standards of the shipping industry." This is a welcome statement, and hopefully such meetings by IACS' Council will help eliminate IACS' Achilles' heel.

Safety at sea and protection of the marine environment must be a relentless effort by those involved in the design, construction, maintenance, and operation of ships. It has been suggested ship safety can best be enhanced by improving prescriptive regulations, and the shipping industry has, for sometime now, been participating in a great deal of international regulatory activity aimed at making commercial shipping safer. In a complex and secretive industry such as shipping, however, there are no simple answers. Knowledge, experience, professionalism, dedication, and transparency are of the utmost importance. It makes no sense to introduce rules, regulations, codes, and protocols if the structural design of a ship is flawed. On the other hand even the most perfectly designed ship, in the hands of an incompetent crew, will not survive the hazards of the seas.

References

"1983, The year of Implementation. MARPOL/SOLAS/Intertanko." July 1983.

ABS/Activity Report. Various Issues.

Alman, Philip, et al "The International Load Line Convention: Crossroad to the Future." *Marine Technology.* SNAME, October 1992.

"Anchor and Balance." Det Norske Veritas, 1984–1989.

Anderson, Kurt. *European Shipbuilding—Modernization, Automation and Politics. Sea Japan Conference,* March 1996.

Barr, W. and C. F. Tipper. "Brittle Fracture in Mild-Steel Plates" *The Journal of the Iron and Steel Institute.* London, October 1947.

Bea, R. G. "Ship Structural Maintenance: Recent Research Results and Experience." presented in London at The Institute of Marine Engineers. University of California, June 1993.

"Condition Evaluation and Maintenance of Tanker Structures."—*Tanker Structure Co-operative Forum.* London 1992.

"Design of the First Generation of 550,000 DWT Tankers." *SNAME* Vol. 85, 1977.

"Dynamic Slosh-Induced Loads on Liquid Cargo Tank Bulkheads." *SNAME* T&R No. R-19, 1975.

"Effect of Rudder Rate on Maneuvering Performance of a Large Tanker." *SNAME* T&R No. R-22, 1976.

Fergusen, J. M. "Oil Tankers in the 1990s." Lloyd's Register of Shipping, April 1990.

Fukuda, J. *Predicting the Longitudinal Stresses Induced on a Large Tanker.* Japan: Fukuoka, 1978.

Grothen D. and K. Londot. "The Construction of the Exxon Valdez." *SNAME,* Vol. 98, 1990.

Grove, T. W. "Modern Tanker Construction—A Classification Society's Perspective." *Spillcon 1992*, Queensland, Australia.

Grove, T. W., et al "Bulk Carriers, A Case for Concern." Great Lakes, Canada, June 1992.

"Guide for Design and Evaluation of Double-hull Tanker Structures." *ABS*, November 1992.

"Guide for Vessel Life Extension."—*ABS*, September 1989.

Hagner, Jr., T. R. "Mid-Deck Tankers."—*SNAME*, November 1990.

Howarth, Stephen. *The Story of Shell's British Tanker Fleets 1892–1992.*

Levine R. A. "Contingency Planning for Oil Spills." *Marine Technology*, April 1988.

Liu, Donald, "Design Requirements for Double-Hull Tankers." *ABS*, October 1990.

Liu, Donald, et al, "Dynamic Load Approach in Tanker Design."—*SNAME*, 1992.

MacCutcheon, E. M. "Rivet Slip, Stress Distribution and Deflection of Ship's Hull." *SNAME*, Vol. 57, 1949.

"Maneuvering of Large Tankers." *SNAME* Vol. 80, 1972.

Mano, Masaki. *Detail Design of Hull Structure.* Tokyo, 1983.

Mano, Masaki. *Some Considerations for Better Hull Structural Design.* Japan: Kinki University, 1970.

Marcus, H. S. "Integrating Environmental Impact into Future Tanker Design Philosophy." *Marine Industrial Technology Monitor*, Issue No. 5. United Nations Industrial Development Organization.

Melitz, D. T. et al. "Structural Performance Management of VLCC's: An Owners Approach" *SNAME* 1992.

Mitsubishi Heavy Industries, Ltd. "Tanker Design for Pollution Prevention." *Skaarup Oil Corporation*, April 1993.

National Research Council. "Tanker Spills: Prevention by Design." Washington, D.C.: National Academy Press, 1991.

Office of Technology Assessment. "Coping with an Oiled Sea—An Analysis of Oil Spill Response Technologies." Congress of the United States; Washington, D.C.: U.S. Congress, March 1990.

Oil Companies International Marine Forum. "Prevention of Pollution from Tankers." Position paper. January 1993.

Okamoto, Kenji, et al. "Deterioration Measurements of Ship's Hull and Application to Design." *I.H.I. Engineering Review,* January 1993.

Overaas, S. and E. Solum. "The Load on Top System for Crude Oil Tankers." *SNAME.* Vol. 82, 1974.

"Practical Guide to the Design and Installation of Crude Oil Washing Systems." *SNAME,* Vol. 88, 1980.

Rutherford, S. E. et al, "Ultimate Longitudinal Strength of Ships: A Case Study."—*SNAME* 1990.

Seaman, M. A. "The Identification and Control of Major Hazards in Industry." *IESS,* January 1992.

"Seatrade Review," August 1993—London, U.K.

"Ship of the Future, 2000." Workshop proceedings. *SNAME,* May 1990.

"Spill Containment and Cleanup—Research and Development" *Marine Technology,* Oct. 1981.

Spyrou, Andrew G. "Designing The Environment-Friendly Oil Tanker."—. Tokyo: *Society of Naval Architects of Japan,*—May 1991.

———. *Energy and Ships.*———London: Lloyds of London Press, 1988.

———. "The Million Ton Tanker." *The Million Ton Carrier Conference,* New York, March 1974.

———. "Oil Tankers and the Environment." *IESIS,* November 1993.

"Structural Problems of Recently Built Tankers." *Nippon Kaiji Kyokai,* London 1992.

"Structural Residual Strength of Oil Tanker Designs—A Comparative Study." *ABS,* January 1992.

Tipper, C. F. "Brittle Fracture Problem, 1943–1956." *British Welding Journal.* 1956.

Tornay, E. G., "Tanker Design for the '90s." *SNAME Philadelphia Section,* Oct. 18, 1990.

Wei-Biao Shi; "In-Service Assessment of Ship Structures: Effects of General Corrosion and Ultimate Strength."—*RINA,* 1992.

Wada, Takao and Masaki Mano. *Practical Design of Hull Structures.* New Castle-Upon-Tyne, U.K., 1992.

Wildenberg T. "The Origins and Development of the T-2 Tanker." *The American Neptune* Vol. 52, No. 3, Summer 1992.

978-0-595-36068-0
0-595-36068-8

Woodlands Library   *12/19*

Printed in the United States
73889LV00003B/94-96

9 780595 360680